World Class
Teaching and Learning
in Global Times

World Class
Teaching and Learning
in Global Times

William Gaudelli
University of Central Florida

LAWRENCE ERLBAUM ASSOCIATES, PUBLISHERS
2003   Mahwah, New Jersey   London

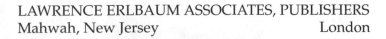

Lawrence Erlbaum Associates, Inc., Publishers
10 Industrial Avenue
Mahwah, NJ 07430

Cover design by Clara Cobb

Library of Congress Cataloging-in-Publication Data

Gaudelli, William.
World class : teaching and learning in global times /
   William Gaudelli.
         p. cm.

Includes bibliographical references and index.
ISBN 0-8058-4078-8 (pbk. : alk. paper)
1. International education—United States. I. Title.

LC1090.G38   2003
307.116—dc21   2002072220
                                                             CIP

Books published by Lawrence Erlbaum Associates are printed on
acid-free paper, and their bindings are chosen for strength and durability.

Printed in the United States of America
10 9 8 7 6 5 4 3 2 1

Dedication
To my mom, Josephine Gaudelli, my first teacher

Contents

III   Alternatives

Preface

The challenges of teaching about the world led me to write this book. As a new high school teacher over a decade ago, I struggled to make sense of the world class that I had been assigned. While talk of globalization was rapidly increasing, I grappled with the globalization that was supposed to be going on within my classroom. How do I "cover" all that students need to know? What do they need to know? What kinds of materials can I use to teach about the world? How do I help students relate to places, people, and events in areas of the world with which they have little or no familiarity? These questions were not unique to my situation or my students, though I remember feeling they were.

I tried to deal with this sense of curricular isolation by talking frequently with colleagues who taught the world class. We shared lessons, went on field trips, invited speakers, and vented frustrations in developing our course of study. We were proud of our efforts, but were also critically reflective in determining what seemed to be effective and what simply did not work. We were able to develop reasonable answers to the questions raised initially, only to find new ones emerging. What is unique about this school context that affects global learning? How should my students negotiate civic obligations that are strongly national with ones that are global? How should we engage controversial issues? How do our identities shape the ways in which we see the world? I consulted the literature in global education and found a number of thoughtful frameworks, stimulating teaching ideas, and provocative debates about the nature of global learning. Lacking in the literature, however, was a variety of substantive accounts of how teachers came to address these problematic areas. This book is designed to address this area of need.

My awkward and stumbling induction as a practitioner to the field of global education led to a more formal inquiry about how other teachers engaged this curriculum area. I wanted to document the ways in which teachers and students at three different schools in New Jersey were learning about the world as a contribution to the existing literature. This book illustrates an ethnographic inquiry into the lives of teachers and students engaged in global education. In these chapters, the voices of the people who teach and learn about the world are animated, contextualized, and analyzed to inform our understanding of global pedagogy.

World Class is written for scholars, practitioners, and graduate students interested in global education. In the conversations that follow, you will hear the struggles and successes of teachers engaged in global education. Rather than simplify these complex experiences and concoct answers to contrived problems, I try to illustrate the complexity of this work and raise thought-provoking questions. I do not intend to provide solutions to global pedagogy in this book, but rather, to pose alternative ways of thinking about these problems, and leave the answers, ultimately, up to you.

This book is divided into three parts: *Contexts* includes chapters 1–3; *Problems* is developed in chapters 4–6; and *Alternatives* is offered in chapters 6–9. *Contexts* allows the reader to consider global education from multiple perspectives: teacher, student, administrator, community, and scholar. *Problems* focuses on pedagogical challenges associated with global education. *Alternatives* provides some reflection points that encourage the reader to consider different ways that we might converse about global teaching and learning.

Contexts is foundational to the rest of this book as it outlines important issues to be addressed. Chapter 1 "Where in the World Have You Been?" briefly traces the roots of global education as a curriculum field. In chapter 2, "Three Schools at the International Crossroads of New Jersey," I argue that New Jersey is an ideal place for examining global education as it is a state whose economy and population are globally integrated. I also provide background about educational policy in the state and tighten the lens, sketching the three high schools in which the study was conducted. Chapter 3, "How Can You Fit a Global Village in a Classroom?" addresses contextually unique issues that teachers face when they attempt to bring global perspectives into the classroom.

Problems illuminates some of the difficulties that teachers have when they encounter the world in their classrooms. Chapter 4, "Global Education as Anti-American Curriculum?" examines the supposed tensions between global education and national curricula. Chapter 5, "Opening Pandora's

Box: Cultural Relativism in Global Education" discusses issues related to cultural relativism and universalism in global classrooms and how teachers and students attempt to walk this philosophical tightrope. In chapter 6, "Conversations About Our Houses of Mumbi: Identity in Global Education," I borrow from a Gikuyu myth about the construction of identity to examine how students and teachers shape their understandings of global learning from their own senses of self.

Alternatives focuses mainly on reframing problems associated with global education. Chapter 7, "Rethinking Nationalism, Cultural Relativism, and Identity in Global Education," offers ways of reorienting pedagogical problems raised in Part II of the book. Chapter 8, "Teachers as Community Intellectuals: Professional Development in Global Education," is a clarion call to invest heavily in the education and professional space of teachers to ameliorate some of the problems examined herein. Finally, chapter 9, "A New Way to the World? Global Times, Global Citizens," discusses the potential of schools to create a dialogue about what global citizenship means in the 21st century. The appendix includes a brief discussion of the methodology used in this study and a reference list. A brief afterword is provided to examine the aftermath of September 11, 2001, in light of the ideas raised in the book.

ACKNOWLEDGMENTS

I owe so much to colleagues and family for their support and encouragement in this process. A special thanks to my editor, Naomi Silverman, for having the confidence in this project from the start and my reviewers, Dennis Banks, Ken Carlson, Terri Epstein, and Stephen Thornton, for challenging me to improve this work. Your insights and encouragement were vital to this project.

To the anonymous participants; thank you for opening your classrooms and giving your time to this inquiry.

To my colleagues from Hunterdon Central Regional High School, especially Nancy Bennett, Bonnie Berringer, Sean Chappe, Vince Damico, Bill Fernekes, Kerry Kelly, Catherine Lent, Jennifer Peck, Lissa Richardson, Will Richardson, John Smith, Maria Sydor, and the social studies department; I miss teaching with you and remain inspired by you.

To my friends at Rutgers, especially Ken Carlson, Al Howard, Ronald Hyman, Carey and Nancy McWilliams, Jack Nelson, Nobuo Shimahara, and Burt Weltman; your teachings remain with me.

To my colleagues from Teachers College-Columbia, especially Beth O'Brien, Margaret Smith-Crocco, and Stephen Thornton; thanks for the opportunity to teach and for the support in this and other efforts.

To my new professional family at the University of Central Florida, including Karen Biraimah, David Boote, Andy Brewer, Douglas Brumbaugh, Jeffrey Cornett, Trish Crawford, Jennifer Deets, Randy Hewitt, Marty Hopkins, Marcy Kysilka, John Manning, Sherron Roberts, Sandra and Mike Robinson, Edmund Short, and Carolyn Walker-Hopp; I appreciate the long conversations over coffee about many of these ideas, your partnership, and fine company.

To my family, Dad, Gina, Fred, Freddie, and Joseph; Angelo, Cheryl, Michele, Angelo, and Anthony; Rita, John, and Michael, thank you for all that you have done, for the love you have given, and the peace that you bring me.

To my Mom, Josephine Gaudelli; thank you for being my first teacher; you have given me life, and I miss yours every day.

To my wife, Elizabeth; thank you for all you have done and for all of your confidence in our many changes; your love feeds and sustains me; you are my home and my life. And to my son, Alexander, you are a gift to the world and I will always be there for you.

Personal Prologue: A Conversation About World Teaching and Learning

> As civilized human beings, we are the inheritors, neither of a inquiry about ourselves and the world, nor of an accumulating body of information, but of a conversation, began in the primeval forests and extended and made more articulate in the course of centuries. It is a conversation which goes on both in public and within each of ourselves … Education, properly speaking, is an initiation into the skill and partnership of this conversation.
> —Oakeshott (1962, p. 199)

The ability to converse is the most obvious expression of the human intellect, the attribute that, in its complexity and diversity, most sharply differentiates us from other species. Humans are social creatures. Conversation is the glue of our sociality, the point at which we interact meaningfully with our world. Infants, speechless wonders, even make utterances that suggest the formulation of thought and a passion to communicate. Children's babble and frustration in not being understood demonstrates how thought and communication are uniquely interwoven. Humans are driven to converse about what they think.

School and homelife typically provide forums where verbalisms and thoughts are organized into a form widely recognizable by organizing and homogenizing conversation, and to a lesser degree, thoughts. Learning in school is typically a matter of engaging with teachers, peers, films, books, journals, computers, and many other forms of media. The extent to which a child can be conversant with sources of information often predicts his/her success in school. Student free time is literally overflowing with conversations. Where did you buy that? Where are you going after school? Do you like her/him? What time is the party? On entering the classroom, teachers direct students to prescribed conversations: the course of study. Schools are fundamentally conversational social institutions.

This book is a portal into the conversations about global education among the two most vital players in schools: students and teachers. Amid the cacophony of a busy school emerge multiple streams of discourse. As a teacher turned researcher, I listened to these conversations in classrooms, hallways, libraries, study areas, and teachers' lounges. I asked students and teachers to wonder aloud about their experiences in learning and teaching about the world, to share their frustrations and achievements in understanding such a vast and complex area as world studies. The purpose of this book is to organize these conversations in a way that will inform, challenge, and provoke those interested in global education.

How does one begin a conversation about the world? The topic is so unmanageably vast, it seems to be an impossibility. In thinking about this question and the study I was about to engage, I found myself pondering my own conversation with the world over my lifetime. How did I come to know the world around me as a child? Recognizing that acts of remembering are always fictional recreations, I begin by recounting my life around the issues at the center of this book: education and globalization (Grumet in Cole & Knowles, 2000, p. 128).

My life began in the sleepy, rural town of Elmer, New Jersey, in the late 1960s. Although this was a time of great social upheaval, places like Elmer were far removed from the tumult. The most notable building in Elmer back in the 1960s, as well as today, is the hospital. There is not much else, except for a small grocery store and a few gas stations. If you blink while driving through, you may miss it. Elmer is not the most isolated place on the planet, but it seems far removed from the rest of the world.

As a child, I lived a fairly remote, parochial life in Millville, New Jersey, just a stone's throw away from Elmer. The city of Millville, a city in name only, was economically dependent on the large glass industry. Many people in town were working poor and our lives reflected to some degree the community's economic state. My father owned a small heating and air conditioning installation business and we lived in an old house that my parents were constantly fixing and remodeling. Although we were relatively poor, mine was not a childhood of deprivation. I had wanderlust as a child, often riding my bike across the nearby town line to say I had been somewhere other than Millville. Watching birds in my backyard as a child, I remember a feeling of awe and envy as they could seemingly travel anywhere they wished, something I wanted to do. We rarely traveled beyond Millville, except for an excursion to Niagara Falls, Washington, D.C., and summer visits to the nearby Jersey shore.

Our trip to Niagara Falls offered me great excitement. Not only was I going on vacation, but also to another country! Leaving a restaurant one evening on the Canadian side of Niagara, I was stopped by a group of Japanese tourists that did not speak English. They were able to gesture for a photograph, however, to which my parents consented. The shutterbugs gave me a yen as a souvenir, bowed slightly, and went along their way. I was so intrigued that they could not speak English, so amazed that they were from a distant place, and so enchanted by this odd piece of money. This simple exchange brought me closer to the realization of a world beyond my hometown.

I recall asking my mom and brother after this encounter if people speaking other languages interpreted what they were saying into English. They had difficulty understanding my question, but I persisted in asking if that was how all people understood the world, in English. The idea that objects may be universal but that the words to describe them were not was baffling to me as a child. I assumed that people spoke other languages just for pleasure or distraction, but in the end, everyone was essentially an anglophone. This purely egocentric view of the world was eventually set right, transformed into the realization that someone could converse with the world in sounds that were seemingly unintelligible. The notion of perspective entered my mental vocabulary, and I began to apply this to all of my understandings. I assumed dogs had the same type of complex language as humans and that a dog from France would not be able to talk to a dog from India. By all accounts, I was a strange kid.

I remember listening to the beautiful melodies of my grandparents speaking Italian. When they wanted some privacy in their cramped home, they reverted to their native tongue to maintain secrecy. I eventually learned to pick out a few words; *Gulliarmo* meant they were talking about me and *mange* signaled the essential conversations about food! Most of these exchanges were lost on my American acculturated ears, as our family's ethnic language had passed away years before I was born. I recall thinking how odd it was that they could speak so fluidly in English one minute and in Italian the next. Italy was a distant place in some ways, but in others, it was right in my grandparents' kitchen.

Most of my access to the world beyond Millville came from the media. My parents modeled intellectual curiosity. Ours was a house filled with stimulating conversations about events of the day. My father ritualized newspaper reading and news programs were the main fare of our family viewing. Scanning the headlines, I read about the end of a war in a place called Vietnam. I was drawn in by the descriptions of turmoil surrounding antiwar protests. The television in my house flashed scenes of what looked to me like the trial of the President, the impeachment proceedings of President Nixon. At a young age, I could not fathom what would make the U.S. President leave his job, but my dad's succinct explanation helped me understand: "Nixon lied to the American people," he said with angst.

Family conversations at the dinner table were often about current events, which politicized my outlook at an early age. I remember talking about a famine in Biafra, a place that could have been on the moon for all I knew as a child. It certainly was not on my globe, although another place called Nigeria was there, in bright green. Biafra seemed to affect me directly, however, because my parents would remind me not to waste food on account of starving children there, even broccoli and lentil soup. On Saturday mornings, I was glued to the television for one of my favorite programs: *The Big Blue Marble*. The show brought the environmental movement into the lives of children. What drew me to watch was that wonderful image of the Earth from space, a new perspective that captured the imagination of many people. I wondered about the marvel that was our Earth.

My childhood global education was more about wondering than traditional learning. I had a globe at home that I adored and an encyclopedia set. I would spin the globe on its axis and stop it with my finger on a new spot: Chad, Indonesia, Chile, and Sudan. Questions would pour forth: Does anyone live there? How do they live? Is it like my life in Millville? Do the kids go to school? I wonder if they lacked for food like the Biafran kids? For lack of information, I would create unbelievable stories about the places I pointed to on my globe, usually based only on the name. Chad must have been a place where all of the people were named Chad, just like a friend of mine. Indonesia was filled with Indians, like I saw in old Western movies. Chile must be where a hot, tomato beef stew that my mom made originated. Sudan was filled with four door vehicles like my dad drove ... and on and on. Thinking about my musings now is funny and somewhat embarrassing, but this was how my curiosity developed, probably not unlike the way most children nonsensibly come to understand their unfamiliar world.

Formal education in Millville offered little about places beyond the United States that I recall, with the exception of my first social studies class in seventh grade. World geography was my first formal exposure to topics beyond the scope of the United States, as we identified countries, cities, and land features on wall maps. Our class enjoyed playing geography bee, where you competed against a peer to be the first person to find an obscure place on the map. I loved this game and was frequently a finalist in the class because of my independent globe wondering. My classmates regarded me as somewhat of a social studies guru as we took great pleasure in identifying each other's academic strengths and weaknesses. My hyper-competitive peers readily conceded social studies maven (read-nerd) to me because, in the words of Dave Fox, "Social studies isn't that important anyway, so we'll let Gaudelli have that one!"

Brunei. Here was a country that I knew nothing about, one that never ended up under my finger in the globe-spinning game. It was also the country that I was assigned to research for an oral report in world geography. I nervously approached the bucket of names and despaired as others shrieked when they pulled Germany, England, and Italy. The pressure was on, as I had already been anointed social studies geek, needing to prove it was a title I deserved. I blindly selected Brunei and my peers laughed derisively. "Brunei? Where's that?! He'll never find that one!" The school library did not have any information on this obscure place. I was amazed that there could be such a place, so distant from life in Millville, about which I could not find information. I went to the local public library and searched for Brunei in vain. My globe offered no solace as Brunei was not there either. *National Geographic,* found in the dusty shelves of our public library, finally rescued me.

I recall being amazed by the photos of Bruneians, thinking they did not resemble people in my hometown. Millville was a fairly homogenous place, a condition worsened by the regimented tracking system in the schools. I did not venture far beyond my small, "A-track" crowd in high school. We were all White, Christian, and mostly middle class. My friends were so homogeneous that I, as a second and third generation Italian-American and barely middle class even by Millville's standard, was considered somewhat different. Ethnic slurs were sometimes hurled in my direction, but they had little power, as I knew Italians were no longer a minority in any real sense. My friends and I knew that we were all very much alike.

My first sustained interactions with diverse people occurred as an undergraduate at Rutgers College. My freshman floor was a varied group of students from throughout the state and beyond. I was one of the token students from the southern part of a state dominated by the north in every respect. In September of my freshman year, Rosh Hashanah and Yom Kippur signaled a mass exodus from the dormitory by Jewish students. I remember wondering where everyone had gone. My roommate, who was Jewish, explained what the holidays signified in Judaism. As a freshman in college, it was my first meaningful interaction with people who did not believe the same things that I was raised to believe.

The approach of Christmas and Hanukkah offered another opportunity for encountering the world among my college peers, this time in a more comical way. We decided to decorate for the holidays, but lacked the money to buy a "holiday tree." Steve Lutens, who was Jewish, agreed to go into the park and cut down a tree to adorn our barren hallway. We could see Steve in the park below our dormitory, cutting down a tree, when the Rutgers police spotted him as well. The tree was already down when Steve realized he had been spotted. We watched as he frantically tried to outrun the police, but was eventually apprehended.

Those remaining on the floor decided that we should go down to the police station and help out our floormate, now a felon. When we arrived, Steve said he must have been the first Jewish kid arrested for stealing a Christmas tree. We joked about this episode for the remainder of our year together. The great Christmas tree caper, which cost Steve hours of community service, had a positive result, however: It sparked a good deal of religious conversations on the floor among Jews, Christians, and Hindus.

Along with interactions with college peers, my course of study offered opportunities for learning about the world. I majored in political science and minored in history while pursuing a high school social studies teaching certificate. I took some introductory classes in international relations, world history, sociology, and anthropology. The ideas and readings interested me immensely as I was constantly being exposed to new information. Professors and students who were passionate about world study from various academic perspectives left a positive impression on me and reinforced my own interests in the world. I enjoyed the wide-ranging discussions, from the split caused by the Cold War, the political and military battlefield of Vietnam, the political history of the Soviet Union, and the cultural variety of humankind. I remember feeling intellectually alive and amazed at the connections that I encountered between disciplines.

My experiences as an undergraduate in the school of education were overwhelmingly positive. Many of my peers were not the least bit interested in their education classes, viewing them as a distraction from the "important stuff," or content, they would have to know as a teacher. I found education courses to be a refreshing change, as they addressed larger issues that cut across disciplines and reinforced my developing understanding of the seamless web of knowledge. I felt at home academically, as someone interested in knowing more about the interconnectedness of the world but not wanting to be limited to one discipline's construction of knowing. Social studies education courses in particular allowed the generalist in me to thrive.

Hunterdon Central High School in Flemington, New Jersey hired me to teach a new required course entitled *Comparative World Studies* that appealed to my inclinations toward being a generalist. The course of study comprised four units: Tradition and Change, Global Security, International Human Rights, and the Global Environmental Challenge. The course caused me alarm and excitement. The wide range of topics that I would now be responsible for was overwhelming. Though I had formal learning in some of these areas, I lacked depth in all of the topics. About 2 weeks before school began, I panicked. After a month of immersing myself in reading for the course and 2 weeks of preservice preparation offered by the high school, I still felt woefully inadequate.

I was offered another high school teaching position where I would be assigned classes in U.S. government and history. I seriously considered walking away from the challenge and seeking a position teaching U.S. history in another high school. Over lunch with Bill Fernekes, my new supervisor and gifted mentor, I expressed my earnest anxiety. He offered comfort, saying, "You don't need to know everything; your conceptual background in social studies will pull you through." I did not agree at the time, but I later found this to be sage advice.

I quickly enrolled in a graduate program with global education as a preliminary focus. The blend of content and pedagogy that I had only just tasted as an undergraduate was again my emphasis. I sought professors and specialists in various regions, with a particular emphasis on African studies. The coursework coupled with the rigors of daily teaching helped to refine my own thinking about world teaching. But it was a daily struggle, trying to guide my students in constructing meaning about a world that seemed so distant to them, as it had seemed to me as a child.

I assumed that students in Flemington, from families that were much wealthier and cosmopolitan than my own upbringing in Millville two decades before, would be open to global study. I quickly learned that we are all to some degree parochial, regardless of economic status; we all live in our own Millvilles. Many students resented having to take the new "world course," complaining that it did not matter to them what was happening in an African country. It seemed that their parents had not insisted they eat their vegetables for the Biafran kids nor were most of them going home to play spin the globe.

I tried two approaches to influence their views about world study, which met with varying degrees of failure. First, I tried to force them to be open-minded about the world. The paradox in this approach is all too apparent to me now, but there seemed to be no other way as a new teacher. During my first year, the Jewish high holy days of autumn came. The experiences of my freshman year of college echoed freshly in my mind, when a student said mockingly, "Yeah, it's that Jew holiday today … damn Jews!" to the laughter of his peers. I remember my response as if it happened yesterday: "That is the type of thinking that allowed the Holocaust to happen and I won't tolerate it in this class!" The class fell silent and the young man bowed his head in embarrassment. I felt righteous that I had "stamped out prejudice," soon to realize the folly in this thinking. I ruined a teachable moment with my righteousness and the class ceased to be about learning, denigrating into a test of wills between students and their teacher.

After repeated attempts and failures using the zero-tolerance approach to student misconceptions, stereotypes, and outright bigotry, 2 years later I employed a different tact. When students made disparaging remarks about "Others," I turned them into potential inquiries for the class. Kyle, a disaffected student with an antiglobal ax to grind, quickly served me notice that studying Africa was not for him. "I don't care about crazy Africans in tribes and I don't want to study this crap! Why do we have to study this stuff anyway?!" Instead of shouting him down, I tried a new way: Kyle's question would become a focal point of our inquiry. I asked the students to brainstorm possible reasons why they, or anyone, would benefit from studying Africa.

Their responses were enlightening. Students wrote about the possibility of visiting or working in an African nation someday, the specter of an African war with U.S. involvement (as the conflict in Somalia later fulfilled), the economic interdependence of the world, particularly the resources located in Africa, and even the fundamental value of humans regardless of national origin. Their responses ranged on a continuum from self-interest to human interest. What was most important for me, however, was the direction of the class. Unlike the class 2 years previously, it was an open dialogue of inquiry rather than a punitive, adversarial climate. I encouraged more conversation rather than compelling students to engage in the types of conversation that I would have liked them to have. Kyle was to some degree validated, and although I doubt he ever pursued a career as an African anthropologist, he was more amenable to the course as a result of our dialogue.

Lengthy discussions with students and parents about why global education is important were a regular part of my rookie teaching experience. Not only was I scrambling to find adequate materials with which to teach and teaching myself along the way, I was often asked to defend specific lessons and, at times, the course of study. I remember a parent expressing her misgivings that her son was being exposed to ideas about how other people in the world lived. I asked her why that idea was troubling. She said that the world beyond the United States was really irrelevant and a waste of time to study. American isolationism, something I had studied in the abstract in international relations courses in college, was tangible in my classroom and the larger community.

Parochialism is a state of mind that can be reshaped through global experiences, which I tried to offer my students. Working with Jennifer Peck, an idealistic colleague and friend, we started an international exchange with a high school from St. Petersburg, Russia. This experience offered a firsthand look at another society and shaped my worldview profoundly. I came back from a month of living in Russia ebullient and overflowing with stories of everyday life in the former Soviet Union, and 15 pounds lighter due to the food shortages in the new Russian market economy. I saw the effect that the exchange had on my students as well as myself, as they returned home with a new perspective about the Other, as well as themselves.

This experience, and many others as a classroom teacher, convinced me that global education is a lifelong process. I continually sought professional growth opportunities in my quest to become more globally educated. It was and remains a daunting challenge. As my interest in African studies grew, I located a summer study program that would help enrich my knowledge and experience. I found the Maryknoll Institute for African Studies, based at Tangaza College in Nairobi, Kenya. There I took classes for a month and engaged in a preliminary field study on education in Nairobi. I returned to school, excited about my experiences, sharing them with students and teachers alike. The resulting interest was so great that teachers urged me to form a tour group, and so I did, returning with teachers and students to Kenya in the summer of 1999.

I found traveling to be a great resource for teaching about the world. A unit of *Comparative World Studies* focuses on the global environmental challenge. An important topic in this unit is that of tropical and temperate deforestation. As we talked about the wonder of these fragile, interdependent systems, I felt drawn to a firsthand study of a rainforest region. I joined a group of fellow teachers in the summer of 1998 and spent 2 weeks on a field-based rainforest program in Costa Rica. Guided by local naturalists and biologists, I was able to explore an enchanting natural resource that I previously only knew in text and film. I found firsthand experiences in different societies a great enhancement to my own teaching. Beyond the multimedia presentations and talks I developed on my travels, the anecdotes and examples that I could bring to the classroom literally mesmerized my students. Personally, I was gaining a more nuanced view of the complexity of our world and realizing how much I did not know in the process.

The study–travel experiences along with continuing coursework and professional development provided me the opportunity to write new courses of study in our high school. I worked with a dear friend and colleague, Nancy Bennett, in developing *Multicultural Studies* in 1994 and wrote *African Studies: Global Issues* in 1998 with the help of Africanist scholars Al Howard and Michael Kirwen. These new electives, along with the required course, *Comparative World Studies*, contributed as much to my own growth as a global learner as to my students. To say that I was a world traveler would be a gross overstatement, but I sought new experiences that left me confused yet curious.

In *Comparative World Studies,* my colleagues and I tried to raise student awareness about the situation of other people, despite some resistance from students and community members. We tried to inform them about their world by inviting guest speakers from various global situations, including a mother whose son was murdered during the civil unrest in Chile, a journalist who witnessed the Cambodian genocide and another who first broke the story about genocide in Bosnia, a student who survived the Bosnian war, a family of Nigerians recently immigrated to the United States, a Japanese businessperson, the wife of an American executed in Chile during the Pinochet military takeover, and an Indian couple who talked about their arranged marriage. Although we did not formally measure and/or study the effects of the class on students over the past decade, anecdotal evidence suggests that students were positively affected. Many students on returning from college pointed to *Comparative World Studies* as a vital part of their preparation to go beyond their small New Jersey suburb. I have had students go on to work with refugee relief in Eastern Europe, teach in South Africa, and work in the Peace Corps throughout the world.

What did I learn from teaching about the world? I discovered that learning begins through a conversation with one's students, starting with their experiences. The world is not something outside ourselves, a distant place far removed from our everyday lives; indeed, we are integrally connected to the global village. Students helped me to realize that I would be more effective if I tried to understand their thoughts and experiences and show how these apparently unique insights have a global dimension. I adopted Dewey's notion that learning begins with the experiences of the self. I also learned that most people live in their own Millvilles; their experiences tend to be locally oriented. This is not necessarily limiting, especially if one recognizes the local–global connections that abound. Some of my students and their parents, however, often treated the world beyond our community with disinterest and disdain, in spite of their economic position.

Parochialism is not a fatal disease; rather, it is an experiential perspective that can be altered. I tried to bring my students to new places in the world, figuratively and literally, to have them see the interconnections around them. I also learned that global study can be controversial and perplexing. Sorting through the tension between relativism and universalism in world study was, and continues to be, an intellectual challenge. I quickly realized that there were no easy formulas or pat answers for the complexities of world teaching. I needed to be a reflective thinker, or in Dewey's terms, "active, persistent and careful ..." (1910/1997, p. 6).

My voice has been the only one heard in the conversation thus far, a very limited monologue. This personal recounting was offered to make full disclosure about my experiences related to the study and to introduce my experiences relative to this study (Creswell, 1998, p. 202; Kvale, 1996, p. 242), but also for the reader to get a sense about how I came to write this book. Examining the thoughts and experiences of other global educators, however, will broaden, deepen, and enrich the story. It will allow the reader to converse and more fully understand how teachers and students come to know the world and themselves: how they engage in a conversation about the big blue marble.

I

Contexts

Much of early educational research was focused on a decontextualized understanding of pedagogy. Early scholars tried to limit the influence of certain variables, viewing those as extraneous detail that hampered a clear understanding of the intended focus. More recently, naturalistic educational scholars have made contextual issues a centerpiece of their work, recognizing that the complexity and elusiveness of context is of primary importance in understanding pedagogy as it occurs in diverse settings (Cornbleth, 1991). Context is an important consideration for ethnographers in particular, as it allows the reader to catch glimpses of dynamic situations and how factors interact differently in unique situations. Rather than extracting ideas and factors from a research setting to ascertain educational theorems or maxims, contextual matters, in their elusive complexity, become crucial elements in our emerging and tenuous understanding of phenomena.

Contexts can be historical, social, and/or economic (Creswell, 1998). Each of these factors will contribute to setting the stage for this study, as the first three chapters detail the history of global education, the global connectedness of New Jersey, its social and economic context of educational inequity, and a profile of the three diverse high schools studied herein. Tightening the contextual lens in chapter 3, we begin to see how the unique situations of each school directly affected the manner in which global curriculum was transacted.

1

Where in the World Have You Been? An Overview of Global Education

The earth's a big blue marble when you see it from out there
The sun and moon declare, Our beauty's very rare
We sing pretty much alike, Enjoy spring pretty much alike
Peace and love we all understand, And laughter we use the very same brand
Our differences, our problems from out there, There's not much trace
Our friendships they can place, While looking at the face
Of the big blue marble in space.

—Redwine
Big Blue Marble lyrics

Efforts to explore space had a profound effect on the human psyche, significantly shaping the way that we saw ourselves on the planet. For the first time in history, people were able to see the Earth as a whole, able to grasp its wonder, frailty, and oneness. *The Big Blue Marble* television program was premised on this image and the implications that lie in this reoriented perspective. The image of Earth floating in space allowed us to see ourselves as a single entity and elevated interest and concern for the planet we so evidently shared. Three decades after the image of the big blue marble was popularized, talk of living as one planet persists. The phrase *global village* has become clichéd, yet the extent of globalization is vast and real, for well and for ill. The food we eat, the clothing we wear, the air we breathe, the fuels we consume, and the media we watch are intertwined with global connections. The global village holds out the promise and peril of a shrinking, interconnected Earth and myriad outcomes that have and will continue to result.

BACKGROUND

World education has existed, in different forms, since Pliny's encyclopedic *Historia Naturalis* published in the first century of the Common Era. This work, which describes the presence of monsters in far-off lands, was mythology written as history that stood for 14 centuries (Willinsky, 1998, p. 23). Columbus' voyages, and a host of other explorers and colonizers in the period 1490–1600, produced an array of firsthand accounts of Others. Though skewed, biased, and contrived, these served as a foundation for world learning in the modern period. Philosophers attempted to organize the world analytically. Hegel, like many of his enlightenment contemporaries, made sense of the world categorically. There were those of the West who were of history, and the rest of the world ("Orientals" and Africans), "a world divided among people who live inside and outside history" (Willinsky, 1998, p. 119). Historical actors comprised (a) those who had agency and (b) those outside the boundaries of history, a-historical people, who were acted on.

Studying the world improved in the 20th century, although many of the issues raised regarding bias, distortion, and making the Other seem exotic and monstrous remained, only in subtler forms. Schools, colleges, and universities incorporated world study, such as world geography, international relations, world history, and Western Civilization, as curricular mainstays. Degrees began to be offered in many of these fields and academic departments were organized around these fields. The Cold War illustrated the real politick need for world study, as a means of insuring hegemony and control, knowing more about an "evil Other" that embodied our compulsive focus. Hegel's bifurcated world continued to have merit during the Cold War. The divide changed in the latter half of the 20th century, however, from "civilized/uncivilized" or "historical/ahistorical" to "emancipated/dominated."

Global education emerged in the late 1960s as a departure from the bleak traditions of world study, a nascent yet decidedly alternative curriculum. In November 1968, *Social Education* published a special issue entitled *International Education for the Twenty-first Century* including a "veritable 'who's who' of international educators" (Tucker, 1996, p. 47). While this collection of articles made reference to previous efforts to understand the world in a variety of educational venues, it suggested a commitment to education that was not so single-mindedly focused on the nation-state and one that recognized the significant global problems of the time that involved yet transcended Cold War calculus. Among the authors were scholars from a variety of disciplines: social psychology, economics, geography, political science, and international relations. Curiously absent were representatives from social studies education and curriculum/instruction scholars, although they soon joined the fold. This journal represented the first collection of global education scholarship in one forum, and arguably, the birth of the field.

Why did global education develop in the 1960s and from what did it originate? A variety of convergent phenomena contributed to the birth of this curriculum field. Beginning in the early part of the 20th century, there was a growing sense of oneness about the planet and its inhabitants. A number of events illustrated the lack of a world community during this past century, such as horrific genocides, devastating world wars, use and proliferation of weapons of mass destruction, and burgeoning human population growth. Institutions were established, many in direct response to these global problems, including the United Nations and countless subsidiary groups, tens of thousands of nongovernmental organizations, international covenants on human rights, treaties limiting weapons of mass destruction, and other agreements calling for a cessation of environmental degradation. Global education emerged against this wider backdrop as a means of preparing young people to live in an increasingly problematic and interconnected world.

Educational institutions and those who peopled them were increasingly attending to the global nature of problems, as "preparing young people to live creatively and cooperatively instead of destructively in this village is a major responsibility of schools" (Nesbitt, 1968, p. 637). Fuller (1969) offered a "manual" for the Spaceship Earth metaphor while Carson (1962) raised alarm over the use of pesticides in her book, *Silent Spring*. Ehrlich (1968) examined the effect of population growth on the planet and McLuhan (1964) coined the phrase *global village* to describe a shrinking planet inextricably linked by communications technology. This early global scholarship, emanating from a variety of academic disciplines, provided the initial thrust behind efforts to move education beyond parochial boundaries of the nation and toward understanding global systems and dynamics.

A much larger, socially diffuse phenomenon was also gaining symbolic popularity in the 1960s. The image of Earth from space had a profound effect on the human psyche, offering "a new view of our planet as a finite system, as one interconnected world" (Merryfield & White, 1996, p. 177). Never before had the planet and its inhabitants been so starkly cast as a single entity than by the image of Earth from space. This image, coupled with the emergent reality of global problems articulated by an interdisciplinary group of scholars, created a rich climate for developing global curriculum.

A comprehensive review of the global education literature has yet to be completed, and this chapter is not intended to fulfill this need. Rather, my goal is to review some of the major themes related to the development of global education over the past 30 years, as the title suggests, considering where the field has been. After examining various definitions of the field, I address six themes related to global education's development: (a) focus on teaching and learning, (b) controversy, (c) rethinking the nation, (d) cultural diversity, (e) civic action, and (f) empirical research about global education. Each theme reappears throughout the book many times in the conversations of teachers and students. This initial chapter provides a wide context for the book, designed to assist the reader in situating the conversations examined herein within the larger development of this vital curriculum field.

DEFINING GLOBAL EDUCATION

Global education scholars have grappled with the obtuse quality of the field since its inception and throughout its development (Anderson, 1968; Becker, 1968, 1982; Case, 1993; Kirkwood, 2001b; Kniep, 1987; Lamy, 1987). Lamy (1987) wrote, "Although global education is not constructed on the assumption of any single discipline, its advocates and practitioners are also struggling with these fundamental questions to define the scope and methods of this multidisciplinary approach to understanding" (p. 1). Global education is often described as an amalgamation, a new field emerging from various loci (e.g., international relations, cultural studies, environmental study, economics). The problem lies in how these boundaries are cast, what is included and omitted, from the field.

A multiplicity of definitions for global education have been offered and most are problematic in some respects. Perhaps it is the potential vastness of the field that makes a succinct yet inclusive definition elusive. Global education could arguably refer to the totality of human thought and action, although such an inclusive definition is unreasonable and meaningless. So what is global education? I have collected a variety of conceptualizations that have currency among scholars in the field. Although this set of definitions does not include all that have been offered since the 1960s, it captures those that are most widely cited in the literature.

As evident in Table 1.1, most of the scholars employed the "borrow and add" approach in developing a definition of the field. Case (1993) based his

TABLE 1.1

Definitions and Conceptualizations of Global Education

Author(s)/Year	*Definition/Conceptualization of Global Education*

Anderson (1968)	Development of students' understanding of …
	     the Earth as one planet
	     mankind as one species
	     international system as one system
	 The curriculum should develop students' capacity to …
	     develop world-mindedness
	     critically consume and process information
	     intellectually and emotionally cope with continuous
	        change
	     accept and cope with the realities of the human condition

Association for Supervision and Curriculum Development (ASCD-Anderson, Nicklas, & Crawford) (1994)	You are a human being. Your home is planet Earth. You are a citizen of a multicultural society. You live in an interrelated world. You need to learn, care, think, choose, and act to celebrate life on this planet and to meet global challenges.
Becker (1979)	Multiple levels of analysis of events (i.e. individuals, nation-state, international organizations) Interdependence Individual involvement Concern for the well being of all humanity Interactions between humans and the environment

Case (1993)	Substantive and Perceptual Dimensions
	 Substantive dimension includes …
	     universal and cultural values
	     global interconnections
	     contemporary worldwide concerns
	     origins and patterns of worldwide affairs
	 Perceptual dimension includes …
	     open-mindedness
	     anticipation of complexity
	     resistance to stereotyping
	     inclination to empathize
	     non-chauvinism

Hanvey (1976)	Five elements of a global perspective Perspective consciousness Knowledge of world conditions Cross-cultural awareness Knowledge of global dynamics Knowledge of alternatives
Heater (1984)	Knowledge about the world and mankind as a whole. Awareness of interrelatedness. Appreciation that people have rights and duties towards each other. Consciousness that one's own perspective on world issues is biased. Ability to view others and oneself empathetically.

continued on next page

TABLE 1.1 *(continued)*

Author(s)/Year	Definition/Conceptualization of Global Education
	Appreciation of others; sympathy for unfortunate, regard for achievement. Skills to critically engage mass information Ability to communicate cross-culturally without prejudice. Readiness to act in a responsible way to help resolve world problems.
Kniep (1986)	Global education as content knowledge Human values Global systems Global issues/problems Global history
Merryfield (1997)	Global education involves the study of … Human beliefs and values Global systems Global issues and problems Cross-cultural understanding Awareness of human choices Global history Acquisition of indigenous knowledge Development of analytical, evaluative, and participatory skills
National Council for the Social Studies (1981)	Teaching students about … Interconnections among cultures, species, and the planet "The purpose of global education is to develop in youth the knowledge, skills, and attitudes needed to live effectively in a world possessing limited natural resources and characterized by ethnic diversity, cultural pluralism, and increasing interdependence"

Pike and Selby (2000)	Uniting two strands of educational thought
	    worldmindedness
	    child-centeredness
	Across four dimensions of analysis
	    temporal
	    spatial
	    issues
	    inner

Reardon (1988)	Global citizenship Planetary stewardship Human relationship
Werner and Case (1997)	Four central themes … Interconnections Perspectivity Caring Alternatives

substantive and perceptual dimensions, especially the former, on the work of Kniep (1987) and Hanvey (1976), for example. Such a process of amalgamation is to be expected, although the potential downside is that global education can become a catch-all curriculum wherein everything fits. If that occurs, then global education may lose a cohesive structure that can be used to distinguish it from other fields. Popkewitz (1980) suggested that "global education" functions as a slogan, designed to create a mood with which people can affiliate particular pedagogical practices, rather than a tightly defined field: "I think I value global education, but I am mired in its linguistic confusion" (p. 303).

How global education is understood vis-à-vis other closely related fields demonstrates the need for greater conceptual clarity. Multicultural education is a closely related field that has had a similar historical development and shares some of the definitional ambiguities of global education (see Grant & Sleeter, 1998; Bennett, 2001). Merryfield (1996) argued, based on a narrative survey of multicultural and global educators, that although the areas are commonly separated in academia, practitioners are likely to make connections between these related fields. Whereas differences exist with regard to emphases, they could best be described as siblings or first cousins in pursuit of similar goals: preparing students to inherit an interconnected world that is complex and diverse.

Some of the more traditional forms of world study, by comparison, are cousins of a more distant variety, perhaps one or two times removed. World curricula that is more closely aligned with traditional disciplines, such as world history, world cultures, and world geography, lean away from an integrated approach, like global education, and toward a discipline-centered inquiry. For the world geographer, for example, issues of place, movement, region, and human–environment interactions take center stage, as world events are cast within this disciplinary framework. Among these different conceptions of global pedagogy, there is a "family likeness" and "family quarrels" as well (Richardson in Heater, 1984, p. 21).

At times scholars in traditional world studies and global education have tried to distance themselves from those in the other area. Woyach and Remy (1989) articulated five approaches to world study (world history, Western Civilization, historical cultures, world geography, and international relations) without ever using the phrase *global education*. Although both have written and been cited in global education, their act of omission is notable. McDougall (2001) similarly lamented the move toward a holistic study of the world when he speculated about the marginalization of world geography: "Is it because geography just seems passé in an era when communications technology, commerce, and ideas 'transcend boundaries' and make the earth a 'global village'?" (p. 12).

The question that lies just beneath the surface of efforts toward definitional clarity remains: To what extent should global education be tightly or loosely defined, exclusive or inclusive? Some have argued that greater uniformity would provide more credibility, particularly for teachers, policymakers, and the general public (Kniep, 1985, 1986; Lamy, 1990). Kniep (1985) asserted, "Until such extended descriptions (of practice) become part of the literature of global education, we will not have a full and convincing answer for those skeptics and uninitiated who ask: 'What is global education?'" (p. 31). Lamy (1990) argued, "The best way to avoid major controversy is to clearly define the substantive focus and the learning objectives of any interdisciplinary program" (p. 49).

Others have advocated a looser conceptualization of global education, seeing it as a potential asset in widening the field (Case, 1993; Tye, 1990). Case (1993) argued, "Loosely defined coalitions ... often permit otherwise disparate factions to ally in pursuit of common goals" (318). Werner and Case (1997) argued, for example, that global education need not exist as a separate curricular entity, but that it should be integrated throughout the existing courses of study. In a sense, a curriculum that examines interconnections, perspectivity, alternatives, and caring is, in fact, global education, instead of including "yet another addition to the crowded curriculum" (p. 192). A tight definition of the field, in this manner of thinking, is unnecessary, because it would permeate all aspects of the school and would not need to exist as a separate, discreet entity.

Still others have sought a middle ground, attempting to amalgamate the disparate elements of global education. "While schools use a great variety of labels to identify courses and units in intercultural studies ... the context for many of those programs increasingly recognizes that we are all members of a single species, living on a single planet and sharing a common fate" (Becker, 1979, p. 51). Kirkwood (2001b) similarly contended that differences in conceptions of the field are not substantive but idiosyncratic, allowing for amalgamation to be complementary rather than incongruous.

Perhaps an adequate definition of global education is unachievable, as it may be characterized as an essentially contested concept, or a conceptual disagreement where many make legitimate, reasonable claims about the nature of the concept. As Gallie (1964) explained, "There are disputes, centred [sic] on concepts which ... are perfectly genuine; which, although not resolvable by argument of any kind, are nevertheless sustained by perfectly respectable arguments and evidence" (p. 158). Case (personal communication, August 1, 2001) suggested that this concept can be applied to global education, wherein the differences that emanate from this disputed field are reasonable and potentially generative.

So what is global education for the purpose of this book? I define global education as a curriculum that seeks to prepare students to live in a progressively interconnected world where the study of human values, institutions, and behaviors are contextually examined through a pedagogical style that promotes critical engagement of complex, diverse information toward socially meaningful action. My task in this book is not to stipulate a definition and prove its merit, but to examine how teachers and students in classrooms interpret global education. I offer my own definition as a means of understanding how I interpret the data in this study, hoping that it raises questions and debate about the nature of global education rather than supplying a definitive answer to this ongoing puzzle. Although examining definitions and conceptualizations can be a worthwhile pursuit, global education takes shape in the real world of classrooms in the lives of teachers and students (Becker, 1982), and as such, receives the bulk of my attention in this book.

FOCUSING ON TEACHING AND LEARNING

Countless initiatives have been undertaken to engage students in global learning, only a small fraction of which is discussed herein. The critical point in this thematic overview is that global education has frequently been aligned with a style of constructivist pedagogy. Doolittle, Hicks, and Lee (2001) contended that three types of constructivism exist (radical, social, and cognitive), each with unique epistemological and ontological assumptions. With respect to this typology, global education is most often manifest as social constructivism, where the individual cannot come to know truth in an absolute way, but can learn socially constructed meanings through the lenses of language, culture, and context.

Most global educators advocate classroom change from traditional, rote pedagogy to constructive, multidisciplinary learning. Scholars argue this pedagogical shift is needed to prepare student skills and aptitudes for an increasingly interdependent world (Pike & Selby, 2000). In this type of global pedagogy, "learning is self-motivated and directed; focuses on aesthetic, moral, emotional, physical and spiritual needs of the learner as well as cognitive attainment; knowledge building entails a dynamic interaction between teachers, learners and multiple sources of information" (p. 143).

Constructivist pedagogy fits well with the broader principles of global education, as the field has and continues to be about transformation.

Hanvey (1976) asserted that in order for students to operate effectively in the new global village that they stood to inherit, a reorientation of perspective was required. This orientation entails:

> *Dimension 1*—Perspective Consciousness, asserting that a person's worldview is not universally shared and that others have worldviews that are profoundly different from one's own.
>
> *Dimension 2*—State of Planet Awareness, involving "getting into someone's head" and understanding their attitudes and behaviors from their perspective.
>
> *Dimension 3*—Cross-Cultural Awareness, related to the diversity of ideas and practices found in all of humanity.
>
> *Dimension 4*—Knowledge of a Global Dynamic, expressing the notion that the Earth is indeed an interconnected system.
>
> *Dimension 5*—Human Choices, suggesting that problems confront individuals and societies that they have the power to act on.

Anderson and Anderson (1979) offered a hypothetical glimpse of schoolwide curriculum globalization at a fictitious 21st-century high school that operationalizes Hanvey's principles.

> I took the opportunity to wander the school plant. I was particularly attracted to the photographic display along one of the hallways. The wall was lined with photos showing human faces, some revealing happiness and joy and others grief and sadness. The display ... was entitled "The Language of Smiles and Tears" and had been created by a student photography club. Later, I met Nobu and we proceeded to her world literature course. On this particular day, they were ending the section of the course that dealt with birth. One of the students had written a short essay dealing with similarities and differences in attitudes toward the birth of children revealed in the literature the students had read, and today the class discussed and criticized the young man's essay. (pp. 28–29)

Global education was created to be accessible to all students. Placing global education within the reach of many students was a significant transformation, as content of this nature (i.e., international studies) had previously been reserved for elite students who wanted positions in the foreign service (Kirkwood, 2001b). Until the 1960s, it was widely held among educators that students under the age of 16 were too young to grasp international matters (Heater, 1984, p. 11).

Little has been documented about how teachers began implementing global curricula in the 1970s. Keehn (1989) found only two states (Michigan and Utah) had a curricular mandate prior to 1980. King (1979) described efforts to introduce global content in Colorado, Connecticut, Illinois, and Maryland, including teacher exchange opportunities, the world in your community activities, and environmental education programs. He characterized the implementation at the end of the 1970s as uneven and sporadic, however, and lacking a national commitment. Weston (1975) suggested that educational institutions in the United States, elementary through university, were doing very little to address the global problems of the day. Konick (1979) pointed to the fact that, as of 1973, only 8% of teachers had a course whose primary foci was international matters. The few educators who were teaching about global problems, systems, and dynamics in the 1970s were associated with nongovernmental organizations like the Consortium on Peace, Research, Education and Development (COPRED).

Leading scholars in global education identified the lack of practical applications of extant theory at the end of the 1970s and collaborated to support "the teacher's central role in brining global perspectives to the classroom" (Remy, 1982, p. 154). Toward that end, *Theory into Practice* devoted an issue to examine implementation of global education in a variety of settings. Woyach and Remy (1982) discussed the Columbus in the World program, a global education curriculum based on the local–global connections in communities. Tucker (1982) described the Global Awareness Program he developed in Miami that established a network of teachers, pre-service teachers, and scholars to globalize curricula. Lamy (1982) described teacher education and material development at the Center for Teaching International Relations at the University of Denver.

Teacher education and professional development were needed to support the transition of theory to practice. Case, Merryfield, Pike, Selby, Tucker, Werner, and Wilson were (and some continue to be) actively involved in teacher education programs designed specifically for global educators. Merryfield, Jarchow, and Pickert's *Preparing Teachers to Teach Global Perspectives* (1997) provided specific suggestions about teacher education programs based on experiences working with teachers at The Ohio State University. Merryfield's contribution illustrated partnerships that can exist between teacher educators, teachers, and school districts in teaching for world-mindedness. At the close of the 1980s, 23 state legislatures required a version of global education for high school graduation (Becker, 1991). Global education was implemented in locally variant ways, as determined by school boards and their appointed curriculum directors, but it was clearly emerging as a centerpiece of curriculum change in a number of states. States that did implement global education often funded teacher in-service to support the initiative, and funding was set aside for material purchase at the local level (Keehn, 1989).

Canada, particularly in the past decade, has been very active in global education practice. Emerging in the early 1990s, the Canadian International Development Agency funded several global education projects, including university centers for global education (Werner & Case, 1997). Pike and Selby's program of the Ontario Institute for Studies in Education at the University of Toronto engages teachers, teacher educators, and preservice teachers in similar global education preparation. Their book, *Global Teacher, Global Learner* (1988), offered teachers hundreds of ideas to teach about the four dimensions of globality: spatial, temporal, issues, and inner. A more recent book by this scholarly duo, *In the Global Classroom: Volumes 1 & 2* (2000), thoroughly illustrates classroom practices that are world minded and child centered.

The transformative quality of global education may have also served as an impediment to wide implementation. In Keehn's (1989) survey of global education implementation in the United States, a recurrent theme in the state-by-state summaries is a lack of a unified definition, a lack of textbooks, and a lack of teacher preparation. Boston (1997) offered, "In spite of years of consistent messages about the importance of a global education at a policy level, most schools still fall short of providing a global education for their students" (p. 169). She indicated that the limited access to high quality curriculum materials remains a fundamental problem in the field with regard to curriculum change. Tye (1999), in his research of global education in 53 nations, found that the lack of teacher skills, training, and interest ranked as significant impediments to implementing global education.

Barriers to global education in the 1990s also included the development of curriculum standards and high-stakes assessment. As Kohn (1999) argued, "The current demand for tougher standards ... carries with it a bundle of assumptions about the proper role of schools" (p. 15). Despite these assumptions, many of which contradict empirically supported teaching and learning practice, a "remarkable consensus" has emerged regarding high-stakes assessment, resulting in winnowed curricular choices (p. 16). Virtually every educational system in the United States is currently operating under a standards and high-stakes assessment policy, where global education is either at the margins of what will be tested, and therefore learned, or nonexistent. What is increasingly evident in schools is trivial pursuit pedagogy, where "drilling and skilling" are the norm and success on standardized tests the goal (Anyon, 1997, 2001; Gaudelli, 2000).

Questions about what is actually happening in global classrooms have periodically arisen within the field. Becker (1982) contended that although teachers and schools throughout the United States had optimistically received general theory, little was known about the quality of what was occurring under the guise of global education. "There does seem to be a real quality problem in this field" (p. 233). Anderson (1982) further suggested, "There is a degree to which looking for global education in schools and classrooms can be likened to watching a classical magic show. That is, things are not necessarily what they appear to be" (p. 168). Anderson used an example of teaching about Japan in a way that promoted stereotypical thinking, making the Japanese seem exotic and disconnected from the rest of the planet.

Efforts have been made to detail more carefully how global education has been engaged in classrooms, although these have been far and few between. Merryfield (1998) examined teacher implementation of global education in a comprehensive study of experienced, novice, and preservice global teachers. She sought to address the need to understand how teachers and students engage global education. "Although there has been considerable rhetoric about the need for global education, little attention has been paid to how teachers are actually teaching about the world, its peoples, and global issues.... We know very little about what actually happens in globally-oriented classrooms" (p. 345).

CONTROVERSY

The lack of documentation about what happens in global classroom has contributed, at times, to misinterpretations of practice. Global education met a great deal of public criticism in the 1980s. In 1979, the U.S. Department of Education created a Task Force on Global Education to support this curriculum field. By 1986, however, support for global education by the federal government was rapidly waning. The Denver office of the U.S. Department of Education published a report titled "Blowing the Whistle on 'Global Education,'" accusing the field of being anti-American, one-sided, relativistic/nihilistic with regard to moral issues, and obsessed with promoting a redistributive economic world order. The inflammatory nature of Cunningham's remarks are illustrated here:

Most globalist curricular materials contain none of the crude anti-American polemics that characterized "new left" denunciations of the 1960's. They have matured into a subtle and sophisticated series of Socratically delivered doctrinal bromides that no longer directly assail the core beliefs and assumptions of our American heritage. They seek, instead, to ridicule our value system by suggesting that we relinquish our economic and political preeminence in the interest of some shadowy "global justice." Their worldview is utopian and pacifist. They are also redistributionists. Although they decry doctrinaire absolutes, they paradoxically strive to replace conventional morality—based on Judeo-Christian principles—with an eclectic, mystical ethos of their own concoction. Their self avowed objective is radical political change, and they intend to achieve it by turning students into activists. (Cunningham in Schukar, 1993, p. 53)

This controversial report was picked up by the mass media and Cunningham's vitriolic diatribe contributed to a "new, controversial image for global education" (Shukar, 1993, p. 53) that has not been completely shed.

The U.S. Department of Education controversy later involved the National Council for the Social Studies, who appointed an ad hoc committee to address the charges. The ad hoc committee found little evidence to support the allegations, although the damage in mainstream public opinion had clearly been done (Ad Hoc Committee, 1987). There were other attacks against global education in the 1980s, such as those against the Minnesota Global Education Coalition and the Iowa Department of Education (Shuckar, 1993). In the 1990s in Tavares, Florida, global education was again publicly attacked with the school board's decision to "recognize other cultures, but as inferior" (*New York Times*).

The shift toward recentering discourse on the nation state, because "conservative groups in the US, with more nationalistic and parochial worldviews see global education as undermining our national identity and as a challenge to our society" was pronounced (Lamy, 1987, p. 1). Lamy (1990) suggested that any curriculum that does not espouse the view that the United States is "the primary world leader and the sole representative of what is good in the international community" will be a source of controversy (p. 54).

The following commentaries excerpted from Keehn (1989) illustrate the nature of the opposition in various states:

- There is strong opposition to "global" education from fundamentalists in the state so it is called international education. (Wyoming) (p. 32)
- There is a negative feeling about global education in the state because it is felt that it distracts from teaching about America. (Texas) (p. 28)
- Global education is a concept of the left. (Alabama) (p. 1)

The public controversy spawned by Cunningham's U.S. Department of Education report created a climate of wariness among curriculum authors. As U.S. Secretary of Education William Bennett's comment illuminates, "When I hear 'geography' and 'history' I am pleased: when I hear 'global perspectives' I'm usually a little nervous" (Rothman, 1987, p. 16). Conservatives saw global education as an affront to "American curricula" and part of the left-wing agenda for social change.

The *New Jersey World History/World Cultures Curriculum Guide* (1988) curriculum framework, which is the focal point of the study reported on in this book, illustrates leeriness about global education even among its advocates. The framework is based heavily on global education's thematic emphasis (human rights, population growth, cultural diversity, peace study, resource exploitation) and cites scholars such as Kniep and Becker. The curriculum guide is titled, however, "World History/Cultures" to avoid the negative publicity surrounding global education in the late 1980s.

RETHINKING THE NATION

Scholars have argued that the term *international,* in comparison to the term *global,* is limiting, failing to capture the interconnections of nongovernmental organizations, tourism, corporations, and individuals (Anderson, 1968; Becker, 1979; Boulding, 1968; Diaz, Massialas, & Xanthopoulus,1999; Kirkwood, 2001a; Tye & Tye, 1992). "From the vantage point of the moon, the facts are so clear that it should not be too difficult to organize a whole curriculum around the concept of the Earth as a total system" (Boulding, 1968, p. 650). Global education theorists generally fall short of advocating world federalism, but they have argued that the nation-state system is an inherently limited construct (Alger, 1968; Boulding, 1968). Despite its limitations, others have noted the controversial nature of examining issues from a global perspective: "The decision to select teaching material on the basis of a global rather than a national perspectives is itself a controversial judgment about priorities" (Heater, 1984, p. 20).

National loyalties have served as "analytical blinders" in understanding the world, especially in the case of "big nations" like the United States (Alger, 1968). Global educators, particularly in the United States, struggle with the tensions between national and world loyalty. "The strong moral tone of the United States foreign policy objectives appears to generate an extreme self-righteousness that inhibits detached evaluation of United State performance by its citizens" (Alger, 1968, p. 658). Global educators were essentially arguing against a simplified, normative discourse about the world, one rooted in the nation-state system. They hoped that global education could problematize assumptions about Others and the world, thereby removing, or at least limiting, the analytical blinder of the big nation.

The extent to which we are a world of nations, a world nation, or a combination of the two resonated throughout the development of the field and remains with us today. Attempting to realign the national–global discourse caused a great deal of hostility toward global education. The controversy of the 1980s was due in large part to a growing sense among conservatives that global education was an "anti-American" curriculum, challenging the superordinate role of the nation-state in curricular formulations. Global education may have been "toned down" to placate nationally oriented policymakers. Parker, Grossman, Kubow, Kurth-Schai, and Nakayama (1998) observed that reform efforts to "internationalize" or make curriculum more global often proceed in ways that are nation-bound (p. 135).

Can students simultaneously "wear different hats" when it comes to abiding national and global identity? Hahn (1984) argued that citizenship is multidimensional and that students can be prepared for this reality if they are given time to address ethical dilemmas and learn from each other through dialogue. Torney (1979) found that students in late elementary school have the capacity to take on the perspective of others if given the opportunity to practice empathizing. Parker et al. (1998) suggested a deliberative curriculum aimed at developing a "global public" be instituted. Six key ideas, offered as questions, would frame the curriculum of schools preparing students for multidimensional citizenship: promoting equity and fairness, balancing privacy and free access to information, negotiating environmental protection, providing for population growth, developing universal values, and distributing power.

To what extent can students be expected to adopt a multidimensional notion of citizenship? Torney (1979) offered two potentially contrasting findings: (a) elementary students have developed a sense of national identity, yet (b) elementary students have the capacity to empathize with multiple perspectives, or "overcoming cognitive egocentrism" (p. 64). Students, if given an opportunity to examine their nation's role in the world, should be able to expand their national orientation and recognize their global place through an emergent empathetic capacity. Blankenship (1990) surmised from his empirical study that "students can simultaneously develop positive global and national attitudes" when they engage in dialogue in an open climate (p. 383). His study suggested that students developed increased senses of political efficacy, interest, and knowledge of global issues from increased exposure to these matters. Kubow, Grossman, and Ninomiya

(1998) argued that multidimensional citizenship may cause role conflicts and difficult individual choices, which can be resolved with a deliberative and reflective framework that allows students to understand their multidimensional identities and negotiate these boundaries (p. 123).

Despite emergent efforts in the field to recognize the multidimensional nature of civics, scholars have generally agreed that global education implementation has been nationally fixated (Hahn, 1984; Lamy, 1990; Parker et al., 1998; Pike, 2000). As Pike (2000) indicated, "The global education movement does not signal a globalization of education; rather it reflects the development of more globally-oriented models of national education" (71). Case (1993) argued that fostering national interests is desirable as long as these do not obscure global commitments. Contemporary scholars blame binary thinking for the perception that global education establishes an antagonistic citizenship model (Case, 1993; Diaz et al.,1999; Tye & Tye, 1992).

CULTURAL DIVERSITY

Human diversity is a core idea in global education and has received extensive attention among scholars, particularly of late (Alger, 1998; Begler, 1998; Bennett, 2001; Cushner, 1998, 1999; Merryfield, 1997, 2001; Wilson, 1982, 1985, 1993). Multicultural education, a curriculum field with parallel and intersecting purposes, theories, and research, has contributed much to our understanding of human diversity in educational contexts (Banks, 1996a; Davidson, 1996; Grant & Sleeter, 1998; Heath & McLaughlin, 1993; Ladson-Billings, 1994; Nieto, 1996; Ogbu, 1991, 1998; Tatum, 1999). Some have attempted to draw boundaries between global and multicultural education (Alladin in Pike, 2000; Diaz et al., 1999; Fain, 1988), whereas others have focused on the fundamental similarity and shared purposes of the fields (Merryfield, 1996; Popkewitz, 1980). Despite distinctions among the fields, there is ample room for overlap, cross-fertilization, and mutual support (Merryfield, 1996).

As interactions across identity boundaries increase, formal education is taking a larger role in addressing issues of diversity around the globe. Nations are grappling with educational policies that address "global" populations in various ways. Cushner (1998) offers findings from 13 national case studies, which yielded the following global commonalities: (a) tension over unity and pluralism, (b) withering of indigenous languages, (c) curriculum design that is restrictive and exclusive of diverse voices, (d) lack of teacher education in handling classroom diversity, (e) attention to multicultural issues viewed as national education priorities (pp. 355–365). Global and multicultural education are curriculum fields designed to prepare young people to live in a global society that is more culturally integrated than ever before, though little research has been done to evaluate their relative effectiveness in this regard.

Questions remain in global education about how to effectively study Others in ways that do not bifurcate any person or group of people from any other. Traditional world studies has been beset by a tendency to "divide the world," or put differently, to think of the world in categorical ways (i.e., developed/underdeveloped, Western/non-Western, Oriental/Occidental, North/South, etc.), whereas global and multicultural educators are attempting to move beyond this divisiveness. Willinsky (1998) poses the question succinctly: "What more will it take ... to break the colonizing hold of the other, especially when the other is, in some sense, oneself?" (p. 157). His answer to the question is that imperialism's legacy has and continues to profoundly shape education in the United States and elsewhere, implicitly informing what students' understandings of the world. As such, the influence of imperialism and colonialism needs to be made explicit as a part of how students learn to understand the world (p. 247). In a sense, Willinsky asserts that the imperial legacy is the manner in which we have all been taught to marginalize or ignore the experiences of countless Others, legitimizing a hegemonic discourse about cultural diversity.

Global education scholars, particularly Merryfield, are trying to move the center of discourse in the field away from a Cold War model that enshrined the U.S./Soviet conflict as all consuming, toward an integrated, multidimensional perspective. Merryfield (2001), borrowing from W. E. B. DuBois, argues that students need to develop a double-consciousness about themselves, or, "always looking at oneself through the eyes of the other" (DuBois in Merryfield, p.187). This coping skill, long engaged by African American students and other minority populations, allows students to see how others are perceiving them as a means of survival. A great deal is known about how identity shapes cultural interaction, communication, and learning (Allport, 1954/1979; Bennett, 1993; Merryfield, 2001; Phinney, 1989, 1990; Phinney & Rotheram, 1987). Global education scholars, however, have only recently connected their discourse to these inquiries and findings. The field can advance with regard to human diversity discourse, but it will need to reach out beyond itself to do so, in a manner similar to the work of some multicultural scholars. Wilson (1982, 1985, 1993) and Germain (1998) have contributed much to the diversity aspect of the field, documenting the work of teachers who bring the world into their classroom through their own global travel/living experiences. Wilson documents the teaching lives of those with extensive experience outside the United States along with people who spent years of service in the Peace Corps. She found students of these global educators reacted favorably to their teachers' efforts; as one student stated, "You learn more because it's the real thing" (p. 96). Germain (1998) generalizes from her study of worldly teachers, or those with extended experiences living in other societies, that "international study affected teachers in their personal and professional lives after they returned home ... they all changed their classroom pedagogy, curriculum, and emphasis to some extent" (p. 214).

CIVIC ACTION

Global education, from its very inception in the late 1960s and throughout its development, has centered on civic matters. Hanvey's (1976) model includes the realm of human choices, or the notion that people need to cooperatively work in societies and as a global community to address common concerns. The phrase "think globally, act locally" has achieved linguistic icon status. Though it is often invoked rhetorically with little "action" to speak of (Merryfield, 2001), the phrase captures the essence of global education efforts.

What does civic action mean? Engle and Ochoa (1988) suggest that civics has three core elements: membership, rights, and responsibilities. Global educators frequently refer to The Universal Declaration of Human Rights (UDHR-1948) and subsequent United Nations human rights conventions as a starting point for studying civic action, as the link between world citizenship and understanding human rights becomes increasingly apparent (Flowers, 1993). The United Nations has declared the period 1995–2004 as the Decade for Human Rights Education. As Shiman and Fernekes (1999) argued, human rights is integral to global education: "Responsibility and caring are core themes for the design of human rights education programs, as well as being essential dispositions for global citizenship" (p. 58).

The Convention on the Rights of the Child (CRC-1989) has demonstrated the importance of the rights of young people within this larger discourse. Teachers frequently use this as a means of drawing students into human rights inquiry, as the issues raised are most pertinent for young people. The CRC includes four broad categories of rights: survival, development, protection, and participation (Pike & Selby, 2000, p. 81). Participation rights are generally those that give rise to student action projects. UNICEF recently opened a web page to facilitate dialogue about what types of action projects in which students can be involved that promote the children's rights globally.

Human rights education has taken an increasingly prominent role, both within global education and as a distinct field over the past decade. Literature in both fields suggests having students examine rights in their own contexts, as schools tend to be rights/responsibility-oriented environments. "The immediate arena for human rights action is the school itself. All schools subscribe to the general ethos of human rights. However, they do not always support this ethos in their relationships and daily organisation [*sic*]" (Cunningham in Pike & Selby, 1988, p. 227).

Global education scholars generally advocate student activism, although evidence suggests that implementation is episodic at best. Diaz et al. (1999) suggested linking students with international agencies and learning from global media sources as a means of promoting activism (p. 197). Pike and Selby (1988) recommended action within the local global paradigm. Their suggestions include teaching language to foreign residents, encouraging local media to provide programs for foreign residents, and setting up a UN club (pp. 222–223).

Global education scholars have also urged teachers and students to explore activism options within the nongovernmental organization (NGO) structure. Boulding (1988) suggested that student involvement in NGO activity can have long-lasting effects on both the world and the individual: "INGO (International ...) activity, such as local ecological and nuclear free-zone projects, very specifically enable people to feel they can participate in the grassroots reshaping the world" (p. 41). Boulding contended there are many people already actively involved in global civic action who can serve as models for students, but she admitted that the process of learning new civic behaviors will take a great deal of time (p. 156). Practicable suggestions for global activism, save few exceptions, are scant in the literature.

Global educators generally agree that civic education is integral to the field. The rationale for activism is generally articulated in this manner: As the Earth becomes increasingly more diverse and interconnected, students need to take a more active role in shaping a just and equitable social order. Some have raised cautions about avoiding indoctrinating youth by presenting them with limited options for action and narrow discourse that does not allow students to reach their own conclusions (Case, 1993).

Defining *activism* is somewhat contentious in the field, as some regard this literally whereas others construe activism as a reflective reorientation of the individual. Case (1993) and Merryfield (2001) seemed less concerned with activism, *per se*, than they were with action that changes the perception of the individual. Case (1993) refers to this change as the perceptual dimension, or "various intellectual values, dispositions, and attitudes that distinguish a parochial perspective ... from a broad-minded perspective" (p. 320). Similarly, Merryfield (2001) talked about action as "sustained and reflective cross-cultural learning" that places individuals in different positions of power than to which they are accustomed (pp. 192–193). She urged global educators to move beyond the empty rhetoric of teaching students to work with diverse people, and engage them experientially and reflectively in these processes.

EMPIRICAL EVIDENCE ABOUT GLOBAL EDUCATION

A great deal of educational theory and practice has emerged since the birth of global education in the 1960s. But what do we know about the effectiveness of this curriculum area? Surprisingly little is known about the effectiveness of global education in helping students to better understand the world (Johnston & Ochoa, 1993, p. 64; Torney-Purta, 1989, p. 209). Due to the broad nature of global education, a variety of studies could arguably be considered part of the field's literature (critical theory, teacher reflection, pedagogical content knowledge/beliefs, cognitive development studies; see Johnston and Ochoa, 1993). In this last section of this chapter, I briefly review some of the empirical studies directly applicable to global education.

Examining the effects of global education courses on student learning has been the primary focus of Torney-Purta's work. In a study on the effect of global education on a sample of approximately 1,155 students from International Baccalaureate (I.B.) schools and internationally oriented schools in nine geographically diverse states (Torney-Purta, 1985), students were given a test that measured world knowledge (global awareness) and world attitudes (global concern) in an experiment/control group fashion, the former being exposed to global education curricula explicitly. A step-wise multiple regression of student scores identified the following variables as the greatest predictors of global awareness: grade point average, reading and/or watching international news, being male, taking more social studies courses, and traveling abroad (p. 20). Similarly, the greatest predictors of global concern were reading and watching international news and grade point average. Torney-Purta (1985) concluded:

> The results of the survey suggest that some programs falling under the general category of global education do make a positive contribution to the global awareness and concern of secondary school students. The effective programs appear to be those which have been established for several years, those which combine curricular with extra-curricular activities, and those which have stressed teacher training. (pp. 23–24)

This research extends Torney-Purta, Oppenheim, and Farnen's (summarized in Torney, 1977) International Association for Evaluation of Educational Attainment's (IEA) Civic Education survey conducted in nine countries involving a survey of 30,000 students. Ireland, Israel, and the United States were more likely to discuss national over international issues, whereas students in Finland, the Netherlands, and Sweden were oppositely inclined (p. 12). This study also found that on measures of democratic values and interest in political participation, scores were highest among students who attended classes where open discussions occurred in open and welcoming atmospheres.

The interaction of class climate and content/attitude acquisition has also been studied in the United States. Blankenship (1990) examined the interaction of classroom climate and global knowledge, attitudes, and civic dispositions. Sampling 202 students in a global education course without a control group, he found that "there was a moderate positive relationship between classroom climate and student global knowledge, global attitudes, and political attitudes" (p. 378). Students who described their classroom climate as more open and flexible demonstrated higher scores in these three categories than those who were in classes that were "less open."

Teachers in various stages of preparation have also been studied in global education. Merryfield (1998) engaged a qualitative observation–interview protocol with 60 participants over 6 years to understand teacher decision making related to global education. Those lacking a strong global education background still recognized the primacy of culture, the need to connect global content to students' lives, and the need to make these connections across time and space. Exemplary global educators employed all of these guiding theories, but added a more sophisticated dimension to their pedagogy. This group of teachers was more likely to teach about global injustices and U.S. hegemony, provide cross-cultural experiential learning, use themes or issues to organize global content, emphasize higher-order thinking and skill development, and employ a greater variety of teaching strategies.

Research has also been done that focuses on the professional development of teachers related to global education. Vulliamy and Webb (1993) examined in-service education and the national curriculum in the United Kingdom. Using in-depth interview data from 26 teachers who participated in a Diploma course in Global and Multicultural Education (DIGAME), they explored how educators negotiated the implementation of a national curriculum. They found that although teachers expected pedagogies such as cooperative learning, problem solving, investigative work, discussion, and self-evaluation would be undermined by national curriculum, most were able to maintain progressive forms of pedagogy (p. 38). The researchers also found that global education was new to many of the in-service teachers, and although they easily adopted constructivist pedagogy, they were generally unable to grasp the holistic, content-orientation of the field.

How teachers respond to efforts to make curriculum more global has been a mainstay of empirical research in the field. Tye and Tye (1992) created the Center for Human Interdependence (CHI) at Chapman College in southern California to provide teachers with the types of global materials that they most needed in their classrooms. Noting that "the resource question is a serious one for the global education movement," the researchers gave teachers an opportunity to engage in dialogue about their pedagogy and seek materials to support instruction (p. 77). CHI was designed to infuse existing curricula with global perspectives, rather than create an entirely new course. Whereas some of the teachers transformed their pedagogy significantly as a result of the grant program, others refused to participate, avoided the program, began and later withdrew, and/or participated selectively.

A number of other studies related to global education could be described here if space and the reader's attention were unlimited (see Barnes, Stallings, & Rivner, 1981; Bickmore, 1999; Germain, 1998; Grant et al., 2001; Hasan, 2000; Schukar, 1993; Torney, 1979; Torney-Purta, 1982; Tye, 1999; Wade, 1994; Wilson, 2001). It bears reiterating that global education has generally lacked a firm empirical foundation through much of its curricular history. A number of areas that deserve attention, such as how teachers negotiate the national–global divide, how school culture and context shapes global teaching and learning, how global educators and their students engage controversial issues, and how students and teachers explore identity vis-à-vis a global curriculum, are developed herein. Although the current effort does not fill all of the gaps in what we know about global education, I hope it provides a meaningful contribution to the existing knowledge about what occurs when teachers and students engage global pedagogy.

CONCLUSION

Reviewing a complex, emergent, and diverse field such as global education is a challenging, but necessary, task. I have briefly discussed definitions and conceptualizations of the field and addressed six themes: (a) focus on teaching and learning, (b) controversy, (c) rethinking the nation, (d) cultural diversity, (e) civic action, and (f) empirical research. The task is necessary as it opens the conversation about global education, addressing issues that are central to this book. Focusing on teaching and learning is present in all of the chapters to some degree, but most evident in chapters 3 through 8. The controversial nature of global education is emphasized in chapter 5, "Opening Pandora's Box: Cultural Relativism in Global Education." Reexamining nation-states and nationalism takes center stage in chapter 4, "Global Education as Anti-American Curriculum?" and chapter 9, "A New Way to the World: Global Times, Global Citizens." Cultural diversity is a recurrent theme in the book, but most prevalently examined in chapter 6, "Conversations About Our Houses of Mumbi: Identity in Global Education." Civic activism is encountered in chapter 9, "A New Way to the World: Global Times, Global Citizens." Empirical findings are cited throughout the book to ground the findings of this qualitative study.

As we begin the journey and conversation of this book, I am reminded of Tatum's (1999) analogy about this type of effort: "Writing a book is a little like putting a note in a bottle and casting it out to sea. You have no idea where or when it will land, who will receive it, or what impact it will have" (p. ix). As an experienced practitioner but a relative newcomer to academic circles, I feel much the same way. The rich and detailed conversations of the teachers and students in this study, and my ongoing commentary, are what I have inscribed in my bottle. I am glad you have uncorked it, and hope you find it engaging, provocative, and informative.

Three Schools at the International Crossroads of New Jersey

There's so much diversity in this school we like to call it the international crossroads high school.
—Mrs. Brandy, Sunny Brook High School

New Jersey has been the brunt of jokes for time immemorial. Aspersions such as "You're from New Jersey? Which exit?" and the like are common-place. A student from Florida, after hearing that a small population of Japanese internees during World War II were relocated to New Jersey, quipped, "So that's how they were punished!" A man from Wyoming whom I met explained that he had been to New Jersey once and left weary because "everyone was in so much of a hurry, I felt like a rat in a maze."

A stereotypical image of the state suggests an overcrowded, hyperdeveloped, urban landscape, crisscrossed by superhighways rising over swampy marshlands. Although this may be an apt description of some areas, those familiar with New Jersey offer a more diverse portrayal. From the suburban sprawl of the north, central, and west, to the rural expanses and pine forests of the south, from the rocky ridges of the northwest to the coastal plains of the Atlantic seaboard, New Jersey is geographically diverse. It is also remarkably integrated into the global village.

The purpose of this chapter is to provide a wide context for the conversations about global education that follow; specifically, the state, its educational system, and schools in which the research was conducted. My purpose in detailing these contexts is threefold: to argue that New Jersey is an excellent "laboratory" for studying globalization due to its globally integrated nature; to illustrate the economic, and therefore, educational gulfs that exist within the state; and to provide the reader with a vivid image of the three different high schools examined in the research. Through this examination of context, the reader will better understand the conversations of the teachers and students about global education and consider how they may or may not apply to various teaching and learning situations.

GLOBAL NEW JERSEY

What social and economic factors demonstrate the extent to which a state is globally integrated? The obvious place to begin is the origin of the people living in the state, or population diversity. New Jersey is the most densely populated state in the United States, with 8.4 million people living in an area of only 7,419 square miles, or approximately 1,134 per square mile (U.S. Census Bureau, 2000). In comparison, the national average for population density is less than one tenth of New Jersey, with 77 people per square mile. A significant number of New Jerseyans, 1.2 million or 15% of the population, are born outside the United States. Additionally, 33.2% of New Jerseyans are themselves born outside the United States or have parents who are immigrants (Wu, 1997). One out of three people living in New Jersey have direct ties to somewhere else in the global village. These figures do not include the large number of New Jersey residents of African American lineage (13%) and early 20th-century European immigrants who peopled New Jersey after processing through the Immigration and Naturalization Center at Ellis Island.

The largest number of immigrants in New Jersey (51%, or one of every two immigrants) is from Latin American countries. Asian-born persons represent 33.5% of the immigrant population, second only to California in the highest population of Asian-born immigrants. Indians make up a substantial portion of that population, particularly in communities like Edison, often referred to as Little India, due to its dense Indian population. An Internet web page called *NJ India* provides voluminous information about Indian merchants in New Jersey, from jewelers to realtors, as well as links to Indian newspapers and information about cultural events in the state. Only four other states (California, New York, Florida, and Texas) have greater immigrant populations (Wu, 1997). New Jersey and New York have a long history of giving refuge to immigrants that dates back to the middle of the 19th century.

New Jersey remains a portal for immigrants due to its proximity to two of the largest international airports in the United States, John F. Kennedy International and Newark International. The difference today is the "huddled masses" now disembark airplanes rather than ships and many are not poor and unskilled laborers like those in earlier waves of immigrants. Since 1980, most of New Jersey's population growth has been due to immigration from outside the United States. Immigrant influx has more than offset the domestic migration out of New Jersey over the same period (Wu, 1997). The pattern is clear: People immigrate to New Jersey from other nations and a substantial portion of native-born New Jerseyans migrate to other states.

New Jersey is also a leader in international travel and trade. Newark International Airport is one of the nation's busiest and has a steadily increasing number of international air travelers. In 1999, 7.7 million international passengers traveled through Newark Airport, roughly one fourth of all air passengers handled there, along with 242,000 tons of international freight, or one fifth of all air cargo (Newark International Airport). The Port of Newark, situated just a few miles from the airport, also is central to New Jersey's global place. Two major shipping lines, Maersk and Sea-Land, are involved in international shipping and represent about $3 billion annually to the regional economy along with an estimated 56,000 jobs (Lavelle, 1999). Secaucus-based Goya foods, a major producer of ethnic food products and large employer, receives the bulk of their products from Spain, Latin America, China, and the Caribbean through the Port of Newark via these shipping lines (Lavelle, 1999). Although these shipping lines have threatened to pull out of New Jersey, they remain, representing a direct pipeline of global commerce in the state.

Former Governor Whitman optimistically trumpeted economic globalization, stating "New Jersey is the eighth largest economy in the United States. We are the fifth leading state in foreign investment, and we are the ninth leading state in exports, with nearly $22 billion in goods exported in 1997, a 12% increase over 1996…. We have used trade to expand our role in the global economy" (Whitman, March 3, 1999). International economic integration has become increasingly commonplace in the state, as New Jersey capitalizes on its geographic location, proximity to the financial capital of New York City, and history of being a global player. As the bridge that connects New Jersey's capital, Trenton, to Morrisville, Pennsylvania, indicates, "Trenton makes, the world takes!" Although this may not be true in terms of manufactured goods today, the spirit of New Jersey's global connections is as true now as ever before.

GLOBAL CURRICULUM

The *New Jersey World History/World Cultures Curriculum Guide* (hereafter, *NJWHWC 1988*) offers economic globalization as a central reason why global education is needed in the state:

> New Jersey is highly industrialized and heavily involved in international commerce. Many national and multinational corporations have their headquarters here; ... thousands of businessmen and women are regularly involved with international trade. This global work perspective creates a demand for a highly educated work force familiar with different cultures. (New Jersey Department of Education, 1988, p. 2)

The *NJWHWC 1988*, written by a team of authors in the late 1980s, was the Department of Education's response to the increasingly global nature of the state. The guide was written at the tail end of widespread implementation of global curricula in the 1980s. Becker and Kniep, leading global education theorists at the time, are frequently cited as the guide uses existing social studies discipline structures and offers themes that unite these distinct academic frameworks.

Local control is a significant concern in New Jersey, as more than 600 decentralized school districts have authority to select text and resource materials, determine curriculum, implement instructional strategies, and fund curriculum initiatives. The recent ballyhoo about New Jersey's failure to teach about the Founding Fathers illustrates a lack of understanding outside the state about the manner in which curriculum is designed and implemented (Sorokin, 2002). In social studies, for example, whereas the state provides a broad, conceptual outline to organize content, the decision about what will be taught rests with local districts. Clearly, New Jersey social studies teachers are engaging study of the Founding Fathers. The Revolutionary Period is unmistakably present in New Jersey. Trenton, Princeton, New Brunswick, and Morristown and other key sites embody this past involvement. The uproar about omitting the Founding Fathers was created by a lack of information among outspoken critics about the curriculum development process in the state. Local control is deeply institutionalized in New Jersey education.

Global education is implemented in a similar fashion, giving school districts significant latitude in shaping how the course of study would be implemented. The *NJWHWC 1988* offers a range of options about how districts might infuse global content, from a fairly traditional world history approach to a course about contemporary global issues. Other options include world cultures, world geography, and international relations, each with a different, yet related, body of content knowledge and assumptions about how the world should be taught. Ferreting out the differences among the various approaches to global education falls beyond the scope of this book (see Woyach & Remy, 1989). Although there is disagreement within global education about what constitutes such a course of study (see chap. 1), the similarities far outweigh the differences (Becker, 1979). The courses, like the ones studied in this research, might have labels that suggest significantly different approaches, such as *World History*, *Contemporary World Issues*, and *World Cultures*. In terms of classroom practice, however, the issues that confront teachers and students in world pedagogy, which are developed in detail in chapters 3 through 6, are remarkably similar.

The backdrop of social and economic global integration, and the curriculum reform that accompany these changes, are foundational to understanding the context of this study. At least two other elements are necessary in establishing a basis for the conversation about global education that follows: the educational system in New Jersey and the three high schools that participated in the study.

TWO NEW JERSEYS: ONE RICH, ONE POOR

Chief Justice Wilentz of the New Jersey Supreme Court, while adjudicating school funding cases, asserted that there are two New Jerseys: one rich and one poor. This is a highly problematic situation in a state where educational funding is generally fixed by local property values and the New Jersey Constitution guarantees that the state must afford each child a "thorough and efficient education" (New Jersey Constitution, 1947/1998, article VIII, section 4, paragraph 1). The problem of unequal school funding is litigated first and legislated second in New Jersey, as in most other states with educational funding problems. In *Robinson v. Cahill* (1976), the New Jersey Supreme Court mandated the legislature to rectify both the funding disparities and the educational content in order to meet the constitutional requirement.

The legislature took a minimalist approach in addressing both needs. The state offered poor school districts "minimum basic aid" in an effort to solve the funding disparities and minimum basic skills instruction with regard to curriculum offerings (Anyon, 1997, pp.136–137). Both initiatives failed to accomplish their intended goals and were later deemed inadequate by the supreme court in *Abbot v. Burke* (1990). Chief Justice Wilentz offered this summary in the opinion of the court: "We find that under the present system the evidence compels but one conclusion: the poorer the district and the greater its need, the less the money available, and the worse the education" (p. 4).

In *Abbot* v. *Burke* (1990), the old system of property tax valuations as a means for establishing educational funding levels was declared unconstitutional. The Supreme Court recognized the municipal overburden that already saddled urban dwellers with high taxes to pay for services unique to cities (i.e., public transportation, full-time fire personnel, and larger police forces; pp. 97–100). The expectation that urban, rural, and suburban districts could be treated the same fiscally, an assertion made in the 1980s by Commissioner of Education Saul Cooperman, was rejected by the Court. The Supreme Court again called for a new funding system wherein (a) funding parity had to be guaranteed by the state in spite of local property value differences and (b) additional funds needed to be available for urban students with special educational needs (*Abbott v. Burke*, 1990, pp. 143–147). The Supreme Court soundly rejected the notion that a minimal education was acceptable for urban kids and unacceptable for their peers in the suburbs. "Thorough and efficient" was interpreted to mean for every child with a high degree of quality.

The New Jersey legislature adopted a $2.8 billion tax package under Governor James Florio to address the court's remedy. This legislation, dubbed the Quality Education Act, was passed in 1990 by a Democratically controlled legislature and signed into law by a Democratic governor. The tax increase was directly aimed at increasing school funding for what came to be known as the "Urban 30," or those districts that were deemed "special needs" by the state. The reaction to the tax increase was vitriolic and fierce, as citizens complained that they were already over-taxed and that this was just another financial burden in a time of a national economic downturn. The legislature responded to the widespread protests by ratcheting down the tax increase to $800 million in what came to be known as the Quality Education Act II (QEA II). This subdued increase had little effect in righting the educational funding debacle in the state and was again found unconstitutional by the Supreme Court in *Abbott v. Burke* (1994). In this decision, the Court charged the legislature to "eliminate the 16.05% relative funding disparity in regular educational expenditures between the wealthiest districts and the poor urban districts" in three school years (1995–1998; Anyon, 1997, p. 146).

The next phase of this saga occurred in the mid-1990s with the passage of the Comprehensive Educational Improvement and Financing Act. Though there was talk of amending the New Jersey constitution to remove the "thorough and efficient" requirement, this was widely viewed as too cynical and counterproductive. Instead, the state developed a common core curriculum that moved well beyond the minimum skills approach of the 1970s, a dollar figure as to what was needed to have all students succeed in this core curriculum, and a broad-based, high-stakes assessment to measure student learning. This funding and curriculum reform was based entirely on a homogenized, hypothetical model school district (Anyon, 1997, p. 147).

In essence, the state was attempting to meet "thorough and efficient" not through the court-mandated requirement of an overhaul of the school funding formula, but by redefining the phrase. Governor Whitman indicated, "We very frankly said we are not looking for parity in spending" (Sciarra in Anyon, 1997). In 1997, the Supreme Court found this approach unconstitutional again, yet the policy continues to be implemented. It often seems in these controversial educational policy disputes that the students are overlooked, especially those currently being educated in a system that is admittedly dysfunctional. As the late Marilyn Morheuser of Education Law Center asserted, "For the sake of the plaintiff children who have 'already waited too long' ... the Abbott II remedy must be enforced" (Plaintiffs Trial Brief, p. 2)

One might ask what place this policy discussion, albeit brief, has in a book addressing global curricula. In order to understand the data drawn from the three high schools, one needs to be aware of the social and economic realities that these teachers and students face daily. These schools truly represent a comparison of apples and oranges, of rich and poor. The schools described in the next section are best understood in the context of the history of inequality that exists in New Jersey's educational system.

In selecting the three schools for this study, I tried to represent the diversity of New Jersey and the socioeconomic realities of its education system.[1] I located a rural school in the south, an urban/inner city school in the north, and a suburban school in the central region of the state. It would have been easier to visit three wealthy, suburban high schools in northern New Jersey, where teachers are adequately supplied with resources, children come prepared to learn, and globalization is an appealing intellectual pursuit. Instead, I engaged conversations about global education in Bart, an inner city high school in northern New Jersey, and Valley, a rural high school in the far southern part of the state. Both are Urban 30 schools, situated in communities where significant social and economic hurdles thwart their children. To demonstrate the contrast of the two New Jerseys, one rich and one poor, I in-

---

[1] The appendix, Methodology, offers more details about site selection and research processes.

cluded one typically suburban high school in central New Jersey, Sunny Brook. These three schools, illustrating the range of New Jersey's educational and economic spectrum, proved to be rich sites for understanding how teachers and students uniquely engage global education.

THREE HIGH SCHOOLS AT THE
INTERNATIONAL CROSSROADS

I contacted approximately 15 high schools and sought permission to conduct the research. I explained in the letter of introduction that the site visits would be extensive and that students, teachers, and curriculum planners in their version of the state-mandated global education course would be asked to participate. I received affirmative replies from Bart High School, Valley High School, and Sunny Brook High School.[2]

The surroundings of the three high schools in this study are indicative of the broader category that each represents: urban, rural, and suburban. High-rise apartment buildings, row homes, an urban park, and an old medieval-style cathedral surround Bart High School. The school is accessible to major highways, a light rail line, and the city bus system. Valley High School is situated at the edge of sprawling farms, orchards, and forested land on the outskirts of a small city. Sunny Brook High School is located on a country road across from a new housing development under construction and about one mile away from a massive, new condominium complex.

Table 2.1 illustrates relevant demographic data of the three communities.

Bart High School is, in many respects, a typical inner-city school. It has a majority Latino population (55%) with a significant African American population (35%), making it somewhat unusual within Urbana because the majority of people in this city are African Americans. The neighborhood is served by frequent bus and light rail service, which I regularly used to acclimate myself to the neighborhood of the school. There is only one working entrance to the school, which is constantly monitored by security personnel. All of the other points of entry are locked as a means of controlling those who enter and leave the building at all times. I was required to show identification and check in each day at Bart. After visiting for more than 2 months, I was not recognized by security. Bart is a place that is uninviting to

---

[2]All of the names of places and people used in this study are fictional to preserve the anonymity of the participants.

TABLE 2.1

Demographic Data

Demographic Data	Urbana Bart H.S.		Farmers' Knoll Valley H.S.		Developmenta Sunny Brook H.S.	
Population (1996)	268,510		55,906		30,716	
Ethnicity	African Am.	60%	White	49%	White	70%
	Latino	26%	Latino	24%	Asian	10%
	Asian, White		African Am.	11%	African Am.	7%
	other	14%	Asian, other	16%	Latino, other	13%
Per Capita Income	$9,424		$12,963		$21,881	
Median Family Income	$25,816		$35,361		$59,264	
College Graduates	5%		8%		23%	
Receiving Public Aid	7%		2%		>.004%	
Persons in Poverty	70,702 (26%)		5,739 (10%)		757 (.02%)	

Note. Data complied from *The New Jersey Municipal Data Book*. Edith R. Hornor (Ed.), Palo Alto, CA: Information Publications. The community names and schools are pseudonyms to protect the privacy of study participants.

enter with a distinct impersonality, a school that feels more like entering an institution of confinement than a place of learning.

A daily ritual at Bart is the intake of students. Students line up each morning to be processed through large metal detectors, enduring this procedure with a matter-of-fact disposition. On my first visit to the school with the district supervisor Mr. Dale, a good friend from a previous partnership, seemed a bit embarrassed as we witnessed this ritual. He explained with a chagrin, "Unfortunately, this is necessary here." Mr. Dale, like many of the teachers at Bart, seemed resigned to the fact that the family situations and larger context of the school undermined their best efforts trying to help these children.

Bart was permeated by a palpable atmosphere of coercion, apathy, and disruption. Students milled in the hallways long after the late bells, recognizing the unwritten rule that you still had 5 to 10 minutes to go to class after the bell. Administrators and teachers tried in vain to get students into their assigned classrooms, coaxing and, at times, threatening them to move. Their actions seemed futile, however, as in many of the classes that I observed, most students did not participate in lessons. When there were worksheets or readings to be completed, a surprising number of the students complied, but their assignments were treated as mere distractions from socializing with friends and listening to music.

During 2 months of research at the school, there were numerous fights inside and outside of the building, during the school day, and immediately following. Student-to-student aggression was a fairly frequent occurrence, manifested in verbal threats, insults in the hallways and classrooms, and physical taunts. During one classroom observation, a female student approached a male student, threatening to attack him for a remark he made. This situation was significant enough to cause the teacher to leave the room and seek administrative support. I periodically witnessed administrators running through the halls to stop disruptions or avert violence. One day a student sprayed the upper hallway with mace. One of the students I interviewed explained that some students did this in hopes of canceling school for the day. Students and staff choked and coughed through the remainder of the day and many were absent the following day due to lingering side effects.

Bart High School, as part of a large, urban school system, implemented the global education mandate in the form of a world history course. *World History* has been in place for over 9 years in the Urbana district and the district supervisor is currently seeking to revamp the course. Urbana is moving toward a world cultures approach, which they began piloting while I conducted research. The rationale for the change, offered by Mr. Dale, was the need to expose urban kids to the diversity of humanity that is increasingly evident in our shrinking planet. Although he thought that goal could be accomplished in *World History,* he felt the *World Cultures* class would be a better way of achieving this goal as it had the potential to focus on social history and contemporary ways of life.

Mr. Dale and the teachers lamented the isolation of their students and thought *World Cultures* was critical in opening them to different lifestyles. I conducted the study in all of the *World History* classes and in the pilot *World Cultures* class. All of these classes were taught to ninth graders, who were generally 13 or 14 years old. Many of the students, however, were taking the course at age 18 or 19 due to course failure and/or school transfers, both common occurrences at Bart.

Teachers and administrators were noticeably wary of my presence in the first two weeks of observations. I was introduced to one of the vice principals and was berated by her for being an outsider who "couldn't possibly understand what it was like to be a teacher in an urban school," who, she added, were the only "real teachers." When I explained that I would be spending 2 months to engage the research, she was somewhat comforted, but remained standoffish. Soon thereafter, as I was working in the social studies office, the business education supervisor entered the room and said, "Who's that?!" gesturing toward me. When the social studies supervisor explained my purpose, the business supervisor said, "Watch him! It's like when you let the government in.... You hold onto your pockets!"

After a few days, the wariness subsided and I was thoroughly engaged in daily life at Bart and my research. All four of the *World History/World Culture* teachers at Bart willingly participated in the research. After the first month, two participants grew somewhat frustrated by repeated requests to observe classes and participate in interviews, so I decided to focus more intently on the two remaining teachers along with the students.

In traveling between the city of Bart and the community of Valley in one day, as I once did, I got the sense that I was in two entirely different places. Driving south on Route 206 to southern New Jersey, one passes large tracts of undeveloped land, some fallow, others filled with crops, and still others with cattle grazing. Passing miles of seemingly endless pinelands with lakes and campsites scattered throughout is a reminder of New Jersey's rural diversity. The rural, bucolic atmosphere of the southern part of New Jersey is a world away from the urban landscape of Urbana. Farmers' Knoll is a fairly isolated community characteristic of the southern region as a whole. Many residents of the northern part of New Jersey have not been to Farmers' Knoll and some are even vaguely familiar with this rural locale. The social and economic isolation of southern New Jersey from the remainder of the state has been the source of tension in the past, as state residents voted 2 decades ago in a nonbinding referendum their desire to divide into two states, north and south.

Despite the pleasant isolation of Valley High School, it is by no means immune to some of the same social ills facing Bart. Valley lacked a check-in desk, metal detector, or strictly enforced procedure for visitors, but had five security guards in the building to assist administrators and teachers. Students were generally cooperative and abided by school expectations for behavior, but there were notable transgressions during my 7 weeks at the site. In one incident, two boys fought ferociously, to the point that one was left unconscious and had to be taken to the hospital via an ambulance. The intensity of the violence was similar to Bart, but the frequency of violence at Valley was noticeably less.

The tragic murders at Columbine High School in Colorado took place in April of 1999 during my fieldwork at Valley High School. Students and teachers were clearly upset by this event, as there were conversations in all classes observed that day and in the faculty workroom. Later in the week, I arrived in the morning to find the building surrounded by police and fire officials. A bomb threat was called into the school that morning, forcing the school to be closed, an incident repeated in many communities across the country in the weeks following the murders in Littleton, Colorado. Despite a feeling of isolation from the world beyond Farmers' Knoll, the repercussions of the events in Littleton served as reminders that no community is truly isolated.

Teachers and students at Valley were very receptive to the idea of participating in research. Mrs. Dilley, a dynamic, intelligent, and well-connected social studies supervisor, led the district, which has a long tradition of being at the forefront of educational innovations. Valley was permeated by a deep and abiding sense of purpose, specifically in regard to teaching about diversity and global connections. The teachers and administrators acknowledged the fact that many of their students were considered "at risk," but they maintained high academic standards and a strong professional commitment within this context. Valley did not suffer from the malaise that permeated Bart, despite their similar student populations and low socioeconomic condition of the larger communities.

While Bart and Valley represent the poor half of New Jersey, Sunny Brook is clearly representative of the rich half of the state. Sunny Brook High School sits amid large-scale housing developments, just a few miles from a major New Jersey highway. Farmland has been converted in large tracts to build new, modern, expensive housing for this quintessential bedroom suburb. Developmenta is a rapidly expanding community, prompting school officials to begin their annual "Report to the Community" with the phrase, "Developmenta is growing. The challenge for the school district continues to be to provide space and programs for the expanding student population while promoting academic, athletic, and artistic excellence."

The growth of Developmenta led to the construction of the new Sunny Brook High School in 1997, which cost approximately $40 million. The facility impressed me with its size and quality. The school is well-equipped, bordering on opulent, with marble floors, a stone carving with the school emblem, and large glass atriums. The cafeteria is organized as a food court that rivals the choices found in some shopping malls. The atmosphere is generally welcoming, relaxed, and informal, but the architecture of the school is oddly corporate. Students were often seen milling about outside the cafeteria, conversing in the outdoor student courtyard, sitting on the floor during class presentations, and interacting with their teachers with an air of affable familiarity. In the 2 months of research at Sunny Brook, I observed no incidences of student violence or significant disruption. When I queried the department supervisor about behavior management, he said it simply was not an issue. There were security guards in this school, like the other two schools studied, but their main task appeared to be shepherding late students to class.

The walls were filled with ads for various activities, including international travel, band, class historian campaign posters, and intramural athletics, to name a few. I was struck by the ethnic diversity of Sunny Brook almost immediately on arrival. As Mrs. Brandy offered, Sunny Brook really looked like an international crossroads school, with so many students of Asian, Southeast Asian, and Latino origin. Sunny Brook is also linguistically diverse, with 21% of the students residing in homes where a language other than English is spoken. These languages include, in order of frequency, Spanish, Gujarati, Cantonese, Hindi, and Arabic. Sunny Brook mirrors the state as a whole with regard to its diversity, with significant Latino and Asian minority populations and a large number of immigrant students and/or immigrant parentage.

Sunny Brook places a great deal of emphasis on academic achievement. Students are offered a wide variety of Advanced Placement courses and these were highly enrolled. The school boasts about the number of students who go on to colleges, with over 80% of their graduates falling into this category. Sunny Brook employs a form of block scheduling. Students attend four 90-minute blocks each day, allowing more time for class activities and prolonged periods between class meetings for extended projects, reading, and writing. Students have a different schedule on A days and B days, alternating between the two throughout the school year. The inordinate emphasis on academic achievement that permeates the school is manifest in significant student competition.

CONCLUSION

The aim of this chapter is to establish a sound basis on which the remainder of the book rests. I have argued that New Jersey is situated at the forefront of globalization in many respects (travel, immigration, population diversity, economics, and international trade) and that it is an ideal location for research about globalizing curricula. I am not suggesting that the study reported on in this book would be inappropriate elsewhere; indeed, research offered by Merryfield (1998) in the context of Ohio, Tye and Tye (1992) related to California, Grant et al. (2001) regarding New York, and Wilson (2001) about Kentucky, significantly enhances our understanding of globalization's effect on teaching and learning throughout the United States.

I also suggest in this chapter that whereas attention to teaching and learning is important, the larger social and economic forces at work in communities should not be overlooked. To depict Bart, Valley, and Sunny Brook High Schools as equals, detached from the political and historical context of New Jersey's disparate and unjust educational system, misrepresents the realities of these schools. Rather, in establishing this educational context, I hope the reader has a clear sense that simply adding a course of study focused on globalization and diversity does not right the wrongs of educational malpractice that have existed in the state. Indeed, a "new course" may exacerbate existing problems. This is a much deeper problem that deserves continued attention and continues to have a profound effect on the lives of children currently in the system.

The remainder of the book focuses almost exclusively on global education and how it is engaged by the teachers and students at Bart, Valley, and Sunny Brook High Schools. How do the three high schools differ in their approaches to global education? What is shared among them? How do student-to-student and teacher-to-student interactions affect learning about the world? What instructional strategies are used and how do contextual factors such as statewide assessment affect teacher choice of methodology? These are the questions to which I now direct the reader's attention, through the conversations of the teachers and students who try to fit a global village into their classrooms.

3

How Can You Fit a Global Village in a Classroom?

The challenge ... is in conceptualizing and implementing a course that is easily taught, academically sound, and politically acceptable to both teachers and community groups.

—Becker (1991, p. 74)

Becker aptly described the reality of all curriculum innovations as the need to recognize the rich and varied contexts of schools and to work these changes into the milieu of the classroom. Teachers in all three schools were challenged and supported by the contexts in which they worked in various ways. Classroom disruptions, state assessments, student interactions, teacher/student relationships, and community values all contributed in complex ways to affect each classroom. I argue in this chapter that "the reconstruction of knowledge and experiences," or the curriculum, is significantly affected by contextual factors throughout the school community (Tanner & Tanner, 1995, p. 189).

Contextual concerns are of central importance due to the ideographic nature of schools: No two schools are alike. Some scholars have argued that there is a "deep structure" of schooling that make them fundamentally similar: classrooms, teachers, students, books, and so on (Tye & Tye, 1992); and yet each school is a unique setting for learning and teaching. The emphasis in this chapter is on the unique setting for pedagogy of the three high schools in this study. Emphasizing the "eye color" or "snowflake quality" of the schools, various factors related to context which make them like no other, the intent is to illuminate the manner in which these districts bring global learning to their students. I propose that "fitting" global curriculum into classrooms is a task that needs to be undertaken with keen attention to context. Only when contextual issues are recognized and addressed can teachers hope to effectively bring the world into their classrooms.

This analysis of contextual factors in global education is built on the work of other curriculum scholars. The popular notion that teaching can be reduced to a standard set of "teacher-proof" techniques applied the same everywhere, regardless of context, is a view widely rejected (Darling-Hammond, 1988; Evans, Newmann, & Saxe, 1996; McLaughlin, Talbert, & Bascia, 1990; Tanner & Tanner, 1995). Individual teachers working in particular contexts shape the quality and quantity of instruction. As Thornton (1991, 2001) has argued, teachers are curricular and instructional gatekeepers through which all pedagogical decisions ultimately flow. Teacher decision making, however, is contextually situated. "The decisions that teachers make about curriculum and instruction in social studies are heavily influenced by contextual factors such as school ethos" (1991, p. 238). Although Thornton recognizes the importance of contexts, he focuses on the role of teachers, with only passing reference to context due to a lack of data in the studies he reviews.

Researchers who ignore the role of teachers in shaping curriculum imperil the validity of educational scholarship, for it is in the classroom where the rubber of curriculum meets the proverbial road (Becker, 1982). Cornbleth (1991) notes that decontextualizing has been the norm in social studies research. McLaughlin and Talbert (1990) contend that a "bottom-up" perspective on teachers' work and workplace is most appropriate in articulating the "embedded contexts and … its contours and substance as *relevant to teachers*" (p.7; emphasis in original).

Teachers are vital players in curriculum construction, but they do not act in isolation from their institutional contexts. What is meant by the term *context* as it relates to this study? Although the history and socioeconomic factors of the schools described in chapter 2 are important, this is a limited lens for understanding schools. McLaughlin and Talbert (1990) defined contextual factors that transcend socioeconomic considerations as "department and school organization and culture, professional associations and networks, community educational values and norms …"(p. 2). These factors may be more difficult to accurately ascertain, but are as much a part of contextual considerations as socioeconomic realities. Teaching about the global village is rightly viewed as actively coconstructed by the thoughts and actions of teachers and students as they negotiate their environments.

Tightening the focus of the lens from the previous two chapters, here is an initial glimpse into global teaching and learning in each high school. In keeping with a more focused illustration of the schools, the data related to contextual issues are presented for each school independently. Although the overarching theme and method of this book is to synthesize all participant conversations, a narrower focus is appropriate on this particular issue because contextual issues are unique to each school studied. The analysis of data for each school is presented in three parts: (a) dominant modes of teaching and learning, (b) key elements of context that support these modes, and (c) students' reactions to the course of study. This chapter concludes with a brief synthesis of contextual issues among the three schools studied.

BART HIGH SCHOOL

Trivial Pursuit Pedagogy and Textbook Domination

Teaching and learning at Bart closely resembles what Goodlad (1984) found in many classrooms: "(Students are) engaged in a narrow range of classroom activities—listening to teachers, writing answers to questions, and taking tests and quizzes" (p. 124). Two excerpts from classroom observations illustrate typical instruction at Bart:

> (Observation) The activity for the day involved students working in their textbooks on the China unit test. Students were asked to use the textbook and do the main idea exercise to prepare for the test. Mr. Ingresso later told me that it didn't matter much what they wrote, as long as they have some answer down for the assignment, they would get credit. He explained to the class, "On page 306 ... now I'm not saying you're going to find all the answers, but some of them are there. Every one of those questions you answer, you get 3 points towards tomorrow's test. In fairness, I said that you could work in pairs. Now, at the end of the period, you hand it in to me."

> (Observation) Mr. Cortez[1] put objectives on the board and said, "Today's the last day we're working on Asia. There will be a test on Asia next week."Mr. Cortez then put five questions on the board:
>
> 1. List the social classes of feudal Japan in order.
> 2. Who were the Mongols? Where did they live?
> 3. Who conquered the land on page 302? How?

---

[1]Names preceded by a title (Ms., Mrs., or Mr.) refer to teachers, whereas first names only (e.g., Aya and Peter) refer to students throughout the text.

4. What are the three parts of the Chinese Dynastic Cycle?
5. What did Japan borrow from China?

As the teacher explained the questions he said, "Don't insert anything more than the question ... don't give me any extra." The class settled in and began copying the questions from the board. They responded in writing to the questions individually while Mr. Cortez circulated around the room making comments to students about their work and/or their behavior.

Bart students were frequently expected to work independently in their textbooks to identify the "faces and places" of various world societies. When I would ask to observe a teacher on a particular day, they would frequently say, "There's nothing going on in class today," which usually indicated students doing worksheets.

Textbooks dominated global teaching and learning at Bart. There were two textbooks used at Bart High School, *History and Life* (1990) and *World Cultures: A Global Mosaic* (1996), for the *World Cultures* pilot course. In Urbana, there was a district-wide directive that teachers should adhere strictly to textbooks, as evidenced by pacing schedules distributed by the central office showing correspondence between weeks of the school year and textbook chapters. Mr. Dale said:

The thing we're seeing now is with all the new texts, a tremendous amount of technology support, CD-ROM, laser discs, and that sort of thing. The ancillary materials are absolutely phenomenal! A teacher could walk into a world history/cultures class with no real knowledge and just use the book and the support material, and they could teach about the world!

Despite the reliance on textbooks, the dearth of books for students was a common problem. When teachers asked students to take out their texts for classwork, invariably some students would claim to have lost their text or left it at home. A few texts remained in the social studies office for borrowing early in the research period, but a month later, even the department office was completely out of textbooks.

Mr. Gordon, a veteran African American teacher, offered an explanation as to why textbooks were always missing:

It is cool to come to school with no books and leave without any books. You have kids here with two sets of books, a book in the locker they take to their class and they have some books home. They don't want anyone to see that they are taking books home and doing homework. It is sort of like a combination of this anti-intellectual thing and the reason why they are doing this is because they are saying, "I don't want to do that! That's the white man's thing!"

Most teachers resorted to having students leave texts in the classroom closet to insure availability every day, which made assigning homework impossible.

Global education at Bart High School could best be described as trivial pursuit pedagogy. Instruction was characterized by a ritualized busyness that emphasized vocabulary identification through repetitive drilling while ignoring value conflicts, uncertainty, and controversy (Hunt & Metcalf, 1968). Teaching about the world in this manner sterilizes curricula to the point that it is reduced to a mundane process of didactic teaching, student passivity, rote memorization, and frequent testing. Conceptual richness, diverse content, and inherent controversy that are embedded in global education are distilled out through trivial pursuit pedagogy. What remains is a pile of seemingly useless names, places, and dates.

Contextual Factors at Bart—Disruptions/Abusive Interactions and Statewide Assessments

What factors explain the preponderance of trivial pursuit pedagogy and passive textbook instruction at Bart? At least three contextual factors interacted in creating trivial pursuit pedagogy: disruptions, abusive interactions, and statewide assessments. Classrooms were regularly disrupted at Bart. Constant interruptions precipitated abusive interactions by teachers and students in an effort to gain control and assert power in Bart's highly charged atmosphere. This pattern justified the need for rote, restrictive classroom instruction so as to prevent an already unstable situation from getting further out of hand. The statewide assessment required for graduation was also used to validate trivial pursuit pedagogy. Teachers interpreted districtwide initiatives to raise test scores as a call to get back to basics and teach skills to raise students' scores.

Teachers and students at Bart consistently reported that issues of classroom management were more important than the course itself. Teachers expressed the notion that classroom management was superordinate and disconnected from the content of the class. Mrs. Lourdes, when asked about her goals for the class, stated:

> To keep the peace ... much of what we do here is not 100% content oriented, it is keeping a reign on the room ... the other day it just exploded in under three seconds. You have to deal with this and anticipate what is going to break out.

Mr. Cortez echoed this concern, "(In) urban education today, continuous interruption of the class is the norm. They expect it (disruptions) and they are ready. The second that it comes up, they add in their two cents!" Rarely did I observe a lesson that was not interrupted, either by student-to-student interactions or from outside the classroom. Aya explained, "Some of the kids don't even care about themselves, they take drugs and smoke ... they are like stray animals."

A notable exception to this pattern was Mr. Gordon, an African American male who apparently had a zero tolerance policy for disruptions. He would not allow late students to enter the class and was persistent and firm in reminding students of appropriate classroom behavior. Fewer than 9 of the 27 enrolled students regularly attended Mr. Gordon's class, however.

One observation of Mr. Cortez' class illustrates a severe outburst:

> A girl had received roses for Valentine's Day and Mr. Cortez was joking with her when a young Latino girl blurted out, "Fuck Valentine's Day!" to which an African American male student said, "That is why you lost your baby!" (referring to the girl's miscarriage at age 15). They began to yell about each other's weight, the boy saying, "You too skinny, girl, lookin' like 85 pounds," to which she retorted, "I'd rather be thin than a big fatty like you!" Mr. Cortez interrupted, "This is not a subway, this is a classroom, you go downtown to do that!" The teacher gave the two students yelling at each other a morning detention, which they immediately refused to serve. As the class grew more unruly and lost focus on the reading pyramid activity about Japanese society, four girls moved to the front to copy notes from the board. A Latino girl (a friend of the one who had allegedly miscarried) then began yelling at the African American male student across the room for the comment he made about her failed pregnancy. Mr. Cortez asked the boy to leave the room, which he refused to do. Mr. Cortez left the room in search of an administrator while the girl got up and physically confronted the boy. He stood up and shouted, "I don't fight girls, go get your brother!" and left the room screaming. Mr. Cortez returned, saying he would need to call security since the boy had apparently left the building. He continued the lesson.

Mr. Cortez spoke to me later that day about his attempts at intervening with this boy. He explained that although he was classified as emotionally disturbed, the student was not receiving the necessary in-class support to address this learning problem. Mr. Cortez' efforts to seek outside help for the child (summoning security and speaking to a school counselor) were in vain and the problem continued.

Students blamed each other for the woes of the school. As Irena explained, "The problem with this school is the students. They're the ones that don't want to learn, and want to be big and all high and mighty. If they were to send good kids, the school wouldn't be so bad." Aya explained the peer pressure to act out in school as a source of difficulty. "I have to fake it.

That's where I'm having problems in my life. I keep pretending to be bad. I don't want to be alone and isolated. I don't come out of school after 2:40 p.m. because there is all this rioting and fights and mobs and the police are always there."

Abusive teacher-to-student interactions were justified as the only way to stop interruptions, despite the repeated failure of this technique. These children, frequently the victims of abuse and neglect at home, found little solace in the schools. One day while walking in the hall, an administrator yelled at a student, "Get to class before I kick you in the head!" Mrs. Lourdes frequently made threatening comments to her students. "Day in, day out, coming in here (at) the end of the afternoon is torture!" and "Gentlemen, let me tell you something, everyday I give you an F and add up enough of them and I will fail the whole lot of you!" and "If I have to stop one more time, you have to go down with Mr. V!"

Going to see Mr. Vorosky was a typical punishment for students who would not behave in class. Mr. Vorosky, Bart's social studies department chair, would humiliate the students when they misbehaved. I observed one of his disciplinary sessions in the social studies office:

> You are a nuisance! The whole world's gotta stop because you've got to act stupid! I'm gonna throw you out (of school) again. I told you one time to cut it out, then you acted stupid all over again! Look at me! I'm sick and tired of talking to you, I don't want to see you! The next time, you're getting out of here and every week I'll throw you outta here. You don't want your mother coming here every week?! Keep your big mouth shut until you get outside and you can go and yell your fool head off! Keep your mouth shut!

Some of the teachers believed that the students had to be reprimanded in this manner for the punishment to have an impact. As Mrs. Lourdes said, "You have to threaten them or they won't do anything. That's what they listen to."

The students, however, tended to view teacher threats as idle. They continually witnessed the lack of follow-through. There was a laissez-faire, "Don't bother me, I won't bother you" interaction in many classroom observations. The number of students wearing headphones during teacher lectures and student work periods demonstrated this attitude. Mr. Ingresso would periodically ask the students to remove their CD players, but to no avail. The students seemed to understand that there were certain acceptable violations of student conduct rules, such as wearing headphones and arriving late to class, but other infractions, like fighting, that would be addressed. As Mr. Cortez explained, "You lose your credibility, there is no type of material consequences for their actions. They are back in your class day after day; so you have to adapt." The adaptation that most teachers chose was to make threats.

Metz (1990) found a similar urban environment in her study. The urban school she examined was a dilapidated, old building that lacked resources, professional growth opportunities for teachers, and was plagued by low student attendance and frequent disruptions. Teachers in her study responded with high absenteeism, reduced effort, low morale, and reduced job satisfaction. The conditions at Bart were much the same. I often had lunch with the teachers and listened to some calculate the number of sick days they had left and the number of weeks of school that remained. Teachers took regular sick days to shorten the workweek.

Trivial pursuit pedagogy and textbook dominance was also perpetuated and validated at Bart by the emphasis on the High School Proficiency Test/Assessment (HSPT/A). Teachers were expected to teach skills, such as finding the main idea and supporting details in a reading excerpt, on a weekly basis. Wednesday became HSPT/A day, as this tended to be the day of the week with the highest rate of student attendance. The teachers complied with this expectation, some defending the validity of a skills orientation. Mr. Cortez stated, "HSPT/A and A skills and lessons designed around a specific skill ... those are important. You have to be aware that as an urban teacher in 1999, the content is structured around the skills, not the other way."

Mr. Ingresso seemed less committed to skill-centered curriculum, saying, "Everything is done to pass the HSPT/A ... everything! The district told me that they want as many students as possible to pass that test, so I go with the flow!" He stressed that global education was "of little importance," but that the HSPT/A was the "real focus." Teachers generally felt "out of control" of the global curriculum at Bart, much like what has been found in research of other high-stakes test contexts (Kurfman, 1991).

The fact that only 12% of Bart students passed all three sections of the HSPT/A on the first try reinforced the widely held belief that this was an important goal for the school. When this statistic is compared to the state average of 75% and the state average of 37% for similar category schools (District Factor Groups), it becomes even more apparent that Bart High School has significant problems regarding academic achievement. Given the intervening factors of the school environment, however, the teachers clearly and understandably felt overwhelmed by the conditions under which they labored.

Bart's deleterious environment is especially problematic for global education. Carl Rogers, in *Freedom to Learn* (1969), contends that "learning which involves a change in self-organization—in the perception of one's self—is threatening and tends to be resisted" (p. 159). Global education places students in the awkward position of understanding themselves in an immense and complex world context. Students may feel overwhelmed by the complexity and novelty of global education. It is natural, according to Rogers, to resist learning about such a diverse area of study, an inherent problem in global curricula (Torney, 1979). Resistance is compounded at Bart by another of Rogers' learning principles: "Those learnings which are threatening to the self are more easily perceived and assimilated when external threats are at a minimum" (pp. 159–160). Bart's environment, as perceived by the teachers and students, maximizes rather than minimizes external threats. An unsafe and frequently chaotic environment does not lead to the openness required to thoughtfully encounter global learning.

Bart Students' Reactions to Global Education

Many students were remarkably positive about the class, despite their relative passivity in learning and the deleterious learning environment. Some indicated that they enjoyed the world course because they liked their teacher's style and efforts. The following are illustrative excerpts from student interviews:

> Mrs. Lourdes, she's great! She's down to Earth and she speaks truly to us and she tells us just like it is. She has no, umm, she puts it in words that we can understand. Like the Holocaust, she puts it plain and simple: Hitler didn't like them (Jews) so he killed them, instead of being like because of this and that, and this and that, blah, blah, blah, no. Hitler killed the Jews. That's all! I like the teacher.

> For me, that's interesting (*World History*), especially Europeans when they colonized, that's interesting. Europeans, they just a small, small continent and they took over a big piece of land, and you're like, "Hey, how did they do that?" You start to thinking. Mr. Cortez, he was talking about the Europeans and explorers and he was saying that colonization is one of those neat words to say they robbed, murdered, and stole. He talked about affairs (sexual) and stuff like that. Everybody was interested in that. Mr. Cortez, he's just plain, just tell you the facts. Mr. Cortez makes it easy.

The students that did enjoy class tended to be academically high achievers and the most actively involved in otherwise moribund classes.

All students did not agree as to the benefits of teachers' emphasizing factual content, however. The students were aware of the emphasis placed on memorization of content and some reacted negatively to this style of teaching. Noreda stated, "Memorization ... for me, ugh! You have to remember things that happened and what year, and then you know that it happened and you don't know the year (sounding frustrated)." Katherine added, "I don't like *World History*. I don't like to read and it is too complicated. I don't remember nothing." Students' reactions were commensurate with their grade performance, as one might suspect. Students who performed better in the class tended to like it more than those who performed poorly.

The students seemed unaware that there were methodologies other than teacher lectures. The students referred to "teacher talk" as synonymous with teaching. They did not mention other instructional strategies in their responses, probably because they had not been exposed to different modes of instruction. When I would ask a question about methodology, such as, "In what ways does the teacher present the material?" the students invariably interpreted this to mean, "How do you like the teacher?" or "What do you think of the textbook? The lectures?" and comment accordingly. The data indicate approbation for the teachers and their lecture-oriented, textbook-based methodology among high achievers and dislike among low achievers.

Students, like their teachers, were sensitive to the contextual issues that negatively affected the learning environment.

> Yeah ... you always thinking about violence ... everything is violence in your mind and school, just constantly, and you constantly think about it and you can't concentrate. It's so shocking! It is a constant struggle to concentrate.

> The biggest problem I think probably is the children who come here have such a negative attitude about coming to school. Seventy percent are here for the mere fact of socialization.

> The attitudes of the kids—disruptive, bad attitudes—they be cursing when they get mad.

> It's not a peaceful place (Bart). You can feel the tension. You know that it's there. Somebody got jumped. They took a boy from this school all the way to where I live and beat him with pipes from their basement. I guess they bored and don't have nothing to do.

Most students felt helpless in correcting these problems and seemed resigned to cope as best they could. Aya's comment about Bart not being a peaceful place is an unfortunately accurate description of the school. Bart's hostile environment hampered the teachers' creative abilities and undermined their effectiveness in making students more globally aware.

VALLEY HIGH SCHOOL

Interdisciplinary, Active Learning

Valley High teachers fit the global village into their classrooms by bringing down the walls, figuratively and literally. *World Cultures* classes were taught to ninth graders and linked with freshman English courses to facilitate interdisciplinary study. Classes met consecutively in adjacent rooms with retractable dividers and teachers frequently removed the wall to engage their students. Students would often come in before class and ask their co-teachers what they would be learning. There was a palpable air of excitement in their learning about the world that contrasted sharply with the atmosphere at Bart.

Mrs. Solotore was the most active in integrating the *World Cultures* curriculum across discipline boundaries. On first visiting her class, I observed she had students working in the library on a Medieval art interpretation project. She encouraged students to find the "facts" of the artwork, but to also dig a bit deeper. "Your conclusion will be your thoughts on the work. What do you think it means, do you like or dislike it and why? What could have been changed about the art?" As students studied the Holocaust in Mrs. Solotore's social studies class, they read Elie Weisel's *Night* in their English class. Mrs. Solotore expanded on the use of literature, "When we do Japan, she does Haiku, and we have more flexibility to do music, cultural foods, and take the kids on trips."

Teaching and learning was activity based at Valley, as compared to passive learning at Bart, as illustrated by the following observation of Mrs. Finberg's class.

> Today was Latino dancing day. Mrs. Finberg and her English co-teacher had arranged for a dance instructor to come in and do a workshop with the students on Latin American dancing. The room was opened in the middle so both of the classes could work together in the activity. Mrs. Finberg began class by taking attendance and checking to see if students had brought in their musical instruments. The students had a number of different home-made objects and some were wearing bright, colorful clothing for dancing. All of the desks were pushed away from the center of the room and the boys were lined up on one half of the room and girls on the opposite half. The instructor took over the class from Mrs. Finberg, explaining the influence of various cultures on the dancing which they would be engaging in today. She discussed the geographic origin of the dances, stating that the Rumba was from Cuba, the Meringue from the Dominican Republic, and the Cha-cha was actually created in the United States. She explained that the dances orig-

inated from old tribal dances that were changed over time as a result of people and cultures moving. The teacher moved students in and out of steps. There was a great deal of laughter in the room and all students were engaged in the activity. A few boys were showing off, clowning around by dancing with each other and screaming. The atmosphere of the room was one characterized by playful joy. Mrs. Finberg had prepared punch and Goya sodas for the students to drink, since it was one of the first days of spring and the room became very warm.

Global education teachers at Valley abided by a set of norms for effective teaching: learning about the world should be interdisciplinary, learning should be active, a diversity of global topics and cultures should be engaged, and positive, respectful student-to-teacher and student-to-student interactions are critical to the healthy functioning of the classroom. These qualities were embedded in most of what I observed at this rural high school, also an Urban 30/special needs district.

The curriculum guide makes explicit the tacit agreement of the teachers about methodology:

> A variety of teaching and assessment strategies, including cooperative learning, modified portfolios, and the use of technology, are used to accommodate the varying learning styles of the students, to help students develop higher level thinking, speaking and writing skills and to encourage creative approaches to problem solving.

Each of the 16 units in the course of study is accompanied by at least four suggestions for activities, such as creating Egyptian myths, tasting Japanese food, student interviews on Latino customs, and a field trip to the Vietnam Veterans Memorial in New Jersey. This pedagogy stands in marked contrast to the enrichment activities noted in the Bart High School course of study guide. The district chair, Mrs. Dilley, clearly stated her preference for active learning in the classroom:

> Well, I emphasize varying the teaching techniques ... (laughs) needless to say that the lecture/textbook turn to page 40 and do the responses is passé ... and most of them (the teachers) are trying different techniques, including the institution of technology. This is all virgin ground.

Some of the activity-based learning at Valley resembled superficial "diversity celebrations" that have been criticized in the multicultural literature (Grant & Sleeter, 1998). Although teachers made an effort to explain the context of the celebrations and rituals engaged, they did not do this in great depth.

Mr. Sidner prided himself on Internet projects that he created for each unit in the course. The projects each consisted of approximately 50 content questions for the students to find in a variety of recommended web pages. In discussing the projects, Mr. Sidner explained, "You can't deny that this is the direction for the future. I can see a day when the kids will each have a computer on their desk." When I queried him as to why there was such an emphasis on recall questions in this active learning strategy, he explained, "because these are general kids and they can't do the difficult stuff."

Mr. Sidner did not deny his general students the opportunity to learn experientially, however. During one observation, he had arranged for a colleague with a background in yoga to instruct his students in this practice. The teacher oriented the students to the philosophy of yoga as an illustration of Eastern spirituality, a noncompetitive orientation. She explained that "instead of 'no pain, no gain,' yoga is completely opposite, completely noncompetitive." The students were seated on the floor of a small auditorium, shoeless and in sweat clothes, as requested by Mr. Sidner. The instructor guided them through a series of deep breathing exercises and relaxation techniques before advancing through various stretching maneuvers. I noted in my field journal the serenity that enveloped the room in this 90-minute period and the high degree of attentiveness for a group of 14-year-old students.

I also traveled with Mr. Sidner's class for one of their fieldtrips to the Balch Institute for Ethnic Studies in Philadelphia. Mrs. Solotore and Mrs. Finberg were also taking their classes to the U.S. Holocaust Memorial Museum in Washington, DC, the same day. The Balch Institute offered students a brief introduction to cultural studies, a video on wedding rituals of Pakistani women, an exhibit about Southeast Asians in the United States, and an artifact display of early 20th-century immigration. The film about Pakistani women engaged their attention and the manipulative aspects of the Southeast Asian exhibit, especially the popular culture items like the Indian CD music, were popular with the students. We later traveled to South Philadelphia to visit and eat in the Italian market. This field trip illustrates the commitment of Valley High School to provide a variety of learning experiences for students to actively engage in their global education through their local community.

Contextual Factors at Valley—Prosocial Interactions and Administrative Support

What contextual factors were present at Valley that encouraged active student learning and interdisciplinary teaching? Students and teachers were remarkably prosocial in their interactions and relationships, a quality present in the formal and informal functioning of the school. Curriculum administrators at Valley, specifically Mrs. Dilley at the district level and Mr. Delatore at the building level, were highly supportive of risk taking on the part of their teachers and provided them with significant material and professional support to enhance instruction.

Prosocial interactions are defined herein as behaviors and communication that promote the well-being of individuals through mutually beneficial relationships in the culture of the school. Valley students and teachers, despite relative economic poverty in the community of Farmers' Knoll, interacted in a mutually and socially beneficial manner. Teachers indicated a sincere appreciation for their students, which manifested itself in a number of ways. Mrs. Solotore would refer to her students fondly as "honey" and "sweetheart." Mr. Sidner was often seen before and after class chatting with students about their plans for the weekend or activities outside of the classroom. Mrs. Finberg would often begin class with a phrase such as, "OK, my dear children, are you ready? Throw out gum, take a deep breath, sit up straight, and you will be pleasantly surprised at how bright you are!" The interactions between teachers and students at Valley had a distinctly positive tone, illustrating a mutual respect and genuine caring that existed. Valley students were recognized for their worth as people.

Classroom management was subsequently a peripheral issue at Valley in comparison to Bart. In the 16 classroom observations, only twice were classes interrupted by inappropriate student conduct. One involved a note being passed in Mr. Sidner's class, which he swiftly intercepted and effectively addressed, and the other in Mrs. Solotore's class, due to excessive student talking. The infrequent interruptions and sense of constructive progress of the classes was remarkable given the age group of the students (ninth grade) and the variety of activities in which they were engaged.

The atmosphere of caring and mutual respect fostered by the teachers at Valley seemed to carry over into student interactions as well. Mrs. Finberg had her students grade a quiz on African geography by exchanging papers. The absence of grade comparisons and chiding was noteworthy. A few students even congratulated one another on a job well done, as opposed to the competitive one-upmanship one would expect to see in this accelerated *World Cultures* class. When Mr. Sidner had students working in cooperative groups, it was clear that even these "general" students demonstrated leadership in the division of labor and set about the research task with a sense of cooperation.

In order to interview students, I had to find them in the cafeteria, because their lunch period was the only time they were accessible for interviews. I had difficulty finding students, as during observations I only saw them from behind. I was impressed with how students knew each other and how they would help me find interviewees. In this rather large 9-10 high school building of over 900 students, the students usually knew who I was asking about and could even tell me at which table they were seated.

Administrative support was another contextual factor that encouraged active learning and interdisciplinary global teaching at Valley. Mrs. Dilley was very active statewide in social studies education and served on the initial statewide social studies curriculum standards committee. Mrs. Dilley was a proactive administrator who identified problems and sought workable solutions to facilitate change. She identified a problem with elementary students not performing well in geography and published a book with her faculty about the history and culture of Farmers' Knoll, specifically designed to engage their students. She was thoughtful, enthusiastic, well-read, and professionally able. Mrs. Dilley also served as the curriculum supervisor for art in the district, which may explain in part her willingness to encourage interdisciplinary teaching in social studies.

Mr. Delatore, the building supervisor, periodically asked for material support from Mrs. Dilley, to which she complied readily. The intensity and sense of purpose that they shared about providing resources and support to their teachers was palpable. The summer prior to the research period, faculty who taught *World Cultures* spent 2 weeks sharing lesson materials, rethinking the course of study, and discussing how to integrate technology. Teachers were paid for this curriculum development work, further illustrating the professional commitment of the school.

Valley, as an Urban 30/Special Needs district like Bart, receives additional state funding to compensate for depressed property values and a weak tax base. Funding for special projects, such as curriculum development, field trips, and technology purchases, is generally available. All of the *World Cultures* students were given at least one field trip to enhance their global learning. Curriculum administrators secured funds for these trips because they valued active learning experiences. Mr. Delatore would often arrange for coverage of classes so teacher could share their areas of cultural expertise, such as teaching about yoga.

Valley Students' Reactions to Global Education

Most students seemed to genuinely appreciate the opportunity to learn about the world in a mutually respectful and caring atmosphere. Despite normal adolescent grousing about the quantity of homework and projects, students were generally positive about the class and the manner in which it was taught. The following comments illustrate this distinct student pattern:

> I like the *World Cultures* class a lot. I like the teachers and how you can combine the classes and you can have more people to work with instead of just one class.

> We do a lot of projects in the class with whatever we're doing. We usually have one research project a marking period. It's fun because we can read novels and have discussions. We have discussions all the time.

> We had a lady come in and explain to us the Spanish dances and culture. I really liked them, the activity, and I know the kids really liked them and I know for a fact that they learned something new.

The unanimity of positive student feedback was most striking. Even students who were currently failing the class or performing poorly claimed to enjoy the class. Valley students were indeed learning "something new" as they engaged the world in their classrooms. Valley teachers fit the global village into their classes in a manner that was active, integrative, and ultimately, engaging. Teachers were supported in their pedagogy by a context that fostered pro-social relationships and administrative support.

SUNNY BROOK HIGH SCHOOL

Individuality and Ability Grouping

Sunny Brook High School is an impressive, new building, rising three stories over sprawling acreage of suburban landscape. Its stone façade, rich marble flooring, and brightly hued lighting and walls create an ambiance of comfort and serenity. Inside the global education classrooms of Sunny Brook, the panoply of different faces reminds the visitor that you are in a place that the teachers affectionately refer to as "an international crossroads" school. Two phenomena characterize the overall thrust of global education at Sunny Brook: individuality and ability grouping.

A unique pattern found in Sunny Brook was the emphasis on the place of individuals as cultural representatives. I repeatedly noted during observations the tendency of teachers to emphasize specific historical and contemporary people as representatives of societies and/or time periods. These individuals were frequently characterized as either heroes or villains, as the following class observations illustrate.

Mrs. Gormley went on to explain that they are having these difficulties (civilian casualties in Kosovo) because they are trying to limit military casualties by using high altitude bombing with computer guided attacks. The boy with a strong Slavic accent than said, "Milosevic is not going to give up!" to which Mrs. Gormley replied, "The original goal is a good goal, you can't defend Milosevic, he's a horrible man and he's doing terrible things."

Mrs. Brandy's class was engaged in presentations on Latin American dictators today. The teacher looked around the room for a volunteer to go first, but no one volunteered. Mrs. Brandy then called on two girls to present on François "Papa Doc" Duvalier. The Chinese girl of the tandem had difficulty pronouncing his name, to which the teacher said "don't worry about how it is pronounced." The Egyptian girl said, "He was a horrible man, he was terrible to his people killing them and everything" in an excited manner. Mrs. Brandy said to her, "She's the cutest in the world!" Another group then presented on Pinochet of Chile. After their brief presentation, which lacked a depth of understanding of the events in Chile, Mrs. Brandy said, "He followed Allende. Why did the U.S. want him out of power and back Pinochet? He committed human rights violations too, but we backed Pinochet ... why? Because he (Pinochet) was an anti-communist!"

I queried the teachers as to their perception of focusing on individuals. They agreed that it was a dominant aspect of their pedagogy and offered a rationale for doing so. Mrs. Gormley, the unofficial leader of the group, said:

Individuals are different and they are more real, they are something that the kids can really latch onto. We do Latin America, the dictators, and they pick somebody to be, and my kids dressed up in costume, they had signs with Latin American dictators. I had enough to give everyone somebody to focus on, you have to give a speech as the character and get into the time period. It (focusing on individuals) gives you a broader scope, I guess, to deal with a range of issues.

Mrs. Gormley also assigned four book reports throughout the year, mostly biographies or autobiographies of exceptional people from the cultural groups studied, rather than the lives of average folk.

Emphasizing individuals in course content also seemed to bleed over into the emphasis on individual ability levels among students. Sunny Brook abided by sharp divisions in ability level grouping, with A (low), B (middle), and honors tracks. The apparent effort to disguise the tracks by inverting the letter order did little to hide the real differences in classroom approaches among the tracks. Three vignettes of classes in each track illustrate the different expectations in each track: honors literature circles, middle-level cooperative group research, and low-level book reports.

Honors students were expected to read and critique four books about various cultural representatives over the course of the year, whereas the A and B tracks were not required to do so. Literature discussions were frequent occurrences in the honors *Contemporary World Issues* class. Students were engaged in higher level thinking, analyzing the purpose of the author in their presentation of characters, and synthesizing these characters with broader cultural images.

Mrs. Gormley lamented the lack of materials that would challenge her honors students:

> You have honors (kids) who are at a higher level and you don't have the kinds of materials to teach them with. The honors, some kids are into *Scholastic Updates*, but I have kids that are brilliant! They are bored with this (*Scholastic Updates*) stuff!

Mrs. Gormley felt a great deal of pressure in providing a rigorous, academic experience for her honors students. Despite her efforts, most of the students did not find *Comparative World Issues* challenging. Pete, an honors student, said, "I've yet to understand why honors *Comparative World Issues* is still honors. The way I see it, I've done a book report each marking period and a project, and that's it!"

Mrs. Wegian's B, or middle level, class had just begun studying the Arab–Israeli conflict when I arrived to begin research. The project was summarized in a teacher-created document, "Whose Israel is it?" This class was divided into five groups, each assigned a 20-year time period to research and develop a timeline about Israel's 20th-century development. The students were required to have at least one primary source and a map to illustrate their time period. The students prepared for two 90-minute blocks in the computer lab, researching their eras on the Internet. They then prepared their timelines in a third block and presented their work in a fourth block. The emphasis in this class, as compared to the honors class, was on the ability to locate, reorganize, and present content, as opposed to analyzing, synthesizing, and evaluating it.

While Mrs. Gormley's class discussed world literature, and Mrs. Wegian's class created timelines of Israel, Mrs. Brandy's low-ability A group did book reports on Latin American dictators. Students worked with a partner and selected a leader to research (e.g., Fidel Castro or Augusto Pinochet). After a week or so of independent research, they didactically presented their reports to the class. Students generally reacted positively to the assignments. Hsong, a recent Chinese immigrant, stated, "When they do the presentations, that's good, because like, when they tell a lot of things that are not related, I think it's good to hear what they did and what they think." Adam, an African American boy, agreed, "I don't like individual things, I would rather work with someone else on a presentation. We work together to solve the problems. We put things together and either it comes out right or comes out wrong and no one is to blame." Interestingly, cooperation such as this was found in the low-achieving A group and the middle-achieving B group. Students in the honors group were expected to complete book reports individually.

The Contextual Factor at Sunny Brook—Student Competition

Why did Sunny Brook teachers focus on individuals in course content and abide so firmly to the constructs of ability-level grouping? Competition was a key contextual component at Sunny Brook that ultimately shaped pedagogy. The students demonstrated peer competition repeatedly in observations, even at a time of the year when students were, by their own admission, lax. Grades were used by teachers and recognized by students as a motivating tool, as evidenced in the following observations.

> Listen up, we have interims tomorrow and I'm going to tell you what you need to do to improve your grade. You still need to turn in written work. If you don't, you will get a zero! You have to do the presentation and if you don't, you get a zero! One boy protested, asking for partial credit for a late paper, whom Mrs. Brandy consulted with privately.

> These are the grade sheets … if you have a problem with your grade, make a note and I'll come back to you (to discuss it). The students quickly crowded around the grade sheets, talking about their scores. The kids compared scores and boasted when their grade was better than that of a peer.

Students seemed to respond to academic threats despite the fact that, as seniors, many of them were already accepted into college, which suggests the depth of competitiveness among Sunny Brook students.

The emphasis placed on grades may have contributed to the competitive environment, but such a complex phenomenon as competition has other sources, including the students themselves. The students added further support to the notion that competition is prevalent and engendered by peer interactions.

> There's a lot of competition between students for high rank in class. I remember last year in physics, the class was full of seniors and three sophomores wanted the highest average. I remember one sophomore made a remark,

"Look at the three highest grades, they are all sophomores!" There's an academic competition, and for sports one person wants to be better than the
other person.

When she (Mrs. Wegian) posts the grades, the people always want to know
the code names ("Hey, who's Rainbow 6?!") so that they can see who had the
high grades, and the kids compare their grades.

Certain kids in class are competitive when report cards come out, people are
like, "Oh look, I got higher than you!" or, "Ha, ha, ha! You got a D in AP English!"

The students usually qualified their perception of competition as endemic
in the school, but claimed not to participate in this type of behavior. Students frequently attributed competitiveness to their peers rather than themselves, but they unanimously agreed that the school was a competitive
environment.

Sunny Brook teachers engendered competition not only in posting
grades but also with regard to the students' college choices. Mrs. Wegian
had a bulletin board in her room with banners of the colleges to which students had been accepted. The students referred to the board in their informal discussions in class, noting those attending Brown and those going to
Raritan Valley Community College. There seemed to be a sort of hierarchical rank ordering in the college banner display, with Yale, Brown, and
Cornell on top, followed by Rutgers, Penn State, Ohio State, and Raritan
Valley Community College and Bucks County Community College on
the bottom.

A bulletin board like this one would have looked positively foreign at
Bart High School. Whereas students at Sunny Brook bragged about their
academic prowess, Bart students were more likely to advertise their academic failure. As Mr. Gordon suggested, it was "cool" to not carry textbooks at Bart. Even though it was generally considered "uncool" to be
extremely competitive at Sunny Brook, students readily engaged in those
behaviors and responded to teacher academic threats.

There may be sociocultural factors present at Sunny Brook that encourage focus on the individual to a greater degree than at Bart and Valley. The
ethos of communities like Developmenta, and similarly, schools like
Sunny Brook, is permeated by individual achievement. Individual
achievement requires a fair amount of competition. An individual
achievement model tends to be zero-sum, wherein the success of one individual means the failure of many others. This is apparent in many other aspects of the school, such as elevated levels of competition for class

offices, emphasis on advanced placement courses and tests, an overt commitment to "excellence," and recognition of the college choices by students. Sunny Brook radiates the values of suburban life: competition, individuality, and achievement. The achievements and failures of famous individuals as a way of understanding cultural diversity and global issues, however limited a perspective that may be, is in a real sense "speaking the language" of Sunny Brook students.

Sunny Brook Students' Reactions to Global Education

Students at Sunny Brook, similar to those at Valley and Bart, were largely positive about their experiences in global education.

> You watch good movies on people's heritages, rather than sitting down, breaking out a book and copying down notes. I don't think there's one person I know that doesn't like this class, not one.

> The class is more fun because people participate a lot and we do a lot of projects in class. I think that it's run really well and I personally enjoy it because we watch a lot of films and stuff and I'm a visual learner. This class is really good because of the way it's taught.

Students were highly attentive in class, eager contributors to activities, and responsive to the various work tasks which their teachers prepared for them. *Comparative World Issues* teachers echoed the feelings of their students, indicating, as Mrs. Brandy did, that, "This is the best course I've ever been associated with!" The three teachers had an esprit de corps that contributed to their enjoyment of the course and the satisfaction of their students.

CONCLUSION—FITTING A GLOBAL VILLAGE INTO A CLASSROOM

The question that frames this chapter seems to suggest the difficulty of fitting so much content into a course of study, the challenge of teaching the world comprehensively and comprehensibly. Global education, however, is less a matter of content as it is a style of pedagogy and a way of viewing the world (Pike & Selby, 2000). In this chapter, I offer the introductory question as a means of examining fit in terms of appropriateness, rather than size or scope of content. Borrowing on the contextual work by McLaughlin and Talbert (1990), "At the most fundamental level, context matters because effective teaching depends on teachers' opportunities to choose materials, objectives, and activities they believe are appropriate for themselves and for their students. Does the curriculum fit the class? Does it fit the interests and backgrounds of the teacher?" (p. 2).

So what are the take-home lessons from this initial glimpse into teacher and student conversations about global curriculum? Contextual factors clearly matter in curriculum implementation; these are features of the school that are often beyond the control of teachers and students acting individually. In Bart, we saw a dysfunctional school filled with disruptions and deleterious relationships, infertile soil with which to grow the seeds of curious minds, let alone the roots of interconnected global life. A socially beneficial environment at Valley engendered teacher professionalism and experiential learning, which generated student interest. Sunny Brook suggests how broader community values can influence the curriculum, as a focus on individuals in course content and homogeneous grouping aligned with a hyper-competitive environment.

Why was global education reform implemented so differently at Bart and Valley? Perhaps the difference is attributable to what Cornbleth (1990) has referred to as the mediation of socioeconomic context. Rather than socioeconomic factors freely passing into the classroom, mediation suggests a sense of agency among teachers and administrators to determine what "passes" into the somewhat artificial environment of the school. Valley teachers created a warm, caring environment through promoting caring social interactions among students while Bart teachers generally had a laissez-faire attitude about how students interacted with each other. Despite the presence of a gate at Bart and none at Valley, the metaphorical gate of mediation was clearly more effective in the rural context of Valley.

Valley teachers and administrators talked frequently about the need to gear social studies curricula to the backgrounds and perceived interests of their students. Valley's social studies department created and implemented a local history unit, developed field trips to augment the global education course, and conducted action research to ascertain student needs. In comparison, little effort was made by Bart to make the broadly defined global education mandate "fit" the needs and interests of their inner city students. Bart was in the process of changing the course of study from *World History* to *World Cultures* because of a sense that the latter would be more meaningful to students, but they did not have a clear vision of what their students needed from this course, other than an opportunity to work on basic skills. By default, the course content and processes became ancillary to the larger goal: elusive success on a standardized test.

The manner in which the global teachers "fit" the school contexts in which they worked was also the source of some friction. Sunny Brook teachers generally shared in the ethos of upward mobility, encouraged academic competition, and sanctified the individual. Not all of Bart's global teachers, in contrast, willingly adopted drill/skill pedagogy or permitted chaos. Mr. Gordon was a notable exception, creating a tight but warm environment in his classroom. He attempted to engage students in global content in ways more personally meaningful. Although he participated in the weekly HSPT/A preparation sessions, he did so indifferently. Mr. Gordon was abiding by the "cover story" of the school, that Bart's efforts should be directed toward a high-stakes test that most students are destined to fail, while creating an "internal" context within his classroom that represented his deeper professional knowledge and commitment (Clandinin & Connelly, 1996).

Clandinin & Connelly (1996) found that teachers construct contexts within their classroom while being compelled to abide by the larger, normative context of the school. The narrative of one of their participants, Stephanie, illustrates how teachers can create contexts within their classrooms that may be incongruent with the larger context of the school. Teachers who work against the grain of the school context, like Stephanie in Clandinin and Connelly's work and Mr. Gordon are viewed as "outsiders" until, or if, the larger school context is reformed to more closely resemble their pedagogy. Sunny Brook global teachers, in contrast, experienced a match between context of the school and the context of their classrooms, each illustrating values of individualism, competition, and upward mobility.

Valley and Sunny Brook global teachers were committed to content as an element of context. Mrs. Gormley of Sunny Brook served as head researcher with her colleagues, constantly seeking out materials to share with her students. Similarly, Mrs. Finberg, with the support of Mrs. Dilley, was committed to enriching the global education course through searching for content materials offered to enhance her students' knowledge of the world. Each of these schools stands in marked contrast to Bart, where content was a tertiary concern, behind standardized tests and establishing order. Grossman and Stodolsky (1995) identified "disciplinary socialization" as a critical aspect of teaching contexts (p. 6). Secondary teachers in their research identified first and foremost as content experts, creating a "'conceptual context' that helps frame the work of high school teachers and mediates their responses to reform proposals" (p. 6).

Global education was generally successful at Sunny Brook and Valley High Schools because it conformed to the existing content area subcultures of the schools. An esprit de corps existed among these faculties, especially at Sunny Brook, as they defined themselves as the social studies experts who welcomed the addition of global content. By contrast, only two of the four Bart teachers were "lifers" in social studies education, which may have contributed to the lack of commitment to content knowledge at Bart. Teaching out of field is a common problem in urban education. Bart teachers were not socialized by content areas and generally did not identify or act with enthusiasm in reforming their existing courses of study. Even though secondary teaching involves a great deal more than content knowledge expertise, Grossman and Stodolsky's (1995) study indicates that teacher commitment to content fields can create richer learning communities for students.

A final lesson offered from this analysis is that students are interested in global education because of the novelty inherent in the content. Global education offers students a unique opportunity to make personal meaning out of novel experiences and knowledge. Students from my study demonstrated interest in how people diversely adapt to and transform their environments and how societies change over time (or, in their terms, "from back in the day"). A corollary to students' interest in global education is that experiential and active learning methodologies enhanced students' experience and enjoyment of the course, as demonstrated in Valley and Sunny Brook.

This brings to a close the first section of this book, Contexts. In it, we traversed a wide range of ideas: a personal perspective on global education, the development of global education as a curriculum field, the global "laboratory" of New Jersey, the failure to achieve a "thorough and efficient" education for all children in the state, an introduction to the schools in this study, and an in-depth analysis of how school context affects global teaching and learning. Part II of this book addresses problems encountered regularly, though not exclusively, in the field of global education: nationalism and globalism, controversial issues and subsequent tensions between cultural relativism and universalism, and the multiple faces of identity in global education.

II

Problems

Problems can be beneficial, the extent to which they encourage us to think carefully about the world we encounter, theorizing about why certain phenomena exist in particular ways. This perspective may be considered somewhat troublesome in our contemporary world, where problems are viewed as ominous situations so challenging as to be ignored, if possible, or addressed limitedly (e.g., the environmental dilemma and the crisis of urban deterioration). If not overwhelming in scope, tensions can encourage our renewed attention and energies in deriving solutions. As Ryan (1995) wrote in his biography of Dewey, "Individuals and societies alike are stirred into life by problems; an unproblematic world would be a world not so much at rest as unconscious" (p. 28). It is in this engaging, reflective, and potentially productive sense that I offer some of the problems associated with global education through the conversation of teachers and students.

4

Global Education as
Anti-American Curriculum?

Global education ... draws from the increasingly obvious concept of interdependence and those human issues which are supranational. Nationalistic
education is a term that fits the process of instructing people in the virtues of
their own country and the evils of those deemed enemies. In a global society
such nationalistic education appears to be dysfunctional.

—Nelson (1976, pp. 33, 47)

Tension between nationalistic and global curricula is a significant issue in global education and in social studies curricula as a whole. Does one engage study of the world as a means for national critique, to identify and change the pathologies of one's own society (Mead, 1943)? Or, does one pursue global education as teaching about the virtues of one's own society and the evils of others to build a sense of national pride and belonging (Anderson, 1982; Nelson, 1976)? Does a feasible middle ground approach exist? This chapter examines the problem of teaching globally within educational systems that promote some version of a national perspective.

I was teaching a global education course during the Persian Gulf War of 1991. In keeping with Hanvey's dimension of perspective consciousness, I thought it would be interesting to see how other societies' news media were portraying the war. I collected articles from a variety of sources and we analyzed the differences in viewpoints. Some students reacted favorably to the assignment as they expressed a genuine interest in how the United States' actions were being viewed around the world. A group of students were reticent even to engage the exercise, however, thinking that it somehow called into question support for the U.S. war effort. In a sense, this "academic" exercise had taken on new meaning in the context of yellow ribbon-tying war hysteria that pervaded the school and the larger community. This lesson captured in a poignant manner the problem of global teaching in national contexts.

My participation in a student–teacher exchange with a high school in St. Petersburg, Russia, in 1992 again illustrates the national/global dynamic. Dima Milkov, my teacher partner in Russia, spent 3 weeks in the fall of 1992 teaching, attending classes, and observing daily life at our school. A ritual that Dima found most surprising and curious was the daily flag salute. He indicated that this ritual was not what he expected to see in the United States, even after a lifetime of anti-American instruction in the former Soviet Union. He said, "Even as a student at the height of the Cold War in the 1960s and 1970s, we were never asked to engage in such displays of nationalism." Though Dima's experience may have been unique in the Soviet era, I was still surprised by his recollection. My perception was quite opposite, as I envisioned Soviet schools actively inculcating pro-Soviet feelings through rituals. It made me wonder about how nationalistic our schools were in relation to others internationally and the extent to which that mattered.

NATIONALISTIC EDUCATION

Nationalism is one of the oldest traditions in U.S. public education. The building of a national identity through public education was a concern in the first half of the 19th century, from the War of 1812 forward. A sense of national identity was emerging and expanding during and after the upheaval of the Civil War era. By the latter half of the 19th century, with increasing waves of immigrants arriving in the United States, promoting a national identity became a primary concern of schooling. Historical events such as the War of 1812, the Civil War, and immigration led to increased attention to teaching a national heritage, particularly in history and civics classes, in order to bind and unify a nation (Barth, 1996; Nelson, 1996).

Teachers were given primary attention in this effort. Pierce (1926) documented the widespread phenomenon of loyalty oaths, as in West Virginia in 1867: "I have not voluntarily borne arms against the U.S. ... that I have not yielded a voluntary support to any pretended government ... within the U.S." (p. 31). By 1890, special interest groups such as the Daughters of the American Revolution, Sons of the American Revolution, Colonial Dames of America, and the American Legion called for and gained the enactment of laws requiring patriotic exercises in schools (Nelson, 1975, p. 4). Homogenization of "an American" character and how best to translate that into curriculum was of utmost concern.

Nationalistic curriculum has been defined as encouraging the cultivation of love and respect for one's country and the prohibition of ideas challenging national image. Engle and Ochoa (1988) argue that classroom celebrations of national rituals (e.g., Thanksgiving and Presidents' Day) are widespread in elementary education and problematic. "Children are repetitively engaged in activities that encourage unthinking national loyalty and patriotism ... perpetuat(ing) the myths about glories of the nation's heritage ... mak(ing) overt use of children's emotions as well as of rewards in the forms of parties ... (to) manipulate the minds of the young" (p. 33). Naylor's (1974) research suggests that younger, less experienced teachers are more likely to challenge the national image of the nation than teachers with more experience.

Teachers are necessarily involved in the manner in which social studies content is taught and the degree to which nationalistic perspectives are promoted. Teachers can adopt a variety of stances with regard to nationalistic pedagogy, ranging from a conservative approach that defends the authority and greatness of the nation-state to a progressive approach that examines national claims to superiority skeptically. Callan (1994) examines the tension between education as sentimental and critical in liberal democratic contexts such as the United States, finding little comfort in either the conservative or progressive traditions. "Sentimental civic education" leads to "an abridgement of reason" that runs counter to democratic values (p.192), while "critical reason in the shape of an implacable skepticism is politically sterile," leading to despair and anti-public sentiments (p. 204). Callan's preferred style of civic, or national, education is one that follows the middle path of the democratic political tradition, "combin(ing) an exacting rationality with a generous susceptibility to those public emotions that bind us to the body politic" (p. 211).

The United States is not unique in promoting a nationalistic curriculum, but is among those nations actively pursuing nationalistic myths through history teaching (Hahn, 1984; Nelson, 1996; Thomas, 1993). Recent empirical evidence suggests that history textbooks in the United States are relatively less nationalistic than those in Indonesia, for example. The Indonesian texts prescribe certain moral values (i.e., love of country and self-sacrifice), whereas the U.S. texts focus on the individual rights governments are obligated to protect (Thomas, 1993). A relationship may exist between the relative age of nations and their commitment to promoting national unity, although this correlation is only speculative.

Global education was attacked in the 1980s as being anti-American, as detailed in chapter 1. Although the charges were deemed without merit by the National Council for the Social Studies Ad Hoc Committee on Global Education, the view that global curriculum potentially challenges, contradicts, and undermines national curriculum is still prevalent (Pike, 2000). At issue is whether teachers can engage world study in a way that allows for national affection while maintaining a commitment to the planet as a whole (Case, 1993). Callan's notion of negotiating a centrist path between sentimentalism and skepticism is problematic in a global context where not all nations abide by a liberal democratic tradition that encourages a debate such as this.

Leung and Print (1998) also suggest a balanced approach, similar to that of Callan (1994), which involves "critical thinking, participatory citizens with affection for the nation" (p. 19). They offer a classification system for the complex manifestations of nationalism, of which three categories are relevant to this study:

- Ethnic/cultural nationalism—emphasizes blood ties, color of skin and ethnic origins; tends to divide along "us/them" dichotomies.
- Civic/democratic nationalism—emphasizes the rights of people to govern their lives and participate in the goals of the nation; an inclusive form of nationalism that unites people regardless of their origins.
- Cosmopolitan nationalism—emphasizes that all people throughout the world are created equal and should be treated with respect; notions of a global village of humanity working towards shared goals are imbedded in this conception.

These classifications can be summarized, "We are all _____-Americans," "We are all Americans," and "We are all humans sharing one planet." The term *nationalism* in Leung and Print's taxonomy is problematic. It suggests a commitment to a nation-state with internationally recognized political boundaries. They refer, however, to a broader conceptualization of nationalism, one where the allegiance to the group within (i.e., group identity within the nation) is more salient than alliance with the group that subsumes (i.e., nation-state). Leung and Print employ a cultural version of nation, rather than a geopolitical understanding.

Global teachers of Valley, Bart, and Sunny Brook High Schools addressed the problem of nationalism in divergent ways that generally fit Leung and Print's (1998) classification while suggesting an additional category: eclectic nationalism. These four approaches, ethnic/cultural, civic/

democratic, cosmopolitan, and eclectic, frame the data about nationalistic conversations in these global classrooms and illustrate how teachers negotiate the tensions of nationalism in global contexts.

ETHNIC/CULTURAL NATIONALISM

Ethnic/cultural nationalism assumes that loyalty to one's ethnic group is critically important. Ethnic pride and cohesion have typically arisen among these groups globally in the face of oppressive circumstances. Ethnic group identity takes precedence over an affiliation with the nation-states in which they reside, although it is not typically expressed in an extremist manner that urges separation from the nation-state. A few examples may help to illustrate the concept. The Nation of Islam asserts that they are an occupied nation of people existing within a larger national system, the United States. Irish-Catholics in Northern Ireland cohere by their ethnic and religious identity affiliation, rather than to the state authority of the United Kingdom. Kurdish people living on the border between Turkey and Iraq are considered a stateless people whose ethnic identification supersedes identity with the nation-state in which they happen to reside.

Mr. Gordon of Bart, while not ascribing to the polemics of the Nation of Islam, did approach teaching about the world from the perspective of being an African American. Mr. Gordon was an accomplished athlete, athletic trainer, and veteran teacher. Throughout our conversations, he consistently talked about the need to bring his students to understand and appreciate their African American heritage in order to prepare them for the challenging world that lay ahead.

> In other parts of the world, you are being treated as a person, and not a black person. If I'm over in France, they are not going to assume that I stole it. But if you are in the United States, and 10 black kids are there, they are going to assume that one of them did it and start frisking them and harassing them.

Mr. Gordon explained that he was unique among the Bart faculty as an African American male, allowing him to talk about his life and travel experiences in a way that resonated with his students. Mr. Gordon taught his students, who were predominantly African American, not only about being proud and committed to their ethnic group, but also to be understanding of others. The global course was a vehicle for introducing the dual message of affiliation and tolerance. "For the kids we are working with they need to learn that there are different groups and different cultures and they need to tolerate it. Kids are more segregated now than they were in the 50s. People don't talk about that, but a lot of poor kids can only go to poor city schools."

I conducted research at Bart during Black History Month. A great deal of attention was paid by the significant African American student population to developing activities for the month. Students began each day with an announcement about famous African Americans, the media center created a special display, and many teachers emphasized black history in their teaching. There seemed to be a contrast in attention paid to Black History Month by the four global educators at Bart. Attention to developing an African American perspective permeated Mr. Gordon's approach to the course, though his teaching had a tone of tolerance rather than exclusivity. Mr. Gordon felt it was his place to teach pride and responsibility to his African American students, as he believed these characteristics would steel them against the institutionalized racism of the larger society. Rarely did he talk about the United States as a nation, and when he did so, it was only as a means of understanding how African Americans and other minorities have been victimized in this context.

Mr. Gordon, despite seeing the world from an African American perspective and encouraging his students to do the same, was also critical of popular versions of African American identity.

> My students tell me they don't want to do this because it's the "white man's thing," because the whites are doing this, you know, African-centric type thinking. But at the same time, they're talking about BMWs and making dollars, and I say, "Who made that? You didn't make that ... I don't see any African people with a lot of money making that (laughs)!" African Americans want money and that seems to be a motivating thing. So, in one instance you are getting into this heavy brother, African thing and in another instance you are telling me that you want to buy a BMW and an Eddie Bauer and I'm going to get this and get that. To me, that's a big contradiction.

Mr. Gordon was both a critic and advocate of his ethnic group, imploring students to know themselves as black people, but also to be critical of the ways in which black identity has been manipulated by corporate media.

Mr. Gordon's ethnic/cultural nationalism seemed appropriate in light of the larger context of Bart. Students who attended were among some of the poorest in the nation: There was little to appreciate in their lives in terms of economic success and educational achievement. The male African American students in particular reacted with bitterness towards the United States, which they equated with "the White man." Katherine, an African American girl, talked frankly about her perceptions of the continuation of racism in the United States:

> I wonder why racism can't be stopped. In some places, there are still prob-
> lems like back in the day. We was talking about this in class, how to this day, if
> we was to ever go to some places in Mississippi, blacks are not allowed. Why
> hasn't our country done nothin' about this?! It's not fair for people on one
> side of the world to have everything, and the other side have nothing and
> have to go to a place according to the color of their skin. I see that some things
> that was back then and looking up until now have not changed.

Katherine's remarks suggest an honest concern and curiosity about the lack of respect for African Americans in "White America" and criticism of longstanding racism in the United States. Her comment also illustrates her conception of the world ("people on one side of the world") as not being bound by the nation-state but defined by the color barrier in her own society.

CIVIC/DEMOCRATIC NATIONALISM

Sunny Brook's global education teachers based their world teaching on civic/democratic nationalism. Mrs. Gormley focused on political issues and Mrs. Bratus emphasized social concerns, but the overarching theme of their work was the same: The United States is an imperfect nation, but it can change through civic action, and it's still a better place to live than any other nation. This line of reasoning was thoughtfully articulated in interviews and repeatedly evident in classroom observations. The teachers had clearly given this premise of the course careful thought, as they had talked about this issue in a unified manner. Sunny Brook teachers called it a "critical pride" approach to nationalism.

Mrs. Gormley's lessons about the Iranian Revolution of 1979 typified the civic/democratic nationalistic approach; evident in this observation:

> We can be very hypocritical when we want to and if there's one thing you
> take away from this class, it's that we don't have a great foreign policy re-
> cord. We have a terrible, terrible record! We funded the Iran–Iraq war! How
> does our culture look to others?!

Mrs. Gormley, interviewed following this lesson, explained the need to talk openly and honestly about U.S. foreign policy, warts and all. She explained:

I have to be honest with the way the government deals with different countries and that can be disillusioning and many kids have told me how disillusioned they were from the course. But, by the same token, I think every unit I teach, you kind of end the unit and the kids come to the realization: Oh my God, thank God we live in this country. In the end, we are all Americans! Even if we disagree with the government, here a public school teacher can stand up and criticize the government. Students come to the realization that this is a great country, there aren't any other countries like this in the world and the kids have a good standard of living.

Mrs. Gormley's reference to the socioeconomic background of her students indicates a plausible explanation for civic/democratic nationalism at Sunny Brook. In a real sense, teachers in this context were engaging the economic "winners," as many of their students came from upper-middle income backgrounds. Teachers seemed to adjust and augment their otherwise harsh criticism of the U.S. actions because they were teaching students whose families had generally benefited from living in the United States. The context of working with an ethnically diverse population may also explain why a civic/democratic nationalism approach was employed. Despite Sunny Brook's "international crossroads" moniker of cultural diversity, there remained an underlying assumption that these students were fundamentally the same: suburban, upwardly mobile, middle-class, and from educated families.

Mrs. Bratus shared a civic/democratic nationalism perspective as evident through this observation of her teaching about terrorism:

You know, some people call it the war of Independence while others call it the American Revolution. Britain saw it as nothing more than terrorism, so even in our own country's actions, you can see terrorism. One man's terrorist is another man's freedom fighter. It's all about perspective.

The phrase "One man's terrorist is another man's freedom fighter" was a mantra often repeated in Mrs. Bratus' class and a phrase she included on student handouts throughout the unit. Her teaching dialogue suggests that the United States can be viewed from an "outsider's" perspective and that the nation is not always "right" in an absolute sense. She talked at length about this approach in a subsequent interview:

When we're looking at the Cold War, I try to get them to do some critical thinking: Were we being humanitarian in helping other nations or were we looking to keep our markets open to sell our goods? And then I follow up with, this is the best place, and they know that this is the best place in the world to ever live. When we finish every unit, the kids take a sigh of relief that we live here because of the oppression throughout the world. I'm not a raving patriot, but I do love this country, and those people who are going to be our future citizens can improve upon it, not that the government is perfect, so they can improve it. These kids are adult enough to understand that all countries have their faults, yes we can criticize it, but there's no place else that's like it in the world.

Imbedded in Mrs. Gormley's and Mrs. Bratus' approach are three key elements that fit the civic/democratic nationalism categorization: willingness to critique the nation, belief in the unity of all people in the United States, and an underlying reverence for the assumed "unique greatness" of the nation. The clashes between these incongruent beliefs often manifested themselves through teachers' conversations.

COSMOPOLITAN NATIONALISM

Valley, despite its rural setting and atmosphere, exuded cosmopolitan nationalism in its global curriculum. The informal leader of the global faculty of Valley was Mrs. Finberg. In many respects, she set the tone for the way the course would be taught. Her outlook on the interplay between national and global loyalties was based on her ardent belief that people are fundamentally the same. In talking about her goals for the course, she related:

> No matter how different we all appear, we're still the same. We're of the same species, our values systems usually are the same, we have the same desires and expectations out of life that other people do. So I like to foster that sense, so that kids leave the course saying it's great that we have these differences because they make life more beautiful and exciting.

Mrs. Finberg frequently made statements about the need to be concerned for the protection of all people, regardless of their national origin. She explained:

> I have this video on African women and we talk about how hard these women work and how even the poorest American is wealthier than the average African. I have a powerful video on children in Pakistan making carpets, and I stand up there and say, "Do you know where your clothing comes from? Should you get involved? You bought your clothes at Wal-Mart and people are being exploited in a Third World [sic] country and that's a place where the kids could get involved. I tell the kids I was about to buy a carpet and I love them, but I can't buy it because I could not walk on something that a child slaved to create. I hate to make my course about suffering, but I try to uplift the kids and tell them they have so much power. You know, you're an

American, you can say things about these problems, you can write letters and influence world leaders.

Mrs. Finberg was deeply passionate about human rights abuses and used the *World Cultures* class as a vehicle for raising these issues with her students. As the child of Holocaust survivors, she dealt with the lack of action on behalf of Others, because it fell beyond the realm of "national interests." Her commitment to a cosmopolitan nationalism where the rights of all global villagers are equally valued clearly resonated with her familial experiences. Mrs. Finberg's orientation also shaped teaching among her younger colleagues. Mrs. Solotore adopted a similar, if less strident, viewpoint in her teaching and Mr. Sidner's approach blended cosmopolitan nationalism with his military background to form an eclectic nationalistic perspective.

ECLECTIC NATIONALISM

Mr. Sidner of Valley, a young man with varied military experiences including a tour of duty in the Persian Gulf War, best exemplifies the eclectic nationalism approach. Eclectic nationalism cannot be neatly fitted into Leung and Print's (1998) classification but deserves attention. I refer to his approach as eclectic in that he seemed to draw from two nationalistic frameworks: civic/democratic and cosmopolitan. During my time at Valley, the NATO-led conflict in Kosovo was well underway. Mr. Sidner spoke frequently about the conflagration. Students would ask him what he thought of America's actions in Kosovo, to which he replied, "We're fighting for peace and I have to support it." He talked about the fact that Serbian leader Milosevic had perpetrated genocide against the Bosnian Muslims and "he had to be stopped!"

Loyalty and love of country were key values for Mr. Sidner. "If they called me up, I would go in a second to defend freedom, because you're loyal and (should) love this country!" He would admonish students about their lax attitude toward the United States: "If you don't say the pledge because you're lazy, then shame on you. If it is because you disagree, I have to respect that difference of opinion in this country."

Mr. Sidner was overtly nationalistic in his teaching, but was at the same time critical of the nation in the way he approached *World Cultures*. More than his Valley colleagues Mrs. Solotore and Mrs. Finberg, he encouraged his students to critique the United States with regard to cultural practices and even foreign policy. During one lesson, he said, "The CIA was killing

Latin American dictators and putting our puppet governments in their place!"

Mr. Sidner saw a direct and important relationship between national and religious identity. "That's why people are in conflict in Israel, Palestine, and Kosovo and everywhere else, because of this view that I am better than you because my god is greater than yours and my country is better than yours." He encouraged his students to discuss their own religious beliefs in light of what they were learning about world religions and professed a genuine reverence for Buddhist teachings. He explained that "Buddhists are pacifists, they are against violence" while talking about the Columbine High School tragedy. The organization of this lesson implied a contrast of cultural style, between U.S. aggression and Buddhist pacifism. Mr. Sidner's eclecticism was evident in his urging students to adhere to the ties that bind one nation in the ritual of flag saluting (democratic nationalism) and his willingness to critique the United States from the perspective of Others (cosmopolitan nationalism).

CONCLUSION

Global education has been criticized as being anti-American in orientation. Based on the conversations of the teachers in this study, it is clear that this accusation is both exaggerated and overly simplistic. Asserting that global education is anti-American suggests a dichotomization of curriculum, an intellectual trap of the worst kind (Callan, 1994). To emphasize one aspect of the human experience does not necessarily detract from another aspect. Curriculum choices are not best understood as "either/or" choices, and the same applies to global-national tensions in curricula (Case, 1993).

To divide issues, political and otherwise, into national and global domains is meaningless (McWilliams, 1999). Perhaps this is where the problems associated with nationalism and globalism begin, in the tendency to create an intellectual boundary around the United States through which nothing global can enter. Seen in a different light, the United States can and should be treated in curricula in a manner that recognizes its global past, present, and future in a manner that is thoughtfully critical.

There is a common element of national critique in all four approaches examined through these conversations, lending credence to the notion that global education is not blindly "pro-American." The intent of those critiques, however, differs significantly. Mr. Gordon's ethnic/cultural nationalism at Bart was an ongoing criticism of the U.S. failure to address race discrimination. The purpose of this approach was to build a stronger sense of ethnic cohesion among African American students, not necessarily to undermine the United States, although cynicism was probably an unanticipated outcome. Mrs. Gormley and Mrs. Bratus' civic/democratic nationalism at Sunny Brook also encouraged students to criticize the United States. The ultimate purpose of "looking out/looking in" at the world, however, was to demonstrate the unique and superior qualities of life in the United States. Mrs. Finberg's cosmopolitan nationalism at Valley subtly criticized the United States for not doing more about global human rights abuses. The intent here, however, was to encourage students to become active defenders of human beings regardless of their national origin. The eclectic approach of Mr. Sidner was an attempt to help students identify a middle ground between loyalty to humanity as a whole and to one's national family.

Leung and Print's (1998) assertion that nationalism is too complex to allow simple prescriptions in curricular considerations is an important point in this discourse. Their classification system, while not all encompassing, is a useful framework for understanding how teachers make sense of this issue. In the foreseeable future, the construct of nations will continue to merit consideration in popular and scholarly conversations. Though nations are clearly being transformed in the era of the global village, they are not the dinosaurs that some in the past have prophesied. As such, it seems appropriate to engage students in a thoughtful and sustained dialogue about their loyalties to the nation and to the planet (Parker et al., 1998). To move beyond that problem, however, teachers need to engage students in conversation about the legacy of "dividing the world" (Willinsky, 1998) and the parallel need to recognize the emerging whole.

5

Opening Pandora's Box: Cultural Relativism in Global Education

What do you make of little Bobby Hefka in the 11th grade admitting to Mr. Jaslow that he was a racist and if Mr. Jaslow was so tolerant how come he couldn't tolerate Bobby?

—Levine (2001, p. 855)

Mr. Jaslow struggles with a problem that confronts global educators on a regular basis: What are the limits of cultural relativism? Bobby Hefka is a typical adolescent who enjoys exposing apparent contradictions. Bobby is asking a question that Mr. Jaslow might prefer to avoid, a query that many teachers hope gets lost in the din of classroom chatter. Bobby challenges us to consider the extent to which we can accept differences that contravene deeply held cultural values, prying open the Pandora's Box of cultural relativism.

I once found myself in Mr. Jaslow's shoes as a new global educator. My class was studying the Yanomamö of Venezuela. They were shocked by the details of the Yanomamö way of life. Wife beating, hallucinogenic drug use, grub eating, and cross-cousin marriage surprised and disgusted some of my students (Chagnon, 1992). I intervened, hoping to curb what I perceived to be their intolerance and promote a culturally relativistic way of seeing the Other. They seemed to play along with my wishes for the rest of the unit of study. We later studied state-sponsored violence in Chile and now I hoped my students would be outraged at the torture and disappearances perpetrated by the Pinochet regime. They were not overly incensed and some were unsympathetic, which gave me pause. Was I doing something wrong, trying to direct their moral outlook? Why weren't they responding the way I hoped they would? Wasn't it my job to teach them right from wrong on global issues?

I felt that they should be more empathetic to the plight of Chileans and other victims of state-sponsored violence and told them so. I exhorted them to judge those that would deny the rights of others. One shrewd boy retorted, "But why are we supposed to judge Pinochet's behavior and not the Yanomamö men who beat their wives?" I should have been excited that he was clever enough to make such a connection, but instead, I was dumbfounded. I had not quite put these two issues side by side in such a way before and I was confronted with a glaring contradiction in my own thinking. Bobby Hefka was in my class and, at the time, I hoped that his comment would just go away. I had too many other responsibilities, too many burdens of being a full-time teacher, that I did not have time to ponder such philosophical dilemmas, let alone resolve this seemingly irresolvable paradox.

The purpose of this chapter is to explore the diverse conversations about which global teachers and students address problematic moral discourses. The following themes emerge from these dialogues: teacher sensationalization and/or avoidance of moral discourse, teacher and student ambiguity about the limits of cultural relativism, teachers as ethical universalists, and the search for a middle ground in the cultural relativism–universalism continuum.

BACKGROUND

Cultural relativism, defined as a premise where "the values expressed in any culture are to be both understood and valued only according to the way the people who carry that culture see things" (Redfield, 1959, p. 10), has been the source of great controversy among anthropologists, educators, and at times, the public at large. Despite claims that cultural relativism is a "drained term and yesterday's battlecry" (Geertz, 1984, p. 263), the frequency with which it appeared in the conversations of the teachers and students in my study suggests that it has a great deal of currency.

Cultural relativism quickly became a flashpoint in the education diversity debate of the early 1990s. With the publication of the report, *One Nation, Many Peoples: A Declaration of Cultural Interdependence* in 1991, a vigorous debate ensued about multiculturalism; specifically, how cultural differences are understood and valued. The report, commissioned by the New York State Department of Education Report on the New York State

Social Studies Curriculum, asserts that knowledge is a social construction and must, therefore, be treated as tentative, rather than absolute. Hence, "because interpretations vary as experiences differ, a multicultural perspective must necessarily be a multiple perspective that takes into account the variety of ways in which any topic can be comprehended" (*One Nation*, 1991, p.7). The report was widely criticized on the grounds that it emphasized differences that would undermine the unity of society and would promote an "anything goes" belief among children (Nelson, Carlson, & Palonsky, 1993).

The Quincentenary of Columbus' voyage again raised the issue of cultural relativism. Breitborde (1993) suggested how teachers should address cultural relativism with regard to Columbus and the Arakawa natives. In presenting both the advocates' and opponents' positions regarding cultural relativism, he falls short of a solution to teaching about historical cultural clashes, which have the added complication of different ethical standards temporally. However, he asserts that despite the difficulties of suspending moral evaluation, "our own culturally defined humanity is thus affirmed through a culturally relativistic approach" (p.108).

The debate about cultural relativism surfaced in the mass media when two articles from the *Chronicle of Higher Education* were summarized in *U.S. News and World Report* in 1997. Simon (1997) asserted that in 20 years of college teaching, he is encountering students who "believe themselves unable morally to condemn (the Holocaust), or indeed to make any moral judgements whatsoever" (p. B6). He calls this phenomenon "absolutophobia" and suggests that current college students are great proponents of this nonjudgmental philosophy. Haugaard (1997) described teaching Jackson's *The Lottery*, which involves the random selection of a person in a Texas community for human sacrifice. She was appalled when the students refused to condemn the ritual. She reports that one of her students defended her reasoning, saying, "Multicultural understanding ... if it is part of another person's culture, we are taught not to judge" (p. B4).

Although Simon and Haugaard's reports are anecdotal rather than empirical, they suggest a socially diffused notion that cultural relativism, of a nihilistic variety, is presumably running rampant in modern classroom discourses. As Hall and Lindholm (1999) contend:

> Telling anyone what to do, Americans feel, would be asserting moral superiority—a cardinal sin in an egalitarian ethos. In other words, the 11th commandment is "Thou shalt not judge." It may seem paradoxical that one of

Americans' strongest moral values is a reluctance to impose moral values, but a moment's reflection will show that this is simply an expression of an individualistic faith that all persons ought to have the freedom to make their own fates without restraint from their neighbors. (pp. 95–96)

CHARACTER EDUCATION

Character education has increasingly gained attention as an umbrella strategy for exploring morality in schools. Character educators of all types recognize the richly moral circumstances of the school and attempt to locate moral issues in curriculum. Deriving from the values clarification movement of the 1960s, but with quite different assumptions about learning and human nature, character education is increasingly being implemented in schools and advocated by policymakers (Leming, 1993; Robinson, Jones, & Hayes, 2000).

Character education efforts can be roughly categorized on a continuum from imposition to critical reflection. Most scholars writing in this field tend toward the imposition end of the spectrum, defining values that should be taught and advocating ways in which they can be engaged. Bennett (1993) suggests that children must be taught who they are in a moral sense through stories so that they may enter the "community of moral persons" as defined by their society's history and heroes (p. 12). DeRoche (2000) suggests that character education can only be accomplished when a school community decides what values it wishes to teach, or what constitutes a "good student" in a particular context. Kirschenbaum (2000) described his personal journey away from a values clarification approach, where moral foundations were taken for granted, toward an imposition model of character education. He sidesteps the presuppositional question that nags those who advocate an imposition model of character education: To what extent are human beings fundamentally oriented in a moral sense? or, Are our moral selves predisposed to good, bad, or are we blank slates (Egan, 1978)?

Opponents of contemporary character education efforts are generally those on the critical reflection end of the spectrum. Kohn (1997) suggested that the character education movement is driven by "a stunningly dark view of children" coupled with a learning theory that is tantamount to indoctrination (p. 431). Purpel (2000) argued against more character/moral education in schools, per se, as schools are "inevitably implicated in ideological matters" which have been ignored through a normative process (p. 253). He suggested that moral education is not about inculcating values of what it means to be a "good person," but about interrogating normative educational practice with a moral lens.

Scholarly contributions to the character education literature have come from others interested in the development of moral individuals. Leming (1993) is noted for his research about the effectiveness of character education programs. His review of research studies suggests some of what we have learned in the moral domain of identity development: exhortations are ineffective, ability to reason about moral matters does not affect moral conduct, character is contextually situated, and moral development is time-consuming (p. 69). Noddings (1984, 1992) has also contributed to this ongoing discussion, problematizing what she believes are overly simplistic contentions about moral education. She contends that moral education occurs through an ethic of caring, where modeling, dialogue, and practice are integral elements.

GLOBAL EDUCATION AND MORALITY

Moral issues have long been recognized as fundamental to social studies education, and global education in particular, though studies of teaching about controversial topics have been limited. Hahn (1991) found in her meta-analysis of the social studies literature that research into teaching about controversy suggests three patterns: (a) opportunities to discuss controversial issues exist, (b) students want to study issues of moral import, and (c) civic aptitude results when controversial issues are engaged in schools (p. 476). With respect to global education, Schukar (1993) asserted that it is impossible to avoid controversy when teaching about the world.

Global education is fertile soil on which to survey the moral landscape of relativism and universalism, as the study of human diversity is a core of the field. Teachers, scholars, and teacher educators have been searching for a middle ground position that satisfies the apparent contradictions within culturally relativistic inquiry. Asher and Crocco (2001) documented the tension between cultural relativism and ethnocentrism when teaching about gender issues cross-culturally. They contend that teachers should "name and problematize" the tensions inherent in cultural relativistic teaching and inform students that culture informs but does not constrict gender systems (p. 148). "Teachers ... will map the terrain of the middle ground according to their own values and professional judgments" (p. 148). The middle ground articulated by these authors is more about process than product, where teachers "resist facile judgments" about cultural differences.

An-Na'im (1992) believed that relativistic thinking should be maintained to the extent that other societies are not condemned. He suggests, however, that constructive discourse about issues of controversy across cultural boundaries is a valuable endeavor. An-Na'im asserts that cross-cultural dialogue takes advantage of the evolving nature of cultures and attempts to influence their direction without imposition. According to An-Na'im, female genital cutting should be the focus of an ongoing dialogue among people of different views within and outside the communities where it is practiced. Kilbride and Kilbride (1990), who have conducted extensive fieldwork on family issues in East Africa, suggested a blend that they dubbed "relativistic universalism." Rather than accept a detached, cerebral position vis-à-vis another culture, they interact as they research to assist in their self-awareness about "improving dysfunctional social orders" (p.8). Like An-Na'im, Kilbride and Kilbride assert that there needs to be a dialogue about how a society "best" functions, believing that this is facilitated through heightened self-awareness rather than external imposition.

Gutman (1993) argued that deliberative universalism is philosophically sound and practicable. She contends that there are many issues which have no basis in any human system of justice, such as "routine murder of innocents, arbitrary arrests, systematic deception," whereas other issues, such as monogamy and abortion, have legitimate and reasonable justifications on both sides (p. 195). A better way of addressing moral controversies, according to Gutman, is through a process of deliberation among "reasonable perspectives in forums well-designed for deliberation" (p. 198). Deliberative universalism suggests a middle ground approach similar to An-Na'im (1992), where "reasonable" voices are encouraged to debate moral issues on the grounds of justice and fairness.

Bullivant (1989/1993) suggests splitting moral decision making into public and private spheres in search of a middle ground:

> What should a teacher do if he or she comes across a Turkish boy giving his sister a severe beating outside the school gates because he saw her talking to boys during the morning recess? In Turkish culture, a very strong value is placed on a girl's honor, and the boy was putting into effect the norms and sanctions associated with such a value. However, Western societies are not so strict, and this kind of situation can place an Anglo teacher in a dilemma of not knowing whether to intervene and criticize such a traditional practice in the interests of the girl, or to ignore it and allow a harmful situation to continue that might even lead to serious injury. (p. 43)

Bullivant argues that privacy dictates allowing cultural behavior to occur unabated away from public view, but that once the behavior is found in a public place, like a school, that the "rules of the public action system must surely apply," or that of universal standards for human conduct (p. 43).

The situation posed by Bullivant is generally different for global educators in terms of the context in which the judgment is being made. Imagine that the case of the Turkish boy hitting his sister was being studied as an illustration of Turkish culture, as opposed to witnessed by a teacher. How would the teacher and students work through this controversy? The difference for the teacher and students studying Turkish culture in comparison to the teacher witnessing the action is that they are detached completely from the action. The case becomes, in a very real sense, purely academic. What then? Should the rule of "normative equivalence," or cultural relativism, apply when studying a cultural controversy? Or, should the "rules of the public action system" apply when studying the episode of the Turkish boy? How have classroom teachers addressed this problematic issue?

SENSATIONALIZING AND AVOIDING MORAL ISSUES

Teacher participants in the study demonstrated two distinct modes of addressing issues of moral saliency: Some sensationalized whereas others avoided topics with a moral dimension. An intrinsic dilemma of teaching is engaging the curiosity of one's students. Some of the teachers in this study attempted to capture the attention of their students by capitalizing on interest in seemingly exotic practices. The following excerpt of an observation from Mr. Cortez' classroom at Bart High School illustrates the attention-grabbing technique of moral issues:

> Mr. Cortez said, "Who wants to hear a gross story?!" The students were moving around the room and chatting informally with each other. After approximately one minute of student inattention, Mr. Cortez reiterated more loudly, "Who wants to hear a gross story?!" Mr. Cortez then used the countdown method for all students to return to their seats. The teacher said, "Do you remember where the foot-binding term came from?" Mr. Cortez said, "It is so gross." He explained foot binding as a way that women's feet in China were broken to make them smaller. The teacher said, "Have you ever seen when women walk around with itty-bitty pity feet and the man who would say yeeahhh!" (sexually suggestive). Three girls yelled, "Eeww." Once students exclaimed, "That is disgusting!" which was followed by general indecipherable loud chatter among the students. The bell rang signaling the end of class.

Mr. Cortez used this story as a means of involving the students in class and having them pay attention to the lesson, which focused on cultural sharing between Japan and China. He was able to capture their attention, but at the cost of making the Chinese appear more strange and exotic than they may have already appeared to his students.

Mr. Ingresso, a colleague of Mr. Cortez at Bart, talked about how he focuses on cultural differences and controversies to capture the attention of students:

> Well, one of the problems is getting students' attention, with this kind of work, it doesn't grab them. Except, if you can somehow relate it or personalize it where they can really understand. So you talk about how each sex is viewed in a particular country as compared to here in the United States, you're more likely you can get a rise out of them, at least the female students. But in many cases the boys too, because it is something that they can comprehend, it is not an abstract concept, it is something that you can deal with. For example, foot binding, how that was a sign of beauty. And that is fascinating because they (the students) don't understand ... well, how can that be!? they will say. That's something that will catch their attention every time!

World History/Cultures teachers at Bart were sharing a video, *Samurai Warriors*, which they used as part of a unit on Japan. The video was extremely violent and graphic, glamorizing the violence of Samurais without providing a context for understanding feudal Japan. The teachers joked in the faculty room about how the students were titillated by the extreme violence in the film. The teachers assured each other that the students would "like this one!" and found it to be a way of "covering" feudal Japan easily while keeping the students' attention.

As Mr. Sidner from Valley indicated, what interests the students is "Death, dismemberment and sex ... basically conflict. I can guarantee it will get their attention every time." He did not seem happy that his students were interested in these aspects of social life, but played to their interests. Mr. Sidner provided a detailed description of what he referred to as a model lesson wherein he employs the shock quality of cultural differences:

> I have a lesson that I've done before and it's called the "Women of Iran." It is a list of 20 things that a man is allowed to do to his wife if she doesn't do what she is supposed to do. I can say, "Well, listen to this ... these things that happen in Iran" because I've got that interest and I can say, (with unction) "Can you believe this?! The way that they treat their women???" So the reaction is, "I can't believe it!" "I would ... I 'd hit him! I'd knock him out!" And I say, OK, that's good of you to say, now let's do a little role-play. Then I'll do a role play and I'll say, OK, come up here (to a female student) and I'm your husband, and I get intense on them, and I'll say, I want you to cook my meal, and

why isn't that laundry done!? The girl (student) then goes like this (ignoring me) and I go, Don't you ever talk to me!!! (screaming) ... like that, and it scares the crap out of them. I kind of go like this, I raise my hand, and at first some girls will react like this (gesturing to fight back) which is good, and some girls cower, you know, and I say now you know what it feels like to have to go through that. What I normally do, the last thing I do, I show about 5–7 minutes in the class, and I end it with a movie clip from *Not Without My Daughter*. Then I say, What would you do (dramatically)? I end the class on that note. So it all hits home, because I try to show adaptations of real events. You know it's shocking for them, it is, it's shocking for them, in a way that they are removed from it.... I try to get them to feel compassion, you know, for these people.

WG—Is that the goal?

Mr. Sidner—Yeah, that's the goal.

A minority of teachers in this study tended to avoid moral controversies. Their reasons for self-censorship were mostly related to a perceived lack of maturity of their students. Mrs. Finberg said:

I deal with controversial issues, I don't want to say often, but when you need to deal with them. I try to present both sides as fairly and balanced as I can ... I will express my opinion, when asked, but I will state that it is (only) my opinion. You can't avoid controversy, you know.

Mrs. Solotore, a colleague of Mrs. Finberg at Valley, also expressed some reservations about addressing issues of controversy. She employed a more didactic approach in her teaching, as evidenced by the frequency of worksheet instruction, drilling, and quizzes in her classroom. She indicated that controversies came up tangentially in class, but that she did not usually make a conscious effort to put disputatious issues before her students. She was more concerned with teaching students the "basics" about the world that "college prep students should know," such as geography and famous leaders of nations.

Mrs. Gormley, a teacher in ethnically diverse Sunny Brook High School, proposed a compelling reason for avoiding controversial cultural practices, such as female genital cutting. She said:

I don't get into female genital cutting as much as Brandy (a colleague) does. I think that's a touchy subject and an uncomfortable subject, you know? Because of our diverse population, I don't know who has been subjected to that. You know, I would guess that there are people who have (been subjected to it).... and, so ...

WG—Do your students know about it?

Mrs. Gormley—I don't think so. That's one (issue) that I don't talk about.

TEACHER AND STUDENT AMBIGUITY ABOUT CULTURAL RELATIVISM

Ambiguity about relativism was a consistent pattern found among most participants in the study. Teachers, like Mr. Jaslow in the poem, generally would have preferred not to talk about this contentious issue, despite its ubiquitous presence in the course. During the initial interview with Mr. White, department chair of Sunny Brook, the ambiguity that characterized his thinking about cultural relativism was apparent:

> It (the cultural framework for the class) was some consistent way of making sense of culture and being able to analyze culture ... analyze, make sense, I'm very leery of using "compare," that's one of the things we try to get away from which is the idea that there are differences. Let's understand the differences, but be careful about judging difference.
>
> WG—Can you elaborate on this idea?
>
> White—(after extended pause) Well ... so many of these kids, well they're not alone, people will say because it is not my way, it is wrong or bad or inappropriate or silly. I want to be careful, though.... We just didn't get into the idea that anything is ok. I mean we look at infanticide, and can you say that's the way they do it so that makes it ok? I want to raise that issue.... Are there values that are better values? That leads to some fascinating discussions, and you put it in quotes ... "What makes a value a better value?" When I was teaching (*Contemporary World Issues*) I would do similar things in some of the countries. I want to be careful to not say because they do it that way, it was ok ... there weren't right or wrong answers, but I wanted kids to be able to answer those questions.

Teachers throughout the study echoed Mr. White's comments. Mrs. Wegian commented on teaching about African women from a culturally relativistic perspective:

> We deal with female circumcision or female genital mutilizations [*sic*] or whatever you want to call it ... we look at that. We talk about, do we have the right, does anybody have the right to go into another culture and tell them this is wrong and this is right. I don't know if I can answer that question. The kids are very much, because of who they are and how they were raised it is very difficult for them to think that we should go over and do something. Thank goodness (the students say that)! For me, that's always good to look at

a wrong no matter where it is and say, gee, you shouldn't be doing that. Do we have that right? I don't know.

Teachers were leery of being seen as culturally insensitive, as reflected in Mr. Wright's discussion of infanticide. They seemed conscious of the cultural relativism dilemma, as evidenced in their interview comments, teetering between nonjudgment and condemnation, searching for a defensible middle ground.

Students also reflected the ambiguity of their teachers in conversations about cultural relativism. The most pronounced example of this was by Wayne of Valley High School, talking about the practice of having more than one wife. He said:

> I feel as in (pause) in your life, I think that I ... I ... I would judge that (polygyny), me personally, I would judge that as something that I don't think that's right, and I think that's something that all races and all cultures you don't do, that you have respect and respect means you respect someone's feelings and you try to make them feel the way you want to feel. I would judge someone about that, I would judge someone for that, but I don't feel it would be right to judge someone for their faults, because I know that I do wrong too. I don't know if it would be right, but I would judge them and I think everyone else would too, but I don't know if that would be right. I know that men before the Ten Commandments had many wives, but then you couldn't do it anymore. So, as a Christian, I believe you should stay faithful to one partner and that you should have one wife and one wife only. Multiple wives isn't the way to go, so, I would (judge that), I wouldn't, I wouldn't be right to judge someone under those kinds of things, but I would judge them, because I don't feel that they're right, but I'm not sure it would be right for me to judge someone else for that ... yeah.

Wayne believed that it is improper to make a judgment about various family patterns, and at the same time, faulted himself for having those sentiments. Wayne's apologetic tone, demonstrated when he offered a judgment, was echoed by other participants.

Wayne's comments also illustrate the private versus public tension on this issue, resonant with Bullivant's suggestion to split the controversial issue into private and public realms. A powerful dynamic at work in the moral reasoning of students was an expected response that was readily made public, or, "What I should say," and a private response, or, "What I want to say." Public responses tended to be culturally relativistic, whereas private responses tended to be universalistic, or even ethnocentric. Wayne indicated that his own religious beliefs discourage polygyny but that it still would be inappropriate to judge others in a public manner, based on his beliefs, which should be held privately. He, like the teachers, struggled with putting his personal beliefs aside when studying and publicly discussing controversial practices.

RELIGIOUS STUDY AND CULTURAL RELATIVISM

Comparative religious study caused the most ambiguity with regard to cultural relativism. Teachers approached religion gingerly, trying not to offend students of various denominations, abiding closely to the principle of cultural relativism. Students, however "polite" in the public sphere of the classroom, often revealed their utter disdain for religious groups other than their own in the private setting of an interview. Mary, a devout Coptic Christian who attended Sunny Brook, demonstrates the extent to which a negative personal reaction to a cultural group can be publicly withheld and privately expressed.

I observed Mary's class studying Islam and later interviewed her about the course. During the 2 weeks of observations, Mary made no comments, evaluative or otherwise, about Islam. When I raised the topic of Islam during an interview with her, however, she offered this viewpoint:

> I really hate the Muslim religion. I really hate it. Everybody just practices their religion, but the Muslims want to kill you if you don't accept their religion. They just want to make the whole universe Muslim, so I think OK, maybe we could just drop a bomb to kill all the Muslims. But if we do that, we destroy the ancient history of the Muslims, so we don't want to do that. Or, like, gas the people (laughs). I know that the Americans could take all the Christians out of the country and kill all the Muslims (laughs). Another solution is to have the Christians give too many births … are you writing this exactly?
>
> WG—I will when I type it.
>
> Mary—Oh (with nervous laughter).

I was surprised by Mary's comments, which I believe she exaggerated in order to amplify her love for Egypt, her country of origin, and Coptic religion. The moment in the interview that is illustrative of the tension between private hatred and public acceptance of cultural differences is when she queries me as to whether the interview will be taken verbatim. I got the sense during this interview that she became exceedingly comfortable about sharing her views. She seemed at this moment to realize that this was somewhat of a public interview, despite the sense of privacy that she had in the setting, seated alone with me, away from other students in the library. Mary's reaction lends further support to the finding that, despite teachers urging students to be tolerant of others, students in this study tended to maintain their own beliefs about Others.

Some of the students were confused by the principle of cultural relativism as it might apply to their own religious beliefs. Marge, a student at Valley High School, expressed her confusion about being nonjudgmental with regard to religious differences. She said:

> It's weird how we believe in one God and some people just think, oh there's a god of the sun and a god of different things … it's weird. I don't know (laughs) kind of, you know, like, it makes you wonder if we're believing in the right God, you know what I mean? Or, if they're just crazy or something?
>
> WG—What do you think?
>
> Marge—Well, I'm kind of confused about it actually (laughs). That's a hard thing to think about.

The confusion that Marge expressed illustrates a subtlety in studying religions in global education with a culturally relativistic stance. The students felt uncomfortable because they believed accepting the potential validity of a different religion called into question their own faith. Mr. Sidner talked about the difficulty in teaching about religion in a culturally relativistic manner.

> I want to develop an appreciation for other religions and make them understand that their own religion is always a dilution of other religions, and unfortunately that's why people are in conflict in Israel and Palestine and Kosovo and everywhere else, because of this view that I'm better than you because my God is greater than yours. They do a certain ritual say in India, the Temple of the Rat, where they worship the temple that has rats everywhere and they saw men eating out of the same dish as the rat, and they say, "Oh, aww my God, these people are crazy!" and they laugh at them and so forth. But I say it's no more crazy than you walking up and taking communion and eating a bread wafer from someone else's hand or slaughtering a cow to have some beef tonight. They (the students) panic when I try to make comparisons. I think religion is a tough issue for kids to understand, and it's hard for a history teacher to teach about it and you have to show diversity of points of view, and a lot of teachers are afraid to tackle that issue.

Students at Sunny Brook also exhibited negative views toward religious differences presented in the study of Islam. Two of the classes were watching the controversial film about the Iranian Revolution, *Not Without My*

Daughter. Some students responded negatively to Islam, specifically as it is practiced in Iran and particularly in the negative manner in which it is portrayed in the film. Mrs. Gormley explained:

> When you show the movie (*Not Without My Daughter*), people get all worked up about it. They get very worked up about that movie. First of all they get very upset with the violence, the beating, that he beats her. That is the most controversial part of the movie. They say that is anti-Islamic, it is not common in Islam to do that, it is against the Qu'ran. Not to say that men don't beat their wives in every culture, but that it would be frowned upon. That's one of the things that the kids object to and, the coverings, the chador and the scarf, and umm, that I try to bring in this idea that this is cultural, that's Persian, not Islamic.

Mrs. Gormley attempted to steer her students away from making judgments about Islam based solely on the film, ironically encouraging them to view Persian culture negatively instead. Despite her pleadings, however, many of the students maintained stereotypically negative views about Islam and Muslims.

Mr. Gordon's students at Bart High School also reacted negatively toward Islam, which Mr. Gordon described as a "fantasy type opinion." He frequently blamed the media for these stereotypical impressions, about Muslims and others, because they tended to portray cultures as monolithic and simplistic rather than dynamic and diverse. He said, "The kids think, 'I heard it somewhere, so it must be true!'" in developing negative attitudes toward people outside of their own experience. "The kids don't look any further than what is being shown to them."

Despite the generally negative views about Muslims and the lack of cosmopolitan experiences of Bart students to counter these prejudices, Mr. Gordon's class had a rare opportunity to confront their own stereotypes. One of his students, Beba, was a Muslim girl who recently emigrated from Guyana. She appeared to be of Indian origin, as that is her family's ethnic descent, but she was indeed a Guyanian. Mr. Gordon explained that her peers in class assumed she was a Hindu from India and were surprised to learn that she was a Muslim from South America. I asked Mr. Gordon how the students responded when they learned of her background. He replied:

> What came out last week, it just goes to show you they don't have a good idea of what is happening in the world. They think that everyone who is Muslim is either Arabic or black, until we did the section on Islam and Beba knew more than all of them put together. They said in disbelief, "Are you Muslim?" and she said, "Yea." They just assumed she was Hindu because

she looks Indian and they associated Hindus with India and don't know about Muslims in India.

WG—How did they react to this knowledge about Beba?

Mr. Gordon—First, it was like shocking to them, and then it was like more delightful, because they look at her as being more positively. She's a senior and she is in a freshman class and they think of her as being studious, kind of like an egghead, standoffish. But once she brought that out, they had more respect for her.

The tendency for students to respond positively to differences that they encounter firsthand is surprising in light of the fact that Beba was not a well-liked member of the class. She was fairly isolated from the other students, due to what her peers interpreted as feelings of superiority. The first-hand experience and dialogue, however, promoted a greater mutual respect, which is especially noteworthy given the widely diffused intolerance present at Bart High School.

TEACHERS AS ETHICAL UNIVERSALISTS

Teachers tried to walk a fine line between appreciating diversity, such as religious differences, and not offending students of various backgrounds or faiths. Privately, they were more willing to discuss their own perspectives about the issues addressed in class, including religion. Teachers tended to be ethical universalists in their views about moral issues. Ethical universalism is a philosophical position which asserts that there exists a "moral unity of mankind" (Jarvie, 1984, p. 67), based on secular beliefs. Universalists contend that there should be standards of treatment that cut across all societies, irrespective of culture, creed, ethnicity, and gender.

Uplifting human dignity and establishing respect for the rights of the individual are a paramount concern for universalists. Assumptions about what is right and wrong are often central to the universalist position. Universalists contend that principles of fairness and justice evolve over time, guaranteeing people everywhere standards of treatment. Universalism emanates from the principles of fairness and justice articulated in such human rights documents as the *Universal Declaration of Human Rights* (1948) (Buergental, 1995).

Most of the teachers in the study (10 of 13) privately maintained ethical universalist notions, despite their public display of culturally relativistic inquiry. Those with universalistic tendencies were somewhat tentative in their acceptance of this premise and noticeably private in declaring their sentiments. The following teacher comments illustrate the tentative and private nature of ethical universalistic beliefs:

> Mrs. Wegian/Sunny Brook—But in my gut, I think it (female genital cutting) is horrible and I wouldn't want to see it practiced in the United States in any-way.

> WG—How about in Nigeria?

> Mrs. Wegian—Would I want that? (long pause) No.

> Mrs. Gormley/Sunny Brook—My gut feeling is that we do have the right to get involved in (stopping female genital cutting). I hate to say it but, education, that's the key. Well, we watch the *Gods Must Be Crazy* and we look at who is more civilized and, who knows?! Does that give us the right because … I'm uncomfortable with saying civilized or uncivilized, but I think because of medicine and science and that stuff, we do have the right to get involved.

These comments are very instructive in the manner in which they are offered. Mrs. Wegian and Mrs. Gormley both state that in their "gut," they believe female genital cutting is wrong. These key phrases illustrate an important theme in their conversations: Global education teachers privately hold judgments about topics encountered in the course, despite publicly encouraging the students to be nonjudgmental.

Although most teachers were reluctant to share their opinions openly with their students, one teacher was particularly outspoken about her ethical universalistic tendencies. Mrs. Finberg, the daughter of Holocaust survivors, made it very clear through repeated interviews and class observations that "suffering is intolerable!" She offered a detailed argument for universalism in global education, excerpted here:

> The kids say … "What do I care about a woman in India, and if a woman gets stoned by the Taliban in Afghanistan!? Why is it my business to tell them what to do!?" But I want my students to be world human beings! Human rights are a big issue to me. We do talk about women being abused, women having more children than their bodies can really manage, being uneducated, being second-class citizens in their own country. (We talk about) the situation in Third World [*sic*] countries where women in India are forced to marry older men, and the dowry situation where a man gets tired and throws gasoline and sets her on fire and the family goes to court and they do nothing about it. Those sorts of things should just not be allowed!

I continued observing Mrs. Finberg and noticed that her teaching was consistent with her ethical universalistic beliefs. In one observation, she showed a video depicting African women carrying water on their heads over long distances. Mrs. Finberg stopped the video at this juncture to emphasize how difficult and unfair their lives were. In another observation, she described children in Pakistan being forced into labor, making soccer balls and weaving rugs, and decried this activity. I followed up on this issue with Mrs. Finberg, asking if she considered herself a universalist. She replied:

> A universalist? Yes, I would have to say yes. Some cultural traditions, while I respect traditions and I respect cultures, there are somethings we know that are painful. There are people that have no voice and don't know that there are other ways to look at it. I think of the women in Africa who go through the genital circumcision and how painful that is and then don't have the basic human right to (pause/sighs) enjoyable sexuality, you know!? They think that this has been imposed generation after generation, and they don't know that the rest of the world doesn't have that.

The tension between public and private beliefs was also evident in interviews with Mrs. Finberg. She did not make any reference to this controversy in her first interview, raised the issue as a "concern" in the second interview, and became more strident in expressing a universalist philosophy in later interviews. During the final interview, Mrs. Finberg expressed her hope that her students would also be universalists:

> The problem you have with ninth graders is that they are not universalists yet. They are so into their own little world. It is enough to get them to be open-minded about what's going on in our own country and to be angry about certain things, to be passionate about certain things, to have a feeling about certain things, then when I have to take it outside of the US you have to work that much harder to get across the picture that we are all human beings. Watching other people suffer, you know, and saying that's not my problem … (that attitude) takes some effort (to change) and it's not something you're going to do in a month or a marking period.

The comparison with most of the other teachers in the study is compelling with regard to the purpose of the class. Most of the other teachers in the study indicated that it was their task to promote global understanding with a strict adherence to relativistic inquiry in public, despite their personal attachment to ethical universalism.

Teachers seemed implicitly aware of the problematic nature of ethical universalism. Ethical universalism has been critiqued on the grounds that it is another means of promoting Western culture, where principles of fairness and justice are imbedded in the legal and political structures of nations.

As Galtung (1994) asserted, "Universalism ... the idea that what is good for the West is good for the world" (p. 13). Universalism has also been criticized as stepping on the slippery slope of cross-cultural judgment. As Geertz (1984) asserted, once you can label an aspect of culture outside the norms of universal codes, it is easy to say an entire culture is aberrant. How did teachers come to terms with this inherent tension in global pedagogy? Generally, they sought a middle ground.

SEARCHING FOR A MIDDLE GROUND

Teachers struggled to find defensible criteria for drawing the line between appreciating diverse lifestyles of other societies nonjudgmentally (cultural relativism) and critiquing particular cultural norms according to universal standards (ethical universalism). The most commonly asserted criterion for teachers as to the limits of nonjudgment was the threshold of harm. Teachers frequently asserted that behavior was acceptable as long as it did not harm anyone. Mr. Gordon of Bart elaborated:

> Yeah ... ah ... tolerance to a point. I would try and explain it that there are degrees of tolerance and you can go and work as long as ... the key rule is that as long as you are not bothering or hurting anyone, then it is ok. But if you see that it (the cultural behavior) is going to pose some type of danger for a particular group or whatever, then you can't go with it. Listen, they have certain rights, but their rights shouldn't go too much further then what a human being is supposed to enjoy. You can tell everyone what you think, as long as you don't bother anybody, but if your group has been proven to be not tolerant of another group, then they should not be tolerated.

Mrs. Gormley of Sunny Brook also believed the threshold for acceptable cultural behavior should be the "do no harm" principle. She attempted to delineate the distinction between a religion and a cult, saying:

> I guess you could say they (cults) focus on the negative, on spells, on hurting people, those would definitely be, you know, where you seem to have gotten off course, self-destruction like Jim Jones, like weapons, David Koresh ... looking for those things that are indications that the religion is not quite a religion anymore.

This distinction was important to Mrs. Gormley because it allowed her to judge those actions that were not religious. Excluding a group from the "legitimate" category to which it belongs leaves it unprotected by cultural relativism and open to critique. I have termed this criterion the *categorical exclusion*.

Various teachers drew the distinction between judgment and nonjudgment on the *categorical exclusion*. When queried about the limits of relativism, some of the teachers suggested that certain actions should not be granted the mantel of relativist protection since they were not part of the "culture" category. The notion of validity undergirds the *categorical exclusion*. Teachers felt comfortable limiting the applicability of cultural relativism as long as the group, event, and/or behavior was not part of a socially recognized category.

The students were somewhat less exact in offering a criterion for limiting cultural relativism. Most of the students did not offer criteria, but those who did suggested that location and context should be the sole criterion, or, like the old adage, "When in Rome, do as the Romans do." The students felt that all societies had particularistic mores and norms and that those were automatically sacrosanct. Pete of Sunny Brook, reacting to the film *Not Without My Daughter,* said:

> I'm not saying I believe in it, but in their life, they've lived like that for hundreds of years, there's nothing wrong with wife beating in that situation (Iran). In America, on the other hand, I think there is something wrong because people have been brought up to know they're not supposed to do it, but in Iran, where they are allowed to do it to a point, I don't think there's anything wrong with it. I think it all depends on where you are and the culture you are in.

Ham`al of Sunny Brook also offered place as a criterion for limiting relativism. He said:

> If wife beating is part of a culture, I wouldn't say anything. You can't change their culture, that's the way it is going to be. You can't go there and expect them to change and they can't come here and expect other people to think differently. They can't expect us to accept that. If I go to Iran and that's the way it is, then I won't have any right to say anything. They (Iranians) should be in control of what they do.

The few students who offered a rationale (2 out of 27 interviewed) focused almost exclusively on place and situation as the criteria. The teachers, however, suggested criteria such as "do no harm" and the categorical exclusion, which transcend place and time, and are in this sense, more universal.

CONCLUSION

Teacher and student conversations about cultural relativism offer a number of important issues on which to reflect. We see in their conversations an

honest grappling with the tension between a public expectation of culturally relativistic teaching and a private tendency toward ethical universalistic thought. Teachers and students were both aware of and ambiguous about
this tension in their studies. The study of religions, a staple of global education, was the most difficult tightrope for teachers and students to traverse.
Some students feared that accepting the validity of a different belief system
would invalidate their own beliefs. Teachers, aware of this tendency, tread
lightly, if at all, on religious comparisons. Privately, however, teachers engaged in moral reasoning about what they taught from an ethical universalist frame. Some teachers sought a middle ground between their culturally
relativistic public stance and their ethical universalist private position,
seeking criteria that would draw this boundary line fairly.

So how should Mr. Jaslow respond to little Bobby Hefka when he is challenged to accept Bobby's racism? And what should the teacher do when he
sees the Turkish boy hitting his sister in defense of "cultural" honor? These
problems may be resolvable if we begin to address controversial issues
without the simplistic dichotomies that have so often characterized controversial teaching in social studies. What seems to be lacking in terms of the
practice described in this study is sustained, reflective dialogue based on
narratives from multiple perspectives. Beyond that, a framework of caring
is needed to implement global curricula and address moral issues with attention to the emotive and social self, along with the rational one. The appli-
cation of Care Theory to the dilemma of cultural relativism is addressed in
detail in chapter 7.

Mr. Jaslow can begin by caring for Bobby Hefka because caring for students is fundamental to the work of teachers. Bobby needs to be responsive
to being cared for and practice his own caring with his peers, thereby promoting a caring school community. Mr. Jaslow can also find a way out of
the Pandora's Box of cultural relativism by modeling a caring attitude toward Others he encounters in course content and by promoting dialogue
among his students and their global counterparts. The dialogue that Mr.
Jaslow promotes about moral controversies will allow his students to practice caring, and affirm other members of his communities and the world.
Their moral controversies, seemingly so exotic and strange in the abstract,
will become situated and contextualized when discussed in terms of real
life problems rather than as abstract, hypothetical matters that are to be dis-
tantly and "rationally" condemned.

6

Conversations About Our Houses of Mumbi: Identity in Global Education

I shall never leave the House of Mumbi.
— Gikuyu pledge (Gakouo, 1995, p. 4)

The Gikuyu people of Kenya make a pledge to the House of Mumbi as their progenital mother, a symbolic statement of heritage, publicly proclaimed as a badge of identity. The Houses of Mumbi folktale offers Gikuyu people an explanation of their group's genesis, a master narrative of their history, and an explanation of existing social norms, all offered in their mother tongue (Isaacs, 1975). The Gikuyu folktale is not unlike many other stories that bind social identities in the United States: Jewish people gather and tell stories of the exodus from Egypt during Passover Seders, Christians celebrate the story of the birth of their savior at Christmas, and Muslims recount the stories of Mohammad's life through sharing the Hadith. Identity narratives are universal, rich in diversity, but unified in their purpose: to establish a sense of connection to a social group. It is through these stories, and their accompanying ritual, values, and roles, that we come to know our Houses of Mumbi.

I am indebted to my own students for raising my awareness about identity issues through their poignant questions. A White South African boy who immigrated to the United States challenged my use of the term African American, asking "Am I an African American?" A group of White males and females questioned why we were not studying more about their ethnic cultures. A young Jewish girl argued that in teaching about human diversity, I was in fact promoting stereotypical thinking by relying on generalizations about ethnic and religious groups. A White male thought it was silly to bring in guest speakers as representatives of cultural groups. A group of African American teens argued that White people could never understand their perspective so there really was no need to try. Recalling these situations now, I am reminded of how thoughtful and provocative adolescents can be when given the opportunity to express their honest thoughts and feelings. These questions linger in my mind today and have informed this current project.

The purpose of this chapter is to illustrate how teachers and students construct their understandings of identity in the context of global education classrooms. "Who am I?" is the most fundamental of all human questions, one with particular significance to adolescents. I was struck by how often issues of "Who am I?" arose in the conversations of global students and teachers in this study. Participants talked openly about themselves and their experiences, both as individuals and within larger social categories.

A number of important patterns emerge from the conversations of teachers and students about their Houses of Mumbi. Teachers perceived identity development as important, seeing their students in terms of social identity categories. The manner in which teachers taught was influenced both by the social identity categories apparent among students and by the teachers' own sense of self. Students, however, were not quite as definitive in their sense of self, with most having unexamined social identities or engaged in the beginning stages of self-searching. Most students were not personally invested in their social identity; however, they did cluster according to their Houses of Mumbi when given the option.

Why is identity discourse so prominent in global education? I offer a social psychological analysis to help explain the prevalence of social identity in global classrooms. Two specific phenomena will be articulated toward this end: (a) the tendency for people to rely on *human kinds* competence of sorting people (Allport, 1954/1979; Hirshfeld, 1996) and (b) the tendency for people to act on a single feature of their environments automatically, or in a *click, whirr*, fashion (Cialdini, 1988). I hope that by problematizing identity conversations, the reader will have a clearer understanding of how our social selves may affect learning about the world.

THREE CONCEPTUAL FRAMEWORKS OF IDENTITY—FORMATION, ACCULTURATION, AND CONFLICT

What is meant by "identity"? Identity is a multidimensional, abstract concept operating on a variety of levels. Phinney (1990) offers three conceptual frameworks for understanding identity: identity formation, acculturation and cultural conflict, and social identity theory (p. 501). Identity formation focuses *on* the self (Who am I?), acculturation and cultural conflict models address identity groups *in relation to* other groups (With whom do I fit in?), and social identity theory speaks to the self *as part of* social groups (What does it mean to be a _____?). While these domains are frequently treated as distinct elements of identity, the cross-fertilization of ideas is apparent in most identity scholarship. Social identity focuses on those categories commonly identified in the social sciences: namely, ethnicity, race, gender, religion, sexual-orientation, and class, or "aspects that identify an individual with the group (or cultural context) to which he or she belongs" (Schwartz, 2001, p. 38).

Identity formation, or ego-identity framework (Who am I?), is rooted in psychoanalytic perspectives and psychology. Erikson, building on the psychoanalytic work of Freud, developed ego-identity constructs in a foundational manner, albeit in broad strokes (Schwartz, 2001, p. 9). Marcia, a "neo-Eriksonian" identity theorist, offers a definition of identity grounded in the notion of self-structure: "an internal, self-constructed, dynamic organization of drives, abilities, beliefs, and individual history" (1980, p. 159).

Marcia (1980) extrapolates from Erikson's work two independent dimensions of ego-identity: exploration and commitment. "Exploration is the sorting through of multiple alternatives, whereas commitment is the act of choosing one or more alternatives and following through with them" (Schwartz, 2001, p. 11). According to identity status theory, articulated by Marcia and refined by many other psychologists, there are four categories: (a) identity diffusion (low commitment & low exploration), (b) identity moratorium (low commitment & high exploration), (c) identity foreclosure (high commitment, low exploration), and (d) identity achievement (high commitment, high exploration). Identity status theory contends that individuals are at different stages of identity achievement and that these stages can be externally and objectively measured (Marcia, 1980).

Acculturation and cultural conflict represent a theoretical framework rooted in the relations among social identity groups (With whom do I fit in?). As Phinney (1990) contended, "Ethnic identity is meaningful only in situations in which two or more ethnic groups are in contact over a period of time" (p. 501). Studies in this framework have focused on a linear model, which examines identity along a continuum of strong ethnic ties to strong mainstream ties. Scholars in this paradigm seek to understand how people's ethnic identities are changed when they interact in larger social contexts with other groups.

Social identity (What does it mean to be a _____?) examines how the individual understands who they are in relation to their defined social identity. Erikson (1968) saw the interplay of ego-identity and social identity as integral to the process of identity development, "for we deal with a process 'located' *in the core of the individual* and yet also *in the core of his communal culture*, a process which establishes, in fact, the identity of these two identities" (p. 22; emphasis in original).

Phinney (1989, 1990) offered an intriguing blend of identity formation (Who am I?) and social identity status (What does it mean to be a _____?). She contends that ethnic identification can be categorized in a manner similar to Marcia (1980) suggested. Phinney (1989, 1990) offered a three-stage progression of ethnic identity development: unexamined ethnic identity, ethnic identity search, and achieved ethnic identity. Phinney's model is particularly useful in light of the data collected in this study and serves as the foundation for understanding the participants thoughts and actions.

IDENTITY IN EDUCATIONAL
THEORY AND RESEARCH

Education and identity have become nearly synonymous over the past decade, due in large part to the increased attention to issues of human diversity in schools (Davidson, 1996). Gee (2001) offered a rich analytical tool for identity, including four dimensions: nature-identity (N), institution-identity (I), discourse-identity (D), and affinity-identity (A). Identity, in his typology, has to do with our nature (Nature), how we are defined by institutions (Institution), our individuality recognized through discourse (Discourse), and experiences with like others (Affinity) that constitute our sense of self. "There is a growing body of work that studies children and adults as they are mutually and simultaneously impinged on by all of the aspects of identity …" (p. 120).

Ogbu is a leading contributor to identity scholarship in education, analyzing immigrant and involuntary immigrant minorities and how they have performed differently in educational settings (1998; 1991). Employing a comparative cultural framework, Ogbu contends that the cultural incongruence of certain minority populations and the values and norms promoted in schools makes academic success unattainable for many (1991). Whereas Ogbu allowed for individual diversity within any social group, or the exceptional individual (1998, p. 163), he also offered compelling, cross-cultural evidence that the social identity of involuntary immigrants (i.e., African Americans and Burakumins in Japan) matters in terms of school achievement.

Ladson-Billings has also made important contributions to understanding how identity shapes individuals, again from an assimilation and comparative cultural framework. Ladson-Billings (1994) is probably best known for her examination of culturally relevant pedagogy, or the act of "empower(ing) students intellectually, socially, emotionally, and politically by using cultural referents to impart knowledge, skills, and attitudes" (pp. 17–18). Ladson-Billings (1995) argued the need for teachers to teach in a manner that values otherwise marginalized voices. The "psychic preservation of marginalized groups" is an integral element of Ladson-Billing's critical race theory, through the use of storytelling intended to ease the pain of racial oppression.

Heath and McLaughlin (1993) have also made contributions to the literature of identity in schools. Their comprehensive study of three metropolitan centers and the struggles of urban youth in those settings led them to the conclusion that "embedded identities, or multilayered self-conceptions, represent far more than simple labels of ethnic or racial membership" (p. 7). They found urban kids less inclined to talk of themselves and their situations from the perspective of ethnicity labels (e.g., Hispanic, African American), believing ethnicity and race to be "anachronistic symbols of another generation and political agenda" (p. 222).

Social studies education has long been a focal point of identity discourse in schools, manifest in global and multicultural initiatives. Global education theorists have attempted to discern the boundaries and interactions of local identities vis-à-vis an emergent global culture (Begler, 1998) and how the self is understood within an emerging global context (Alger, 1998; Becker, 1991). Merryfield (1997, 2001) identified the prevalence of discussions of cultural identity in global education courses, indicating the core quality of identity in this curricular field. Multicultural scholars have emphasized the presence and vitality of microcultures operating within macrocultures and the need for culturally sensitive teaching (Banks, 1996a; Grant & Sleeter, 1998; Ladson-Billings, 1994, 1995; Nieto, 1996).

When historians review the late 20th and early 21st century, identity discourse will undoubtedly be one of the intellectual hallmarks of this era. Identity discourse has clearly gained the attention of a variety of scholars in our time, from psychologists theorizing about the manner in which we develop and affiliate our senses of self to educators who theorize about the meaning of the self in classrooms and curricula to moral theorists who are concerned about how the self is oriented toward the good. How did global teachers and students in this study address issues related to identity? How do global teachers and students come to understand where they fit in their own Houses of Mumbi? These are the questions to which we now turn.

TEACHER PERCEPTIONS OF IDENTITY

Teachers were aware of their students' diverse social identities. When I was introduced to the faculty with whom I would be working at each site, student diversity, or the relative lack thereof, was the first issue raised by teachers and department supervisors. When I made my initial request of Mr. Dodge to conduct the study in one of the many high schools of Urbana, he selected Bart because it was more ethnically diverse than most of the other high schools in the district. When the teachers greeted me at Sunny Brook, they excitedly and proudly explained that their high school was an "international crossroads." When I traveled to Farmers' Knoll and began working with teachers and students at Valley, Mrs. Dilley explained that Valley mirrored the ethnic and religious diversity of the district as a whole. She also explained tensions between the Italian-American community, a small but prominent group, and the board of education, over maintaining Italian language as a course offering. In all of the schools studied herein, social identity mattered.

> Mrs. Lourdes—There are three groups that I see: Puerto Rican, Black, and Dominicans. What separates them is their cultural differences. The Blacks and Puerto Ricans don't mix but the one on the outside is more the Dominican and their behavior reflects that.
>
> Mr. Gordon—I've been in Bart long enough that I can almost tell the different type of Hispanics by the way they look. I can tell an Ecuadorian now, where I couldn't tell before. I can tell the differences between an Ecuadorian and … (pause) a Dominican from a Puerto Rican. It's subtle differences and if you are here long enough, you don't even have to know the language, but you can start to identify. You can almost tell African Blacks from American Blacks, without even speaking to them, just based on certain attitudes and behaviors.

Teachers viewed the social identities of their students, particularly ethnic identity, as having primary importance in global education courses and the ability to discern student differences as critical to effective teaching. Teachers frequently elicited student knowledge as "cultural experts," encouraging students to speak about their social identities and making personal connections to the social identities of their students, resonant with Ladson-Billings' (1994) notion of culturally relevant pedagogy. Mr. Cortez of Bart explained this approach:

Let's say we're doing the Mayas and Incas of South America. Before you even touch upon a topic, you may want to take an inventory of the class. You know that there are South American people, so you ask them, "What do you already know about this topic before you begin it?" Often they know more about the topic than I will (laughs) especially when I was in Union City, there were a lot of children from Peru, and they knew Incan culture real well. They knew Chitin language real well. They would say, "This means that, this means this ..." and they knew the sons and grandsons of famous emperors. What that does is that it raises the interest level because you are validating the students' background in the class. And that makes them feel that the teacher is sensitive to the students' background.

Mrs. Brandy of Sunny Brook also professed the power of using student identitics in world pedagogy:

I have a kid in my class whose father was a fighter with the Tamil Tigers (of Sri Lanka). That part of the course is so interesting because he came up and told them about individual differences and how his father was in the government as a minority and other Tamils, revolutionaries.

Mrs. Finberg of Valley also commented on the Latino dancing day that she arranged. She said:

The dances that we choose are Hispanic because there's a large segment of these kids in our school. Doing a little bit on Puerto Rico is important not only for the Puerto Rican students but for my other students who know nothing about Puerto Rico, so the others get a better sense of their classmates and where they come from. We just did a unit on South America and the Hispanic kids are feeling good about themselves.

Teachers operated on the principle that in global education, one needs to teach to the social identities of one's students because it is relevant, meaningful, and connected to their experiences and uplifting to their self-esteem (Ladson-Billings, 1995). The extent to which a strong ethnic-identification matters in terms of self-concept and self-esteem is still an open question, but the working theory of the teachers in this regard does have some empirical basis (Phinney, 1990).

TEACHERS' VIEWS ABOUT STUDENT IDENTITY DEVELOPMENT

Teachers concomitantly viewed their students and work in identity categories and believed students needed to develop a strong social identity. In Phinney's (1990) language, teachers felt students needed to reach identity achievement. I observed Mr. Gordon query his students about their knowledge of Catholicism, specifically, communion, confirmation, and reconciliation. He prefaced this series of questions with a blanket statement, "You Catholics should know this stuff!" Ironically, Beba, a Muslim girl from Guyana, responded to the questions posed by Mr. Gordon. Mr. Gordon frequently spoke about how his African American students did not know what it meant to be part of this social identity category, confusing Black consciousness and material gains: "To me that is a contradiction. But, this is where a lot of our African American kids are at."

Mrs. Finberg of Valley also lamented the lack of ethnic identification among her students:

> I'm sad to say this, but I'm Jewish, and while I don't know everything, I'm often surprised about how little African American students know. When you ask "Have you seen *Roots*?" I mean, you ask a Jewish person have you seen *Schindler's List* ... nine out of ten will say yes. It amazes me! Some great movies have been made, *Amistad*, Oprah's *Beloved*, some of my African American students know nothing about Africa as a continent, cultures beyond Egypt. Overall, there should be more African studies on the part of African American students ... Latinos too. Yes ... when I teach Spain as being the mother of all this, they learn things and they don't even make the connection that they are from Spain.

Mr. Gordon (Bart/urban) and Mrs. Finberg (Valley/rural) shared a high degree of ethnic identity achievement (Marcia, 1980; Phinney, 1989, 1990). They spoke reflectively and frequently about who they were in a social contexts, the ethnic groups to which they belonged, and how those identifications shaped their viewpoints and experiences. Not surprisingly, they wanted their students to have a strong connection to their social identities.

The 14 teacher participants had a high degree of ethnic/social identification. When I interviewed the participants and asked them to talk about their personal lives, each participant defined themselves, without prompting, according to social identity categories, ethnicity, gender, and religion the most frequently cited. Participants also spoke of their family roles, occupational situation, and educational background, further evidence that teachers in this study had well-developed, socially constructed answers to "Who am I? Where do I fit in? and What does it mean to be a _____?" These fundamental human questions also emerged in their teaching.

TEACHER IDENTITY AND PEDAGOGY

Teachers' social identities also mattered to the extent that global pedagogy was shaped by the varying social identities of the teachers. Teachers often noted that they taught their courses differently due in part to their identities.

They selected content that resonated with their experiences, designated additional curricular time for pursuing topics "close to home," and characterized course content according to their own Houses of Mumbi. Three teachers best illustrate this common phenomenon: Mrs. Lourdes and Mrs. Brandy with regard to gender, Mrs. Finberg concerning religion and family history, and Mr. Gordon with respect to ethnicity.

Gender

Mrs. Lourdes was proud of her pilot course at Bart, *World Cultures*. She viewed this course as distinct from the *World History* alternative in that it emphasized issues more so than, as she said, "straight history." Similarly, Mrs. Brandy of Sunny Brook boasted that *Comparative World Issues* "is the best course I've ever been connected to" because it offered so much for the students to learn. Although neither woman subscribed to the label of feminist, both asserted that they were personally interested in women's issues. When I asked Mrs. Lourdes what topics she emphasized in the course, she said, "We did a lot of women's rights" because she said it generated student interest. Specifically, her class had done a comparison of the role of women in Saudi Arabia and Urbana to "understand how it is for women over there." Topics such as rape, adultery, and spousal relations in other societies were emphasized throughout her course. I observed a discussion in Mrs. Lourdes class about the role of women in Medieval Europe, emphasizing Joan of Arc in great detail.

Mrs. Brandy also felt a strong personal commitment to teaching women's issues. Mrs. Brandy said, "I always tell the students, for 5,000 years guys have been in charge and we need to change that! You can't have a woman in a man's government, you've got to have all of them in government (laughs)!" During one lesson, a student was making a presentation on Eva Peron of Argentina. Mrs. Brandy spoke glowingly of Eva as a hero to poor people because of her ability to identify with the plight of common Argentinians. She chose to focus solely on female genital cutting in the study of Africa, emphasizing the indignity that it causes women. She addressed the role of women in Islam at great length through the film *Not Without My Daughter* and in subsequent classroom discussions.

Mrs. Lourdes' students detected her emphasis and characterization of women's issues in *World Cultures*. The following excerpt is taken from a joint interview with Randy and Irena, who were students of Mrs. Lourdes:

WG—How often does Mrs. Lourdes tell you her thoughts on topics being studied?

Irena—She does tell us how she feels sometimes. She didn't agree with the girls not being able to go to school in some countries and not being able to go into the army, and not being able to marry who you wanted. That was another thing, that if you disobeyed your family, they would have to kill you in public, because you dishonored them. And if they didn't kill you, they had to send you away.

Randy—When, ah, girls do all the cooking (laughs) ... she talks about that.

Irena—He means stereotypes, when she talks about the women and men. Women have to stay in the house. The women, I mean, the girls in our class argue that they should be equal and the men should help out at home and the boys say, "No, they should have the babies and stay home!"

Randy—The woman should be at home ...

Irena—(to Randy) What you trying to say! Women can't do men's work!?

Randy—Women should be home!

Irena—(gestures to Randy) We talk about this sometimes in class.

WG—Who would Mrs. Lourdes agree with in this debate?

Irena—She agrees with the girls!

WG—Why?

Randy—She be a woman ...

Irena—No, not because of that, because it be her own opinion. There are different kinds of opinion. Sometimes she agrees with you guys.

Randy—No, she only listens to the girls ...

Irena—Because the answers that you guys say are stupid ... like not related to the work that we do.

(Randy shakes head.)

Irena—See, this is the things that happen.

This provocative dialogue illustrates the tension that I observed in Mrs. Lourdes' *World Cultures* class around gender issues. Students sat isolated from one another according to gender, with the exception of an openly homosexual male student who sat with the girls. There was always at least a

6-foot divide in the middle of the room between the girl and boy clusters. Interestingly, Mrs. Lourdes usually sat facing the girls' side of the room and delivered lectures to this area, only making contact with the boys' side when a disruption occurred. The boys perceived, as indicated by Randy, that Mrs. Lourdes was on the girls' side, figuratively and literally, through their frequent encounters with women's issues in the course of study.

Religion and Family History

Mrs. Finberg's emphasis and characterization of issues were strongly influenced by her personal background as well. Mrs. Finberg's parents were Holocaust survivors. She talked at length about how these experiences affected her upbringing, often making her feel appreciative for the life she had, one which her parents were denied as children in Nazi controlled Europe. Mrs. Finberg's parents were being transported to a certain death at Bergen-Belsen after 2 years at a work camp. She spoke emotionally about their liberation.

Mrs. Finberg took her *World Cultures* students to the U.S. Holocaust Memorial Museum in Washington, DC. Mrs. Finberg explained how she used to "hesitate to teach about the Holocaust, but over the years I've become very passionate about it." She had completed the unit on the Holocaust just prior to my arrival. She recounted the students' motivation to learn about the Holocaust, the first topic that really excited their interest. Mrs. Finberg also relied on her Jewish identity in teaching about Judaism. She recounted:

> In the beginning of the school year, when we got to Judaism, I did a Shabat with them and they got totally into that. I was the mom and they were the children, and they asked, "When's dad coming home?" We role-played it and they were totally interested … respectful and interested. They went along with it very affectionately; there was a bonding. Everything that you do that you share with them, that you're not just this person behind the desk. I just think it helps break the ice a little bit.

Mrs. Finberg was aware that she drew on her identity to teach the course and saw this as a great advantage to her global pedagogy.

Ethnicity

Mr. Gordon believed that he could connect with his students in a special manner because of his background as an urban African American. He often compared what it is like to be a Black person in other societies and in the United States. He explained:

> I have traveled all over the world many times and I can bring the African American angle to this course. When I go to China, they see all these wealthy Black people in the media, like athletes and entertainers, so they have a different impression of me in China. It is good because I can come back and tell my students, well listen, in some respects, racism is different, because the racism you experience in the United States, some of it is institutionalized and it has been here for years, and some people don't know any different.

Mr. Gordon spoke with great passion about his students, concerned for their ability to cope in an information-based economy, products of a deleterious educational system. He believed that these deficits, coupled with being an African American, doomed many of his students to dead-end jobs at best and hopeless poverty at worst. He felt stifled by what he believed to be a negligent school administration who did not direct the wealth of state funds to help students.

Teachers tended to see their students in social identity terms, teach to those social identity categories, and emphasize their social identities in curricular choices. I have already alluded to potential explanations for the prominence of social identities in global education classrooms. The social psychological analysis of *human kind* competency and the tendency to act on these categories in an automatic manner (like a cognitive tape recording, or in a *click, whirr* fashion) figure prominently in teacher thinking about social identity. I return to this analysis at the end of this chapter as the manner in which students responded to their teachers' emphasis on social identities is my primary concern.

A TYPOLOGY OF STUDENT IDENTITY—UNEXAMINED, SEARCHING, AND ACHIEVEMENT

A majority of students interviewed for this study generally had not reached Phinney's developmental stage of achievement; they were either searching for social identity (7 out of 27) or their social identities were unexamined (18 out of 27). Only two students could be said to have reached social identity achievement. These findings roughly parallel Phinney's (1989) study of 91 high school students in Los Angeles, where she found 56% unexamined, 23% searching, and 21% achieved (p. 43).

The majority of students were in an unexamined social identity stage, as determined by the following criteria:

- Failure to self-identify with a social identity category.
- Lack of knowledge and understanding of social identity category.
- Primary focus on family situation as defining self (i.e., sister/brother).

Many of the students articulated an ethnic, religious, or gender identity, but it typically did not occur in their self-explanation. Marge, for example, when asked about her ethnic background, replied, "What do you mean? What is that?" More typically, students offered information about their families, parents' occupations, and number of siblings. Many students of Christian background did not understand the sectarian differences within Christianity. As one girl offered, "I think we were Catholic, or Christian, but I don't remember."

The second group of students are those that were either searching for a social identity (7 of 27) or had achieved social identity status (2 of 27). What characterizes those in the searching category? Students in the searching for social identity category displayed three main characteristics:

- Use of social categories to self-identify.
- Public demonstration of a strong connection to their ethnicity or religion.
- Voicing of uncertainty about their social identity.

Of the eight individuals whom I categorized as identity seekers, five (more than 50%) were from Sunny Brook High School, where global education is offered to graduating seniors, as compared to the ninth graders who took the course at Bart and Valley High Schools. Although there is limited empirical support for the influence of age on social identity formation, it is widely assumed to be a factor in developmental models (Phinney, 1990, p. 510). Perhaps this may explain why the majority of students who were 18 years old were either searching for or had reached a developmental level of achievement status.

The students seeking social identity were thoughtful and open about how they came to understand themselves in terms of social categories. Each day during Black History Month, a student would end the announcements with stories of famous African Americans. This celebration permeated the school prompting one girl on the announcements to exclaim, "You should know by now it's Black History Month, unless you got your head in a hole!" Aya, a freshman born in Puerto Rico, talked about how her teachers were making a point to teach about "Black people":

> At the beginning of the year, we got a book about African Americans in English. There's nothing wrong with it, but every year we do the same thing and I don't like that. My English teacher emphasizes that a lot. I wished that she would pick different pieces. We usually do African American stuff. Her room is all decorated with African American stuff. I don't have a problem with that, but every year they emphasize that in school, like Black History Month, and you're leaving out other people, like me!

Aya's comment clearly illustrates that students see themselves through the lens of social identity in the curriculum.

Wayne of Valley also took offense at the omission of his identity group from the course of study. As an African American male, he seemed acutely aware of the ethnic and religious groups which were getting more attention, specifically Jewish Europeans, in contrast to Africans and/or African Americans. When I asked him what problems he perceived in the *World Cultures* class, he said:

> Like I don't know a lot about the slave trade. When we do Black History Month, it's the same people every year, Dr. King, Harriet Tubman, and Sojourner Truth. That's all we study about is the same people over and over. It gets boring learning the same things over and over. I know there are more interesting people than that. But we spend a month on the Holocaust and we learn about different people, the SS soldiers, the camps, we go on the trip, we watched the movie on it. In the Holocaust we watched a movie about someone who went back to the camp. But we've never heard of anyone tell of their emotions about slavery or going back to the farm or plantation where their great-great-grandfathers were or anything! I feel that is a big part of my culture and they don't teach you in school.

Wayne publicly expressed his concerns to his teacher, Mrs. Solotore. He explained that she responded by saying they had studied Africa and that there was not unlimited time to cover all of the areas sufficiently. Wayne clearly felt confident enough about his social identity to confront his teacher, yet he is unsure of the details of his ethnic heritage and wants to learn more. Aya is curious about Puerto Rico, yet lacks the resources, beyond her own experiences and family, to investigate her ethnic affiliation. Wayne and Aya are apt illustrations of students who are not unknowing or apathetic about their social identities (unexamined stage), but have also not yet solidified a sense of their social selves.

Sherry and Beba, late teenage Muslim girls from Egypt and Guyana, respectively, are the only two students categorized as having reached social identity achievement. Both of these individuals, like most of the teachers in this study, were able to:

- Frequently talk about their social identity.
- Demonstrate a depth of knowledge about their social group identity.
- Reflectively think about how those identifications shaped their viewpoints and experiences.

These two individuals were willing to articulate information about their social identity and critique the manner in which their group was being portrayed in class.

The most intense and public offense taken by a student over the portrayal of identity was at Sunny Brook. All of the *Comparative World Issues* classes were shown the film *Not Without My Daughter*. The film, based on the book by the same name, portrays Iranian Muslims as being religious zealots who will do anything for the Ayatollah.

I was observing the last day of the film in Mrs. Gormley's class, which she had planned a discussion to debrief the movie. Sherry, a Muslim from Egypt, became irate during the course of the discussion because of the film's portrayal of Islam and subsequent comments made by her peers about her religious beliefs.

> Mrs. Gormley cautioned the students about marrying someone from another background with which they were unfamiliar, pointing to the ignorance of the woman from *Not Without My Daughter* in what she was getting into. One African American female student commented, "The roles of a man and woman are very different in Islam ... the man controls every aspect, he tells her what to do, she's there to please him ..."

> This comment prompted the ire of Sherry, "See I don't know if I should ... I have a lot to say about this movie, so maybe I'll wait until later." Mrs. Gormley said, "Go ahead, talk." Sherry continues, "OK, Robin said I get too defensive but you don't understand how it is to live your life ... ok, ok, my friend, a boy, I won't mention his name, but he came up to me the other day and said, only half-kidding, 'I'm going to become Muslim so I can marry my wife and beat her!' I can't believe it! People feel sorry for me because I am a Muslim! The beating thing is not religious, it's not about Islam, it's cultural, it's for Iran!" Mrs. Gormley interrupted, "I don't even think it is about

Iran...." Sherry continued, "Yeah, in Islam you think men have all the power, but women have all the power, women have the power ... they make it seem like she's a slave but it's not like that! Islam is a religion, ok, there's no such thing as a Muslim country! I want to cry because I hate this movie! I get so upset! And you, Mrs. Gormley, you show this movie as our study of the Middle East, and that's how people see the Middle East ... it's wrong!"

I subsequently interviewed Sherry about this incident, and she said that she was tired of being treated as a curiosity because she was a Muslim.

Categorizing individuals according to a typology of social identity achievement is problematic. This approach assumes that the researcher can uncover enough data to accurately categorize an individual. As a researcher, I cannot assume the "objective-knower" stance of determining the developmental stage of these individuals. My purpose in offering these categorizations is for exposition, helping the reader organize the student conversations in a manner that is digestible, but not absolute. I offer these categorizations tentatively, with a steady recognition of the variability and fluidity in social identity development (Aboud, 1987).

Student Identity Clustering

One of the most striking and repeated patterns in class observations was the identity group clustering that occurred. Whenever students were given an option, they tended to sit with peers whom they perceived, sometime consciously and often unconsciously, as being like them according to their social identity. The students and teachers were somewhat aware of and perplexed by this pattern. The following student excerpts from all three schools indicate their relative awareness about identity group clustering:

Beba (Bart/urban)—All the Blacks are together, the Puerto Ricans together, the Dominicans together. I don't see much of a mix of the different ethnic groups. Most of them stay with their own groups. It was how they were brought up, to stay with their own groups. They believe in it.

Marge (Valley/rural)—You know how we have two cafeterias? Mr. Sidner ... made a point that how when we're sitting in lunch, we sit with our race. If you ever sit in the lunchroom, there's one side with Puerto Ricans and African Americans and on the other side there's Whites. It's kind of weird that when you sit with the people at lunch, they're all your same race and you don't realize that. You want to stick together with them and hang out with the crowd. I didn't really think of it until he mentioned it, but there's a lot of Puerto Ricans and African Americans where I sit.

Pete (Sunny Brook/suburban)—In my English class, it's funny, we're really open about stuff like this (ethnicity). There are about four Black kids, three

Indian kids, two Korean kids, and a bunch of White kids. We joke around because it's funny that all the Black kids sit together and all the White kids sit together. We joke about it because the other day our teacher made us switch seats and we said, "No, you're sending us to the ghetto!" but we know the kids can joke about it.

Funderburg (1999, p. 87) and Hansot (1993, p.202) similarly found that when students had the freedom of choice about with whom to sit and talk, they selected like people on the basis of ethnicity, race, and gender. Tatum (1999, chap. 4) explains that the tendency to seek affiliation with similar people is a normal and necessary part of adolescence. Most of the students were unaware of the social identity divisions, evidence of their unexamined stage of identity development. Students aware of the social divisions viewed the clustering as a paradox, as did some of the teachers. Social separations seemed to conflict with often expressed beliefs about being indifferent to supposedly superficial aspects of identity, such as skin color.

Clustering did not occur strictly within socially defined ethnic or gender groups. Depending on the situation, students created their own groups. In Sunny Brook, the international crossroads high school, some ethnic groups were so limited in numbers as to preclude a true cluster. Immigrants, such as those from China, Thailand, and Egypt, were not large in number. In such situations, students often based their ethnic group affiliation on their being different from the majority White population of the school. Mary and Hsong of Sunny Brook, immigrants from Egypt and China, respectively, affiliated with the "international group." Mary commented on what they had in common:

I have all immigrant friends. We talk about cultural information, since I have friends from all over the world. If you have an American friend, there is just nothing to talk about because it is the same old, same old and you don't really fit in. But with your immigrant friends, you really fit in because you are an immigrant and they are like your real best friends. The American kids don't want to be with us.

The same situation existed for Beba at Bart High School, where she was one of two students in the school from Guyana. Most of Bart's immigrant students were from the Dominican Republic, and as such, created their own group. The smaller national groups were so few in number as to impede the development of a hybrid group. Students like Beba were, therefore, generally alone and informally unaffiliated.

One cannot ignore the dynamic of power in student identity clustering. Pete, a White suburban male, jokes about being sent to the "ghetto" in his classroom yet does not seem fazed by the phenomenon of student separation. It has little real significance for Pete as he treats it as a curiosity. Mary, a Coptic Egyptian immigrant of minority religious background, however, has a very different perspective. Her comment that "the American kids don't want to be with us" suggests an imposition of separation coupled with a willingness to create an immigrant social group. Inverting the comments is revealing, as Pete is not saying "the immigrant kids don't want to be with us," assuming that his is the "in group" and the alternative, the disparaged "ghetto" people. Mary does not view being integrated as a "step down," or, into the "ghetto." Rather, Mary demonstrates a subtle desire to be assimilated along with a recognition that those sentiments are not reciprocated by her White, nonimmigrant peers.

The presence of identity in global classrooms is clear from the data presented herein. Teachers recognize and teach to student social identities, teachers themselves are influenced by their social identities, believe it is important for students to recognize their social identity, and demonstrate to their students the global connections inherent in their social identities. Students, particularly younger adolescents (age 14–15), are generally either uninterested in social identity or are seeking a social identity. Students of all identity development types tend to cluster according to their various Houses of Mumbi.

IMPLICATIONS

The most obvious implication of these findings is that there is a certain disconnect between global teachers and their students around issues of social identity. Whereas teachers tend to have reached a level of social identity achievement, the majority of their students have not, particularly those around the age of 14. Despite exhortations to "know thyself" in a social identity sense by teachers, the majority of students, especially the younger ones, were not quite ready or willing to heed the message. The majority of students remained in an unexamined stage of social identity development.

Empirical findings clearly indicate that students can recognize human differences at a very young age, probably between 4 and 9 (Aboud, 1987). The ability to be conversant, knowledgeable, and reflective about one's social identity, or as Phinney (1989, 1990) has coined, identity achievement, is a decidedly different matter. Global education courses provide students with an opportunity to confront questions of human diversity explicitly. The long-term effects of studying Others, and by implication, oneself, is not revealed in this study. Perhaps global courses of study assist in the attainment of identity achievement over time, but this is the focus for another inquiry.

A Social Psychological Analysis of Identity in Schools

Why is identity so prevalent among the participants in this study? While this chapter has illuminated the rich conversations of teachers and students about social identity, one is left to speculate about why social identity has such prominence. Much can be said for the importance of identity discourse generally in our society (Heath & McLaughlin, 1993), particularly as it relates to schools (Davidson, 1996). The emergence of multicultural and global education as curriculum fields clearly contributes to this phenomenon. In reviewing the data, however, I wonder if there might be other ways of explaining the presence of identity in global classrooms.

Social psychology offers insights into the human psyche that may help explain why social identity is so prevalent. In general terms, sociologists are concerned with how people are in groups and psychologists are interested in how people are in themselves. The merger of these related fields offers insight into how people think in social settings and how their patterns of thought affect the social situations in which they engage. Two theoretical constructs seem to be most relevant to the influence of social identity in global teaching and learning: (a) People have a tendency to rely on human kinds competence of sorting other people (Allport, 1954/1979; Hirshfeld, 1996), and (b) people tend to respond to a single, salient feature of their environments automatically, or in cognitive tape machine, *click, whirr* fashion (Cialdini, 1988). Each of these principles is offered in light of the conversations unfolded in the beginning of this chapter.

Human Kind's Competency

How do we see the world and other humans? Humanity is so diverse and complex as not to be readily understood. To come to terms with incomprehensible diversity, we readily and naturally categorize people to make them understandable. Our cognitive structures are designed in such a way as to think in categories. As children, for example, we learn about the category of "things that are round" by playing with a ball, drawing circles, and seeing round shapes in our environments. We come to categorize countless things according to their fit in the "round" cognitive group. Once we have established categories, we begin to prejudge on the basis of those constructs. "A new experience must be redacted into old categories. We cannot handle each event freshly in its own right" (Allport 1954/1979, p. 20).

Categorical thinking is a necessity, but it has obvious limitations. We tend to assimilate as much as possible into clusters in order to simplify our lives. We rationalize our categorical thinking when confronted with contradictory evidence ("Yes, but they are just an exception …"). Furthermore, we assign value to the categories we create ("I like Jewish people because …" or, in the negative, "I dislike Chinese people because …"; Allport 1954/1979, pp. 21–23). The tendency to categorize the world around us has also been referred to as the principle of least effort: "To consider every member of a group as endowed with the same traits, saving us the pains of dealing with them as individuals" (p. 173). What emerges from this tendency to categorize human kinds is a tendency to essentialize, or the belief that people have an essence. "There is an inherent 'Jewishness' in every Jew … 'the logical Frenchman,' 'the passionate Latin'—all represent a belief in essence" (p. 174).

Hirshfeld (1996) extended Allport's analysis, arguing that the tendency to think in human kinds categories is illustrative of an innate tendency to categorize according to race and/or ethnicity. He is not suggesting that race or ethnicity is innate, but rather, that race and ethnicity feed on the innate tendency to categorize people in human kinds. As Hirshfeld notes, "Race may be parasitic on a domain-specific competence for perceiving and reasoning about human kinds" (p. 72). In other words, the human mind tends to think in a categorical manner and race/ethnicity is one of the most facile and observable human categories. So, the human mind latches onto these categories easily.

The aptitude for human kinds categorization was apparent in these global classrooms. Teachers demonstrated the tendency to "see" their classrooms in ethnoracial terms (e.g., "There are three groups that I see: Puerto Rican, Black, and Dominican"). Teachers exhorted students to understand themselves in social categorical terms (e.g., "You Catholics should know this stuff"). Some students, those toward the achievement end of the social identity development spectrum, wanted more of their category included in the course of study (e.g., "You're leaving out other people, like me!"). Participants were evidently comfortable with these social categories as they had deep meaning in their cognitive frameworks and social interactions.

Automatic Responses (Or, the Cognitive Tape Recording, Click, Whirr)

It is hard to find something written about education currently without coming across the need to be reflective. Indeed, in *reflecting* on my own use of the term in this book, I too have used the term repeatedly. Although it is a desirable goal for how we should conduct our human affairs, some evidence suggests that it runs counter to the innate tendency of humans. Rather than think reflectively, or as Dewey (1910/1997) said, in a manner that is "careful, thoughtful, and persistent," people tend to do quite the opposite (p. 9). Whereas Allport (1954/1979) and Hirshfeld (1996) referred to this tendency to think in terms of human kind categories, Cialdini (1988) described a human tendency to recognize one salient element of our environments (e.g., race and ethnicity) and turn on the cognitive tape(s) that we have related to that feature. Instead of reflecting on the unique aspects of novel situations and different individuals, we revert to the automatic responses that are programmed into our cognition, playing our "one size fits all" cognitive tapes (*click, whirr*).

The phenomenon of playing the cognitive tapes of identity provides an additional explanation for the actions of participants. Cialdini (1988) identified some basic social psychological cognitive tapes that are culturally imbued and readily reverted to when information becomes too vast and complex. When confronted with a variety of product brands, for example, our cognitive tapes revert to the "expensive = good" rule (p. 5). When we are given a gift, our cognitive tapes play the "gift = obligation" rule (p.21). These fixed-action patterns are numerous in human cognition and increasingly necessary, as we "exist in an extraordinarily complicated environment, easily the most rapidly moving and complex that has ever existed on the planet" (p. 7).

With regard to social identity in the classroom, I suggest at least one corollary cognitive tape, that is, "social identity = different thoughts and actions." I am suggesting not only that people are inclined to think of Others in terms of a human kinds approach, but also that people *act on* these thoughts in a manner that is simplistic and automatic. The appearance of human diversity is quickly and easily substituted for the reality of human diversity, and with it, assumptions are acted on about how people think, what they value, and how they are likely to behave on the superficial evidence of how they physically appear (*click, whirr*).

What did the cognitive tape players, *click, whirring*, sound like in this study? Teachers focused on the social identities of their students (e.g., "I can almost tell the different types of Hispanics by the way they look") and altered curricular offerings accordingly (e.g., "The dances we choose are Hispanic because there's a large segment of these kids in our school"). Students illustrate the *click, whirr*, automated responses of social identity, as they "stuck together" with people who shared in some of their Houses of Mumbi (i.e., ethnicity, race, gender) without being aware of this tendency (e.g., "They are all your same race and you don't realize that").

I am not asserting that these two phenomena (the tendency to think in human kinds *and* to act on these thoughts in an automatic fashion) are misdirected; rather, I offer these two social psychological theories as ways of understanding the larger dynamic of what is happening in global classrooms. If Hirshfeld (1996) was correct, the construct of ethnicity is parasitic on our cognitive tendency to think in terms of human kind categories. Thus, it is deeply rooted in our minds, and therefore, not easily ameliorated or altered. Similarly, if we are to believe Cialdini (1988) that we easily slip into tape recording like cognition and action when information becomes overwhelmingly complex, there is a valid need for thinking categorically.

CONCLUDING THOUGHTS

We all belong to various Houses of Mumbi. These Houses, rather than buildings of wood and concrete, are mental constructions that provide us with a sense of affiliation, fulfilling our human need to belong. I have tried to illustrate the complexity and dynamism of these Houses, all of them at various stages of completion, by retelling and analyzing the understandings of the various participants.

What do we know about the construction of Houses of Mumbi in global education from this study? We know that teachers emphasize the social identities of their students through course content, believing that the development of a strong connection to social groups among students is vital. We know that teachers also accentuate their own social identities in the manner in which they approach global teaching. We know that students are at various developmental stages of social identity achievement, most unexamined in terms of their social identity, with a minority actively searching, and just a few having achieved a firm social identity. We know that students tend to cluster according to their social identities, often unknowingly, in an automatic fashion that may be indicative of the tendency to see the world in terms of human kinds.

If we accept the argument that the patterns of human cognition (category-seeking and automatic) are real in our identity discourses, then we need to increase our awareness of these dynamic processes. The answer is not to exclude categorical thinking, as it is a necessary and helpful aspect of human thought. Similarly, expunging the focus on particularities is also undesirable because exceptions inform our conception of the whole and suggest new, emergent patterns otherwise unseen. The key is to articulate these cognitive processes in such a way that people can contextually and judiciously decide when one type of cognitive process is more appropriate than another (seeing the whole vs. seeing the particulars; Gaudelli, 2001a).

This chapter concludes Part II: Problems. I have attempted to present some problems in teaching globally (nationalism, relativism, and identity) in ways that are productive and provocative. Illuminating the difficulties that teachers and students face when they teach about the world leaves us with a number of lingering questions and some important insights about how to address these dilemmas. How can teachers resolve the inherent tensions in global education between national loyalty and global responsibility? How might teachers and students come to terms with ambiguities in cultural relativism? How can teachers and students engage in meaningful conversations about our Houses of Mumbi? These questions frame chapter 7 of Part III: Alternatives, to which I now turn.

III

Alternatives

Educators have long been searching for the holy grail of curriculum and instruction, the most effective ways of teaching that will produce the highest quality learning. Much education reform today is based on the assumption that there is a "best" way to teach and learn, and that we simply need to replicate these "best practices" so that "success for all" will be achieved. Although these are admirable sentiments, as a teacher, I find that what works with one group of students can be ineffective with another class; what motivates one student leaves another unmoved. What is often overlooked in these "best practice" formulations is the unique dynamics of each group of students and their teacher.

The book's focus thus far has been on describing the unique contexts and problems related to global education in three schools. What follows is an exploration of how teachers might rethink dilemmas, equipped with the insights of teachers and students in this book and elsewhere. My purpose is not to prescribe a set of "tried and true" methodologies in a "one-size-fits-all" manner, but rather to explore how problems that lie within the curriculum field of global education can be fruitfully reexamined and to raise questions toward that end.

Rethinking Nationalism, Cultural Relativism, and Identity in Global Education

The problem fixes the end of thought and the end controls the process of thinking.

—Dewey (1910/1997, p. 12)

The scope of problems presented in the previous part has fixed our attention on the complex dilemmas associated with global pedagogy. The "ends" presented in this chapter are really not ends at all, but rather alternative ways of looking at pedagogical problems in global pedagogy. Rather than contribute to a limited "problem = solution" discourse, I seek to offer alternative ways of looking at extant problems in three areas that many global educators face regularly: nationalism, cultural relativism, and social identity.

NATIONALISM

Nationalism and Globalism

How can teachers resolve the seemingly inherent tensions in global education between national loyalty and global responsibility? Global education is a curriculum that uniquely stresses the role of the student in the global community as well as the national setting. The teacher conversations from my study clearly indicate tensions between national and global affiliations, with teachers seeking a way to justify these apparently dual and juxtaposed commitments. Some chose to emphasize subgroup cohesion, others asserted that the United States is not perfect, just better than all other nations, and still others argued that all people should be treated equitably and justly, regardless of national affiliation.

Case (1993) and Diaz et al. (1999) have argued that supposed tensions between global and national loyalty are purposely misconstrued by detractors of global education. They suggest that the problem lies not with competing allegiances to the world and nation, but in falsely dichotomizing the world from nations and vice versa. Curriculum guides are typically founded on geographic divisions, usually dichotomous ones: United States and the world. Secondary students, depending on their state of residence, typically take 2 years of U.S. history, one year of world study, and one year of government/civics and/or economics. The most prominent feature of this curricular scope and sequence is the misleading U.S./world division that persists.

A deeply held assumption in the dichotomized curriculum is that the United States is a unique social, political, cultural, and economic entity that deserves special attention and is fundamentally unlike the rest of the world. This idea has been referred to as the doctrine of American exceptionalism: "Project(ing) onto a nation ... qualities that are envied because they represent deliverance from a common lot" (Appleby, 1992, p. 419). Not only is the United States *different* than other nations, according to American exceptionalism, it is fundamentally *better*. American exceptionalism suggests a master narrative that ignores or minimizes embarrassing events or shameful episodes (e.g., Japanese internment and the Atlantic Slave Trade), despite our awareness that "more complete perspectives result in a closer approximation to the actuality of what occurred" (Banks, 1996a, p. 8). Call it national hubris, the inertia of institutional history, or simply the perpetuation of traditional curriculum, the fact remains that the United States is treated as a study set apart and vigorously defended as such (Ravitch & Finn, 1987; Schlesinger, 1991).

Children are taught to believe that the U.S. political system, for example, *uniquely* promotes freedom and equal opportunity. By omitting the discussion of other political systems, children are indirectly taught that the rest of the world is subjected to lives of bondage and oppression. "Our history lessons have plotted the progress of freedom and nationhood as a Western rite of passage; modernity has been set against the primitive and despotic ways of the rest of the world" (Willinsky, 1998, p. 121). The messages are less blatantly nationalistic today as they were in during the Cold War when students in Florida, for example, were required to take a course that instructed in the evils of communism and the righteousness of capitalism (Diaz et al., 1999; Nelson, 1976). The ideas of American exceptionalism, however, continue to have profound, if more subtle, force in curricula.

Whereas there is a legitimate and necessary place for study of the United States, why remove it from the global context in which it emerged? Everything about the United States, past and present, has global connections: economic commerce, peopling, cultural mores, political ideology, and language, to name a few. In order to teach about the United States with accuracy, one is driven to examine the global connections that are inherent in its development. The diversity of the United States, illuminated in countless stories told and those yet to be known, create a national heritage that is as problematic as it is diverse.

Do we truly want to promote a global perspective? If so, global learning requires us to rethink our assumptions about how the world can and should be studied and how the United States fits within these conceptions. Willinsky (1998) details the manner in which people in the West are miseducated around the concept of human difference, how we learn about the world through dividing it up:

> We are schooled in differences great and small, in borderlines and boundaries, in historical struggles and exotic practices, all of which extend the meaning of difference. We are taught to discriminate in both the most innocent and fateful ways so that we can appreciate the differences between civilized and primitive, West and East, first and third worlds. (p. 1)

"Othering" in education, or the construction of human categories as the out-group, thereby making people of these groups appear "exotic" and "foreign" (Banks, 1996b, p. 81), is an unfortunately well-established practice. McNeill (1963), for example, offered an epic historical account that emphasizes the rise and fall of "great" civilizations, omitting "uncivilized" societies and/or historicizing Others as having once been great (Chinese, Egyptian, Mayan), with the implication that they are no longer worthy of study. Thinking such as this, deeply imbedded in curriculum formulations that separate the West from the rest, promotes chauvinistic assumptions among children, fortifying misleading stereotypes about Others that are fundamentally counterproductive to global learning. American exceptionalism is part and parcel of this mindset, as it Others the world, setting in sharp contrast the differences, or divisions, that undermine multicultural and world-minded perspectives.

Rethinking Nationalism, Revising Curriculum

Nationalistic curricula of the sort just described is incongruent with global pedagogy. Willinsky (1998) contended that we need to unpack our assumptions about learning a divided world and search instead for the intersections of human societies throughout time (p. 86). How might this be accomplished? Rather than limiting study about phenomenon to the United States, students can be encouraged to see various social problems as shared and global. Table 7.1 provides some suggestions for how typical curriculum standards might be altered to incorporate a global perspective.

Curricula designed in this manner challenges the Othering notion of American exceptionalism, promoting a global orientation for learning. Empirical research suggests that students who take courses where study of the United States is accomplished in a global manner are more likely to adopt an internationalist perspective than students in classes that emphasize American exceptionalism, who tend to adopt a nationalistic viewpoint (Benitez, 2001).

Cooperative inquiry is another means of unpacking assumptions about divisive global learning. As a teacher, I often ask students to define problematic terms in global education (i.e., *ethnicity, race, nation, civilization, civilized, uncivilized, first world, third world, tribal, developed, develop-*

TABLE 7.1

Global Curriculum Standards

American Exceptionalism model	Global model
Understands the military and economic events of the Civil War and Reconstruction	Understands the social dimensions of the United States Civil War in light of another global case study of insurrection: French Revolution, Nigerian Civil War, or the Chinese Communist Revolution
Understands the social and cultural impact of immigrant groups and individuals on American society after 1880.	Understands the global phenomenon of immigration, its social effects on the host and country of origin, and the increasing phenomenon of refugees.
Understands the social and economic impact of the Great Depression on American society.	Understands the period between World Wars as one of global economic depression and upheaval through a comparative case study of the United States and one of the following societies: China, Germany, or the Soviet Union.
Understands the role of the citizen in American democracy (to) develop and define his or her own political beliefs and tendencies.	Understands that citizens are defined by national legal status, that global political belief systems are diverse, and people have the ability to choose political affiliations to varying degrees around the world.

Note. Examples from Florida's Sunshine State Standards in Social Studies (2001).
Note. www.firm.edu/doe/cgi-bin/doehome/menu.

ing, underdeveloped, traditional, modernity, and *indigenous*), particularly when they arise in class discussions. After defining these terms based on their own experiences, knowledge, and course materials, I engage them in a discussion of each term, using the following prompts:

- What is the history of this terminology (e.g., *ethnicity*)?
- How are these terms used today (i.e., in media, vernacular, advertisements, textbooks, conversations)?
- What are the connotations of the terms—positive and/or negative?
- Why are terms that describe similar human phenomena (i.e., *civilization* and *tribal*) used differentially? By whom? For what purpose(s)?

This cooperative inquiry promotes a great deal of critical thinking, encouraging students to make explicit their own assumptions about the world. Further, it challenges them to reconsider the manner in which they implicitly Other, or bifurcate, the world.

Studying the United States from a global perspective is doable and academically defensible, but it remains at the margins (Benitez, 2001; Diaz et al., 1999). Marginality may be a blessing, according to Banks (2001), allowing us to offer unfettered possibilities from the outside in, thereby rethinking the foundations of curriculum. The neat and clean categories of the world and the United States, dualistic and distorting, remain staples of curriculum formulation in schools. I suggest, however, that teachers can work within existing curriculum organizations to promote global learning rather than nationalistic study.

CULTURAL RELATIVISM

Rethinking Cultural Relativism Versus Universalism—Care Theory

How might teachers and students come to terms with tensions between universalism and cultural relativism in global education? Perhaps the alternative lies in a fundamental shift in the manner in which we engage moral controversies, rather than in developing a middle ground approach (An-Na'im, 1992; Asher & Crocco, 2001; Gutman, 1993). Care theory represents an alternative means of engaging moral controversies that does not lead toward the bitter attack–defend spirals that have typified previous discussions in this area. Next, I discuss three interrelated aspects of care theory: definitions and elements, building and linking caring school communities, and applying care theory to global moral reasoning.

Definitions and Elements of Care Theory. Care theory acknowledges the tension between relativism and universalism, yet departs from dualistic thought in coming to terms with moral reasoning. Noddings (1984) rejected relativism, per se, asserting that care is universally accessible (p. 5). Rather than viewing moral controversies as imperatives, however, Noddings argues that rarely are moral dilemmas "sufficiently similar" to require one person to do as another person has done. "The lessons in 'right' and 'wrong' are hard lessons—not swiftly accomplished by setting up as an objective the learning of some principle" (p. 93). Care theory offers a means of rethinking moral problems from a frame that emphasizes affective and emotive capacities without completely disregarding empirical and rational thought.

Care theory is grounded in receptivity, relatedness, and responsiveness (Noddings, 1984; Pinar, Reynolds, Slattery, & Taubman, 1995). Receptivity involves the ability for the one-caring, or the carer, to move beyond empathy and toward duality and engrossment in the lives of others. "I set aside my temptation to analyze and to plan. I do not project; I receive the other into myself, and I see and feel with the other. I become a duality" (Noddings, 1984, p. 30). Relatedness refers to the connections that people have on a continuum of intimacy from mates, family, friends, colleagues, and neighbors. Responsiveness corresponds to the ability of the one-caring to provide care for those in relationships with them. Emerging from a feminist perspective, care theory is not exclusive to women, although women may be predisposed to implementing care due to socialization patterns (Noddings, 1984, 1992).

Caring has four components: modeling, dialogue, practice, and confirmation (Noddings, 1984, 1992). *Modeling* is the way that those in a position of one-caring act towards others, regardless of what they say they believe about caring. *Dialogue* is open-ended and genuine, wherein "neither party knows at the outset what the outcome or decision will be" (Noddings, 1992, p. 23). *Practice* is concerned with the manner in which those who are cared for have the opportunity to gain skills and insights about care-giving. *Confirmation* is similar to the notion of unconditional positive regard, as the one-caring recognizes the fundamental humanity and dignity of the person, regardless of particular behaviors.

Caring and schooling are frequently seen as distant cousins, perhaps those not even on speaking terms (Gaudelli, 2001b; Kaplan, 2001). Dedication to a traditional, liberal education of mathematics, language arts, sciences, social studies, world languages, and other discipline areas frequently supersedes many educators' concern for the child as a human being; likewise, the institution of school. Noddings (1984) contended:

> One cannot dismiss thinking and reasoning from ethical conduct ... it is a matter of emphasis and of origin.... I do not respond out of blind sentiment, but I put my best thinking at the service of the ethical affect. If I exclude cognition, I fall into vapid and pathetic sentimentality; if I exclude affect—or recognize it only as an accompaniment of sorts—I risk falling into self-serving or unfeeling rationalization. (p. 171)

Care theory challenges educators to construct a humane center for emotional and cognitive development that is built on relationships and nurturance.

Building and Linking Caring School Communities.   Establishing a caring community in schools, one based on receptivity, relatedness, and responsiveness where modeling, dialogue, practice, and confirmation of caring behaviors occur, is fundamental to any curriculum, and certainly to global education. What might schools do to create caring environments? The first step is to make caring an explicit, shared goal of the community. Faculty and staff would need to begin the process of care-building with each other. Here are some suggestions, illustrative but not exhaustive, about how to create caring school communities:

- Reduce class sizes to enhance individual relationships among all school participants.
- Create student mentoring programs, where older peers are individually responsible for younger students, providing an opportunity to teach students how to be receptive, related, and responsive in their relationships.
- Encourage teachers to visit families and neighborhoods of their students, spending time with students outside the confines of school.
- Establish small group counseling opportunities for all students, to share their frustrations and anxieties in a safe place (led by faculty with counseling background and supported by the entire community; Gaudelli, 2001b).

Once caring is imbedded in the culture of the school, caring relationships within the school community can be extended, directly and indirectly, to the world beyond. Global education in this setting becomes a lived experience of the school and its participants, rather than solely a substantive course of study to be visited daily for a semester, soon left behind. Global education is premised on the need to recognize global interrelatedness, empathetic consciousness, human and planetary diversity, and the role that humans play in shaping the global society. Caring about the world, as obtuse and challenging a goal as that may be, is central to global curricula. If we can create caring communities in schools, the potential for extending this ethic of caring to the community beyond the school is increased. Globalizing curriculum becomes part of a natural progression of care.

Establishing connections with schools in various nations can make the caring link tangible and meaningful. Many teachers in the United States have ready access to global partnerships with schools via the Internet (Tye, 2001). Despite the digital divide that limits access to technology for many students throughout the world, those who have it can get connected with students from every region of the world. E-mail exchanges, creating on-line dialogue sites, development of student list serves, and other forms of direct communication can serve as avenues for extending care beyond the boundaries of individual schools.

Applying Care Theory to Global Moral Reasoning. Even this somewhat idyllic illustration of a reconceptualized school that is rooted in caring and is globally connected falls short of addressing moral controversies. Critics argue that though creating caring school communities and linking them globally (via technology, travel, and communication), we are still left with encountering differences in moral perspectives. Female genital cutting, euthanasia, infanticide, and abortion are just a few of the potential dilemmas that our global moral discourse faces. What of these?

Care theory provides a way of seeing moral controversies not in absolute terms, but with sharp attention to contexts and situations. As Noddings (1992) offered:

> Women who speak in the different voice refuse to leave themselves, their loved ones, and connections out of their moral reasoning. They speak from and to a situation, and their reasoning is contextual.... that is not to say that caring is irrational or even nonrational.... but its emphasis is on living together, on creating, maintaining, and enhancing positive relations—not on decision-making in moments of high moral conflict, nor on justification. (p. 21)

Care theory is not rule-centered, but situational, differing from rationalistic ethical reasoning that has characterized the debate about universalism and cultural relativism.

Care theory urges global teachers and students to focus on lived human problems as they are differently experienced by participants. Most of the teachers with whom I worked, while articulating a commitment to public nonjudgment, had private reservations about particular cultural practices and beliefs. Teachers tended to understand the world in universal terms; or, "the notion that anything that is morally justifiable is necessarily something that anyone else in a similar situation is obligated to do" (Noddings, 1992, p. 21). Moral education has been founded on the development of moral reasoning, but this premise is rejected by care theorists in that moral considerations are not a search for a fundamental truth about how to behave or what to believe, but caring for those involved or affected by the moral quandary and understanding their situation as unique.

How might a global teacher addressing moral controversies employ care principles? In addressing moral controversies in the classroom, such as polygyny, the teacher would exhibit an openness to inquire about the experiences of people living in this situation. They would ask for more information: How do the women in this situation feel? What are their reasons for being involved in a polygynous marriage? How do the children react? How does the husband treat the wives? How do wives treat the husband? What is beneficial about this relationship? What is damaging about this relationship? How do our own cultural lenses shape and distort the manner in which we view and understand this practice? and on and on. In this quest for more information, the teacher is not only modeling intelligent inquiry, they are also indicating their own tendency to avoid absolutes and seek particulars. Again, the purpose is not to judge, but to understand and care.

Dialogue is perhaps the most crucial piece of care theory as a means of moral inquiry as it allows the students to engage in open, honest discussion where conclusions are not foregone. Noddings intends this dialogue to occur between the one-caring and the cared, but this may not always be possible in the study of global moral controversies. Role play, primary source material, e-mail dialogues, chat rooms, and student exchanges, however, may serve as opportunities to discuss moral controversies. Dialogues about moral controversies with Others, rather than assumptions and inferences gleaned from reading second and third-hand narratives of a controversial issue, would help to create meaningful global conversations about controversial issues that are care based.

Teachers wanting to engage adolescent students in a study of rites of passage, for example, would seek out particular people who have experienced them and gain as much information about the practice before making vacuous statements such as "female genital cutting is wrong." Rather, students

should be encouraged to take the role of one-caring in this moral controversy and develop their caring skills. Inversely, students in the United
States, for example, should be in the role of cared for on moral controversies that face adolescent youths in our society (e.g., premarital sex, abortion, school violence, and poverty) and their global counterparts in the role
of one-caring. Dialogue with people in real circumstances is more meaningful than reading about seemingly "strange and exotic practices of the
Others" that have characterized some studies in cultural diversity.

SOCIAL IDENTITY

Rethinking Identity

Teachers, in their attempt to make meaning of the broad identities in global
education, often use generalizations about Others to simplify the task. In so
doing, they speak of cultures as distinctly demarcated, discernible objects
for study, reifying the notion of culture. Little effort is made to engage in
conversations about cultural information not neatly or easily categorizable.
Teachers tend instead to lump disparate people together into neat categories, illustrated by how they speak about the identity groups studied.

The following excerpts from observations, field notes, interviews, and
documents capture the manner in which teachers and students engage in
identity discourse:

"The Romans believed that they were superior."

"The Haitians ... what do we know about them? They are poor, right?!"

"Hindus ... what do they believe in?"

"Buddhists are a very passive, loving, happy people."

"Africa has resources but it doesn't have the know how to get the resources
and use them. It involves skills and equipment and all of that translates into
money. Many countries in Africa are newly formed, recently under colonial
control, and they don't have the money to put towards social thing. I wanted
you to understand that."

"China doesn't have racism towards Blacks; it is not part of their culture."

"I went to Russia and saw they were so damn poor, they didn't have a way
out of the poverty."

"The beating thing is not religious, it's not about Islam, it's cultural, it's for
Iran!"

"Yeah, in Islam you think men have all the power, but women have all the power."

"Find out what the Iraqis thought about the war."

"For each event, find the Jewish reaction, the Palestinian reaction and the international reaction."

There are indeed elements of validity in all of these statements. The problem arises, however, when these categorizations are portrayed as the way that all Romans felt, what each Hindu believes, and the know-how of every African. Such categorizations are invalid to the extent that they diminish the changing, multifarious condition of all human societies and ignore the individual variability therein.

Appiah (1992) offered an insightful analogy that further illustrates problems associated with human categorization:

> In a sense, trying to classify people into a few races is like trying classify books in a library: you may use a single property—size, say—but you will get a useless classification, or you may use a more complex system of interconnected criteria, and then you will get a good deal of arbitrariness. No one—not even the most compulsive librarian!—thinks that book classifications reflect deep facts about books. Each of them is more or less useful for various purposes; all of them, as we know, have the kind of rough edges that take a while to get around ... there are millions of us ... who can be fitted into no plausible scheme at all! (p. 38).

Burtonwood (1996) further suggested that "labels like Indian, or woman, or Muslims, or American are no more than starting points ... the use of 'them' is a generalization which misrepresents the complexity of the group" (p. 231).

Unpacking Identity

Rethinking identity in global education requires that we unpack our assumptions about race, ethnicity, culture, class, gender, and the myriad other Houses of Mumbi present, literally and figuratively, in global classrooms. Rather than encouraging students to think of humans *solely* in terms of their group affiliations, teachers ought to encourage students to seek diversity *within* social identity groups. In the examples previously offered, teachers might have students articulate the stereotypical understanding and counter those with contradictory evidence. Instead of portraying belligerent Israelis and Palestinians in the current conflict, for example, teachers could show evidence of individuals on both sides advocating a peaceful resolution. A teacher might address the economic poverty in Haiti and Russia, but they should also demonstrate the wealth that exists among certain individuals in each of these societies. Using transformative academic knowledge, global teachers can challenge simplistic notions of identity.

Teachers can also problematize generalizations by discussing a way of analyzing minority group dynamics. Kymlicka (1997) examined the notion of collective rights of minorities. In particular, he identifies two important tensions within minority groups: external protections and internal restrictions. *External protections* demonstrates how a group steels itself against dominant and disparaging majorities. *Internal restrictions* is how the group coheres by limiting the rights of individuals to reshape the group from within (p. 14). Teachers in this study and beyond tend to focus on the external protection while ignoring the internal debate and restrictions that exist within social identity groups. They can approach this issue fairly easily by querying students as follows:

- Why do certain sects within Judaism claim that other sects are not really Jewish?
- What does it mean to be Jewish in these various sects?
- How has Jewish unity been present in the history of Jewish life? Disunity?

Illuminating these external and internal tensions is a more accurate means of examining social identity as it more completely captures the dynamism of social group identity. Another powerful way of making the point of "diversity within diversity" is to engage students in an identity meeting. Students are asked to self-identify with social groups, clustering themselves with similarly identified peers. Once in their identity groups, students explain what it means to be part of each group, to what extent the group identity influenced their lives, and what points of disagreement they found in their conversations. After the caucus, students present their group to the class, illustrating the commonalities and differences within their group.

Teachers may need to rethink calls for students to "Know thyself" exclusively within the constructs of ethnicity, race, culture, class, and gender. Adolescents, as evidenced in this study and elsewhere, are at varying stages of social identity development. Attempting to interest or engage them in an area of study (e.g., global education) through the hook of social identity, though an honorable goal, may be falling on deaf ears. Social identity categories had meaning for a limited number of students, whereas the vast majority did not think of themselves within socially recognizable identity constructs (i.e., ethnicity). As Heath & McLaughlin (1993) found, ethnicity has become passé among many urban youths, tending to define themselves in microsocial terms (e.g., geeks, jocks, skaters) rather than macrosocial terms (e.g., African American, Latino, Catholic).

Social identity is constantly being reshaped and redefined. This is most evident in the evolution of census bureau categories. In the 1950 U.S. Census, three categories existed for race/ethnicity: White, Negro, and Other Races. This classification changed gradually each decade, with the 2000 Census using the following categories: Hispanic/Latino, Black/African American, American Indian/Alaska Native, Asian, Native Hawaiian and Other Pacific Islander, White, and Other Race (U.S. Census Bureau, 2001, p. 2). As the Census Bureau indicates, "Changing lifestyles and emerging sensitivities among the people of the United States necessitates modifications to the questions that are asked" (p. 1). Social identity is clearly a malleable concept with great variation over time.

Young people seem to be at the fore of reshaping social identity. People under the age of 25 were most likely to identify themselves as "of two or more races" in this most recent census (Banks, 2001). This suggests fluidity in the construction of race along with changing demographics among younger people. Census data and other academic studies (Heath & McLaughlin, 1993) point to the emergence of a new youth dialogue about identity, perhaps in its nascent stages. Our constructions of social identity will undoubtedly change in the next 50 years, as they have in the past 50 years, and global educators need to adapt rather than cling to rigid notions of self. Knowing thyself is indeed a valuable resource for global teachers and students, particularly for those who wish to teach in a constructivist manner that is rooted in the experiences and interests of the child. The categories that we use to describe our self-knowledge will inevitably change, but the fundamental questions of identity will remain: Who am I? With whom do I fit in? What does it mean to be a _____?

CONCLUSION

Problems are the wellspring of change and innovation. Educational problems, such as those posed herein related to global education, encourage us to rethink the manner in which we bring the world into our classrooms. With regard to three central pedagogical problems in global education (nationalism, cultural relativism, and identity) I have offered ways of reframing the issues with a few examples of how these reconceptualizations might be practiced. These problem areas are not all those that beset global educators, nor all the controversies in the field (see Pike, 2000). How to address nationalism, cultural relativism, and identity in global education, however, represent significant challenges that raise more fundamental questions about global pedagogy.

There have always been exceptional teachers who problematize pedagogy, research and examine multiple alternatives, participate in professional development, and reflectively implement changes. For teachers to rethink some of these critical areas in global education, however, this process of reflection and revision needs to be normative in the profession. Most teachers with whom I have worked are up to this challenge and interested in partaking, but they need the opportunity to do so. Teachers need to be treated as the community intellectuals that they are and given the space, time, and resources to thoughtfully and critically engage their work.

8

Teachers as Community Intellectuals: Professional Development in Global Education

We will change American education only insofar as we make all our schools educationally inspiring and intellectually challenging for teachers.
—Meier (1995, p. 142)

I recall explaining to my students that I would not be in school for a few days as I would be attending the annual conference of the National Council for the Social Studies. One of my students asked a simple but poignant question: Why are you going? A variety of answers came to mind—to be the best teacher I could be; to bring ideas back from the conference that would enrich my students and the school; to share what I knew from my classroom; to discuss common problems with colleagues. I was unaware of my rationale until that question arose. Instead, like a migratory bird, I was making the annual journey to the national meeting instinctively. Professional meetings were just "what you did" as a teacher. Professional development is more than just attending conferences. Professional development involves all aspects of teacher learning: graduate coursework, institutes, curriculum meetings, informal dialogues, in-service activities, self-reflection, and independent research.

Professional development generally encouraged my excitement about ideas, the lifeblood of teaching. I cannot be sure that all of the professional development activities improved my students' learning. Meetings periodically required time away from teaching, interrupting the flow of pedagogy that teachers cherish. In-service programs rarely were an exact fit for my teaching situation. Graduate courses left me tired the morning afterwards. Taken as a whole, however, professional growth inspired me to be a more effective teacher. Professional development helped me feel intellectually alive and connected to colleagues beyond my school, which allowed some of my students to catch my contagious enthusiasm for ideas.

This chapter is premised on the empirically supported assertion that teaching and learning can be improved by promoting the intellectual development of teachers. This broad philosophical commitment is examined through the scholarship of three areas integral to professional development: (a) *teacher in-service,* (b) *teacher as curriculum creator,* and (c) *teacher as researcher.* Within each of these dimensions of professional development, a brief analysis of connections to global education is offered. I conclude by arguing that teacher in-service, teacher as curriculum creator, and teacher as researcher each contribute to an emergent social role for teachers, that of (d) *community intellectual.* Drawing from Dewey's detailed thinking about what constitutes intellectual activity, I outline the notion of *community intellectual* as it applies to teachers.

The notion of *community intellectual*, though encompassing all aspects of professional development, transcends narrow boundaries of teachers working solely within the confines of schools. *Community intellectuals* are those that model and teach intelligent inquiry with students and freely share their intellectual capacity with larger communities. Prior to exploring three manifestations of professional development (in-service, teacher as curriculum creator, and teacher as researcher), an *a priori* question is briefly examined: Why intellectual teachers?

WHY INTELLECTUAL TEACHERS:
A RATIONALE

Talk of teachers as intellectuals raises eyebrows and suspicions both within and outside the field of education. Teachers often look askance at the idea of being an "intellectual," as many adopt a routine, workaday attitude that is commonplace in the field (Palonsky, 1986). Cole and Knowles (2000) explain that teachers fear being ostracized by their peers if their involvement with a teacher-as-researcher project is widely known (p. 108). Dewey (in Boydston, 1977) referred to the anti-intellectual tendency among teachers as "intellectual subservience," or the urge to find a simple, correct formula for effective teaching that does not require careful thinking (p. 257).

Efforts to diminish teacher agency are all too common in the contemporary policy climate. Standards and high-stakes assessment de-professionalize teaching by forcing local school boards to implement "teacher-proof" curricula that are test-driven (Kohn, 1999; Morse, 2000; Steinberg, 1999). High-stakes assessment saps intellectual activity from students and teachers, reducing pedagogy to test preparation. Perhaps the most disturbing aspect of the entire movement is the implicit messages being sent to students: Facts are the most important elements of learning, smart people are able to retain the most factual knowledge, speed counts, and right and wrong answers are always achievable (Kohn, 1999, p. 86).

Some teachers, drawn to the field for their love of children and ideas, are leaving. Cathy Williams of Seminole County, Florida, for example, left the field because of one-size-fits-all testing and the subsequent lack of respect that is endemic and growing (Bell, 2000, p. A16). Certainly we should have standards and accountability in education, but these need to be premised on sound educational principles of what constitutes effective teaching and learning, rather than on criteria of limiting teacher agency, promoting political expediency, and achieving cost efficiency. Standards and accountability need to be supported by professional development that is funded by local communities and the states that implement them. Standardization and high-stakes assessment in their current forms promote mundane, rote pedagogy that reign in curiosity, dampen inquiry, and encourage student and teacher apathy.

In order for positive school change to occur, a different set of conditions is necessary: (a) elevating the professional status of teachers; (b) promoting the professional, and thereby, intellectual, development of teachers; and (c) encouraging discourse among teachers and students. When intellectual activity sits at the core of education, teachers and students act as co-inquirers and co-creators of curriculum, rather than passive vessels into which the "curriculum" is poured.

When teaching and learning are viewed as intellectual endeavors, teacher professionalism becomes an essential characteristic of the job. Darling-Hammond (1988) defined professionalism as affirming three principles: knowledge as the basis for meeting unique client needs, welfare of the clients (i.e., students) as paramount concern, and collective responsibility of the profession for definition, transmittal, and enforcement of standards (p. 12). The maintenance of a profession is a demanding intellectual endeavor, one that requires rigorous attention to theory and practice. Professionalism suggests reasoned standards of practice to meet changing needs of students, not static prescriptions. Professionalism requires "continual learning, reflection, and concern with the multiple effects of one's action on others as fundamental aspects of the professional role" (p. 39).

Some have raised legitimate concerns about society becoming overly professional. Metzger (1987) has argued that professionalism, in teaching and elsewhere, has deleterious effects on democratic societies. He suggests that as knowledge becomes more specialized, the possibility of tyrannical wielding of power increases; "a society in which everyone is at the mercy of someone more thoroughly in the know" (p. 18). Professionalism in teaching, in this sense, provides teachers with too much authority. Though Metzger raises valuable criticisms, the public nature, and therefore regulation, of teaching by law and school administration is well established. The risk of tyrannical professional teachers, therefore, is unrealistic in the current environment.

Why promote teaching as intellectual activity? Such a mindset encourages curiosity about ideas among teachers and students, illustrating the need for teaching to be organized as a profession. But the notion of what it means to be a teacher intellectual has been only briefly appraised thus far. We now turn our attention to the elements of professional development (in-service, teacher as curriculum creator, and teacher as researcher) that illustrate what it means to be a teacher intellectual.

IN-SERVICE

In-service is defined as the process engaged by teachers toward accruing knowledge, skills, and attitudes over the course of a career to enhance their professional capacity. Three curricular domains are typically the focus of in-service education: content, instruction, and school ecology, or context (Pinar et al., 1995, p. 764). Traditionally, in-service has been viewed as a means of teaching teachers that which they did not receive in their preparation programs (Neff, 1990). Such programs tended to focus on the universal nature of teaching and schools and how they could be improved by offering a generic program of improvement.

A recent trend that has shaped in-service addresses the uniqueness of teaching in specific contexts. This type of in-service is referred to as *phenomenological* as it places the experiences of the teachers in their particular settings as the focus of the education (Pinar et al., 1995). The emphasis in these programs is not offering a set of discreet skills and/or knowledge bases, but providing the tools with which teachers can co-create their own pedagogical solutions to extant problems.

Empirical studies have not determined the extent to which in-service changes pedagogy over the long term, although preliminary evidence favors in-service of a phenomenological variety (Boote, Wideen, Mayer-Smith, & Moon, 1999; Dean, 1991; Goldenberg & Gallimore, 1991; Molseed, 2000). Molseed (2000), for example, led a group of current teachers in developing a contextually specific internship handbook for their school. The process of creating the handbook was arduous and revealing, encouraging the teachers to learn more about their own practices and procedures while preparing to help pre-service candidates (p. 477). Yuen-Kwan (1998) inquired about the "life after the course," or the sustainability of teacher in-service over 6 months. She found that teachers perceived utility in the in-service immediately following the work and 6 months after the course, suggesting that such courses live on in classrooms (p. 7). Leach and Conto (1999) found that short in-service (i.e., ½ day) can be effective in changing long-term teacher behavior if it is accompanied by procedural feedback. Even in this episodic style of in-service, a process of contextualized feedback was required for success in changing pedagogy.

In a study currently underway, I find that teachers have generally negative views toward traditional in-service (i.e., decontextualized, generic teacher training models), viewing them as an imposition from outside that wastes time and does not improve teaching. As one teacher in the study claims, traditional in-service is equivalent to "teacher detention." In comparison, secondary teachers are generally responsive to in-service that is content specific, has long-term goals, promotes extended dialogues, and contextually examines pedagogical applications (Gaudelli, in review).

Global Connections for Teacher In-service

In-service for global teachers is critical for at least two reasons: (a) Teachers lack global knowledge due to the absence of attention to international study in their own education (Heater, 1984; Merryfield, 1998; Tye & Tye, 1992); (b) The rapidity of globalization and exponential growth of information requires constant learning on the part of teachers (Dean, 1991). Global education has received substantial attention relative to other areas with regard to in-service (Adler, 1991, p. 216), due in large part to the inadequate teacher preparation for global teaching. The National Council for Accreditation of Teacher Education (NCATE) noted that "the (teacher education) curriculum lacks adequate content and experiences in global and/or multicultural perspectives" (Gollnick in Diaz et al.,1999, p. 8).

Global education and in-service seem a natural fit, as long as elementary schools, secondary schools, and institutions of teacher education continue to marginalize global learning. In-service is a critical dimension of professional development and the intellectual development of teachers, perhaps the most common of those examined in this chapter. Teacher as curriculum creator, although less common in formal ways, is an equally important element in the professional development of teachers.

TEACHER AS CURRICULUM CREATOR

Curriculum reform has been metaphorically compared to an ice sculpture, a seemingly solid object that quickly begins to melt and change when it is molded. As a result, discussions about curriculum frequently turn into "dealing with objects—like course materials, textbooks, assessments, and units of study" because of the fluid nature of the topic (Hatch, 1999, p. 2). Curriculum is such an obtuse and contested term that defining it sharply is problematic, leading toward reductionist thinking. Jackson urges, rather, that definitions of curriculum be understood within the "rhetorical structures" from which they emanate: cognitive processes (how we think), technological orientation (occupational goals), self-actualization (self-knowledge), social reconstructionist (social justice), and academic rationalist (discipline knowledge; Pinar et al., 1995, pp. 28–29). Our concern is less with defining the dripping block of ice that is curriculum and more with those who attempt to sculpt it: teachers.

Thornton (1991) reminded us that teachers are curriculum and instructional gatekeepers, making daily decisions that shape what is taught and how it is taught. In this sense, all teachers are curriculum creators. Even the teacher who passively accepts the directive curriculum "as is" will invariably add their particular emphases. Imagine a scripted class where teaching is prescribed and perfunctory, with all the lesson elements laid out for presumably expedient execution, a vision approaching reality in some school districts (see Morse, 2000; Steinberg, 1999). Even in this scenario, where a teacher seemingly has no input, the curriculum will be shaped, or authored, by the pedagogue. The inflection of her voice, the attention of her eyes, body movements, pauses, and silences are just a few of the tangible and profound ways that even the most rigid adherence to a prescribed plan are shaped by teachers.

The locus of curriculum creation and reform has frequently been an area of contention in the field. Duncan (1973) suggested that curriculum directors have the expertise to exert their authority, power, and influence on teachers to implement curriculum change. In this early formulation, curriculum change was fundamentally the task of administrators, perhaps working in concert with their staff. More recently, the focus of change has shifted closer to the classroom and the experiences of teachers. Bolin (1987) contended that teachers are creators of curriculum due to the inevitability of teacher choice in the classroom (p. 106). "When a teacher makes decisions … he or she is engaged in a rational, intellectual activity" (Norlander-Case, Reagan, & Case, 1999, p. 27). Teacher thinking *in situ* has come to be known as *critical reflection*, or "think(ing) about what is taking place, what the options are, and so on, in a critical way" (p. 27).

Curriculum creation scholarship has tended to focus more on the design rather than implementation of curriculum, at the expense of understanding implementation and teachers roles as creators. Bolin (1987), in surveying curriculum theory, suggested, "All the thinking goes into design; design is important; the teacher is instrumental" (p. 101). Clandinin and Connelly (1992) offer the conduit metaphor in understanding this phenomenon. They argued that curriculum has been viewed from a means–end perspective that separates teachers from the curriculum; or served by an intermediary, such as a curriculum director (Duncan, 1973). Curriculum reform, in this paradigm, is the work of interlocutors from beyond, rather than teachers from within. The task of the teacher, as such, is to implement the curriculum reform (p. 71; Clandinin & Connelly, pp. 370–372).

Curriculum creation clearly includes classroom implementation and teacher thinking, a fairly recent recognition in the literature (Cornett, 1990; Norlander-Case et al., 1999). Given the recent focus on the classroom environment, apprenticeships and master teachers might enhance curriculum change efforts. Apprenticeships exist to promote the social reproduction of knowledge and skills, where "those who are more knowledgeable gradually help novices develop expertise" (Levstik and Barton, 2000, pp. 14–15). Levstik (1997) applied an altered version of the apprenticeship model to students and teachers, where both are learners in the co-construction of historical knowledge. An apprenticeship model in teaching allows veteran teachers to share their experiences with novices, assisting their curriculum development skills. Identifying teachers who possess the requisite skills, experience, and knowledge to effectively develop curriculum is an important piece. Schools might implement a master teacher model toward that end, encouraging the sharing of intergenerational pedagogical experience (Klein, 1985).

Philosophy and Curriculum Change

Curriculum creation is perhaps best understood on a continuum, including control, consensus, and emancipation (Pinar et al., 1995). Control creation, exemplified by the "teacher-proof" curriculum, is typically organized in a top–down fashion originating from outside schools. Consensus curriculum creation is premised on negotiation (Bolin, 1987). Negotiation allows interested parties within and related to the school community to make divergent philosophical premises explicit and design and implement curriculum that everyone can accept, if not savor. Emancipatory curriculum creation assumes teachers will "develop knowledge, undertake research, change, grow, reflect, revolutionize their practice, become emancipated, emancipate their students, engage in group collaboration, assume power, and become politically active" (Clandinin & Connelly, 1992, p. 377). Emancipatory curriculum creation is clearly the most demanding of the teacher in this taxonomy.

Assumptions about what constitutes the good life and how that is achieved underlie all curricula; therefore, all efforts to create and change curricula are ultimately philosophical propositions. Bolin (1987) recommended the following questions toward making those assumptions clear: "What does it mean to be a human being? What does it mean to educate? What is the purpose of schooling?" (p.103). Dialogue about what constitutes the "good life" will suggest which model of curriculum creation is preferred. If one responds to the question "What does it mean to educate?" by stating "To instill in children the suitable knowledge and skills for economic success," clearly a control model is most appropriate. Conversely, if one responds to the same question by stating "To illuminate examples of oppression for the development of an ethos of social justice and a commitment to social action," an emancipatory model is most fitting.

Curriculum creation has been beset by the failure of those involved in the process to plainly articulate their philosophical foundations (Bolin, 1987). Ideologies that tend to be valued in society during a certain period of time (i.e., progressivism in the 1920s, conservatism in the 1980s) are often reflected in curriculum philosophy (Clandinin & Connelly, 1992, p. 367). The intellectual climate of the era, therefore, often presupposes answers to fundamental questions.

An example of this in contemporary discourse is the prevalent assumption that the purpose of schooling is to provide children with job market skills so they may be gainfully employed in the future. Again, this notion is so deeply imbedded in the cultural climate of our time as to give it the force and weight of canonical truth, particularly among the lay public and policymakers. It is the task of curriculum creators, including teachers, to make explicit those presuppositions about knowledge, human nature, and truth that lie at the core of curriculum debates to promote intelligent dialogue and implementation (Egan, 1978).

Global Connections for Curriculum Creation

Global curricula, according to Pike and Selby (1999), represents the merger of two strands of educational thinking: world-mindedness and child-centeredness (p. 11). Global education, defined as such, is clearly a field with a great deal of latitude with regard to curriculum creation. Acknowledging that schools cannot teach the totality of the world in one course, or in the course of a lifetime, how can they choose which ideas to include and which ones to omit? Massialas (1996) recommended the following criteria in selecting global curriculum topics: *relevance* of the issue, *content* that triggers thinking, issues that encourage *action*, issues that can be *practically* studied, and issues that embed *multiple perspectives*. Theoretical literature can serve as a guide in making curricular decisions, but ultimately the power to decide rests in the hands of global educators in the field.

Teachers with whom I have worked, including participants in this study, tend to emphasize those content areas with which they had the greatest degree of background knowledge, and therefore, comfort level. In a curriculum field as diverse as global education, those preparing or engaging in this pedagogy need significant time to develop those content fields with which they have little familiarity. It is not beyond the realm of reason to suggest that teachers in this field may need additional release time to prepare, at least during initial stages of their careers, to enhance their grasp of curriculum breadth.

Curriculum creation was formalized in all of the districts studied herein, generally adhering to a consensus model and occurring over the summer break. Global education courses were given special attention by department chairs studied, because they recognized the challenging nature of their work. I attended Valley's curriculum creation meeting, which occurred over the course of 2 weeks, in which teachers were paid. During their deliberations, they talked about *World Cultures* and the difficulties they were having in "covering" the course content. Suggestions were made as to what topics to emphasize, omit, and edit. They brainstormed interesting extension activities for existing topics and the development of a common portfolio assessment.

Although I did not visit the other two schools during their summer curriculum work (Bart and Sunny Brook High Schools), teachers shared their experiences from this process and seemed genuinely engaged by the revision process. Bart was piloting a *World Cultures* class to replace *World History*, though most of their conversations focused on the selection of a new textbook. Sunny Brook's *Comparative World Issues* teachers had a great sense of ownership of the course of study. The curriculum guide listed the teachers' names along with the course name ("Gormley and Brandy's Comparative World Issues") and seemed to have a freer hand in course development then their colleagues at Bart and Valley.

Global teachers cited a lack of time during the school year as a major impediment to curriculum development. The lack of time to fully engage global curriculum is similar to what most teachers engaged in curriculum reform experience (Berliner & Biddle, 1995, p. 338). It was evident from the teachers' comments that they were willing to engage in curriculum development, if they had the time, as Mrs. Finberg articulates:

> We have to start rethinking teaching. A teacher can't be the secretary, the typist, the call up the parent person, and the purchase order preparer, all while being creative in the classroom. I need someone to pull something from literature and art to support my cultural study. Instead, I have to do that all myself, and sometimes the task is so overwhelming, I just don't have the time to do it, so the idea goes out the window. It's more frustrating for social studies. Look at the breadth of what we teach! Not just skills, concepts, geography, politics, art, economics, literature, music ... everything plays a role in society!

Curriculum creators need time to develop classroom materials and inquire about content areas in greater depth. They also need evidence, broadly defined, about what works in their unique context and how they can be more effective in implementing global curriculum, so that curriculum creation can be responsive and intelligent. Despite evidence of effective pedagogy widely available on the macro-level, it is the ideographic evidence from the school environment in which teachers are trying to globalize curriculum that is critically important. Toward this goal, teachers can become constructors of knowledge as well as curriculum; they can be researchers.

TEACHERS AS RESEARCHERS

Evidence, in the sense of teachers as researchers, comes in a wide variety of types. *Evidence* conjures up images of professional empirical studies, statistical analyses, and prestigious think-tanks creating "legitimate" or "real research" (Cole & Knowles, 2000, p. 98). Educational research has long been the domain of scholars, typically in colleges and universities, produced in a hierarchical fashion. Researchers *generate* and analyze data while teachers *consume* the knowledge created. Although this process has some value in education, action research offers a complementary means of inquiring about the nature of classroom life from the vantage point of the practitioner.

Cochran-Smith and Lytle (1993) offered a paradigmatic view of educational research that tends to unfold chronologically. Three paradigms of research are identified: teachers as technician, teacher and classroom ecology, and teacher as researcher (pp. 6–7). The technician paradigm is the earliest tradition of educational research, typically associated with quantitative methodology. For the better part of the 20th century, the purpose of educational research was to ferret out principled, empirical truths so that this knowledge could be universally applied to improve pedagogy. The second paradigm, teacher and classroom ecology, recognized the naturalistic and contextual qualities of pedagogy, attempting to capture these nuances in qualitative research, such as case studies, narratives, and ethnographies.

Teacher as researcher, the third and most recent paradigm, represents a significant departure from the other two approaches. In the former, teachers and their experiences are objectified. After the research is conducted, they are expected to be the recipients of knowledge that is created elsewhere. Teacher research, or action research, however, places the experiences of the teacher at the center of knowledge construction, because they "have daily access, extensive expertise, and a clear stake in improving classroom practice" (Cochran-Smith & Lytle, 1993, p. 5). Teacher research is thus defined as "the systematic and intentional inquiry carried out by teachers about their own schools and classroom work" (pp. 7, 24).

Advocates of action research "seek to dissolve, explode, and deconstruct the taken-for-granted and reified forms of curriculum research" (Pinar et al., 1995, p. 491). Some action research forms commonly reported on in the literature include narratives, journals, oral inquiries, observations, interviews, document analyses, and/or modes of knowing yet undocumented. The key elements in action research involve using data from one's own learning environment to develop knowledge of the local environment toward creating local theory (Cochran-Smith & Lytle, 1993, p. 55; Cole & Knowles, 2000, p. 89). Action research emphasizes the process of inquiry, rather than the methodological structure for the sake of reproducibility. As teachers and students are brought into the process of knowledge creation, a "community of inquiry" is established that places knowledge construction at the core of classroom activity (Wells, 2001, pp. 7, 14–15).

Action research is most commonly used to understand classroom dynamics and particular teaching strategies. Feldgus (1993) examined a variety of language arts techniques in the context of their own classrooms. Teachers are frequently drawn to evaluate how changes in their classroom behaviors affect student learning (Kochendorfer, 1997). Collaboration of students and teachers in joint research efforts have also been documented (Chinn, 1998) along with parental collaboration efforts (Feldgus, 1993). Zygouris-Coe, Pace, Malecki, and Weade (2001) discussed the nature of action research in a university setting, particularly the inherently relational and problematic nature of collaboration (p. 410). Sweeney, Bula, and Cornett (2001) examined how a beginning high school chemistry teacher researched the intersection of his personal practical theories and his practice through a teacher-as-researcher process.

Action research, despite hundreds of published reports and frequent citations in educational literature, is supported more in rhetoric then in reality. A series of obstacles prevent a shift toward teachers as researchers, including the isolation of teachers, socialization of teachers as knowledge consumers, and suspicion and contempt of educators for educational research (Cochran-Smith & Lytle, 1993, pp. 86–87; Palonsky, 1986). A supportive environment is needed to implement action research programs. Action research can be nurtured if school districts and the communities that support them value the intellectual capacities of teachers while recognizing the problematic nature of inquiry.

Global Connections—Teachers as Researchers

The potential for action research in global classrooms is great indeed. Global teachers can make use of the autobiographical narrative development recommended in action research literature, similar to the personal prologue in this book. Understanding the manner in which teachers have come to know the world in their own lives is critical as it gives them a way of relating to their students, particularly in the United States, where the overwhelming majority of citizens do not have a passport and lack international experiences. Teachers, perhaps with the aid of Boulding's (1988) *Portfolio of Global Experiences* or Merryfield's (1997) *Tree of Life* activity, can heighten their consciousness of their own global learning process, thereby aiding their students in similar pursuits.

As global education involves reaching out beyond oneself in a metaphorical sense, care must be given to provide a safe, secure environment in which this cognitive reorganization can occur (Pike & Selby, 2000, p. 25; Rogers, 1969). Part of feeling "safe" involves making students have some ownership and agency in the class. Classroom meetings provide an opportunity to make explicit the goals, processes, and problems experienced by teachers and students for the purpose of brainstorming solutions based on the data of shared experiences (Donoahue, 2001). Classroom meetings can also provide teachers with important insights about how to make their classrooms safer, more inviting environment where students feel comfortable to intellectually stretch themselves.

The study reported on in this book is an example of the ecological research paradigm. As a high school global education teacher, my presence was perhaps less threatening to participants, as I was a peer rather than a "university researcher." Despite the similarities in our roles, a certain distance remained in our relationships as they were aware that this was a research effort. In conversing with colleagues over extended periods of time, I became increasingly convinced that they could be doing similar studies themselves, if they had the time and support to do so. Though I was not in a position to advocate systemic changes in any of these schools, this experience helped to persuade me that teacher research holds great potential for global teaching, and indeed, all pedagogy.

COMMUNITY INTELLECTUALS

The final section of this chapter addresses the overarching notion that imbeds each of these areas of professional development: in-service, teacher as curriculum creator, and teacher as researcher. Teachers' latent roles as community intellectuals subsumes all of the ideas presented earlier, offering these in a new light that emphasizes the connectedness of the teacher to the multiple communities they serve.

Community intellectuals are defined as people in the process of developing their capacity, and that of others, to reflectively frame inquiry, garner evidence, make claims, and draw tentative conclusions about experiences toward common interests. Community intellectuals, specifically teachers, have the ability both to model intelligent action and guide others in the development of their capacities. Community intellectuals not only have the responsibility of modeling and teaching others in the pursuit of intelligent action, but also in offering their capacity to various communities in guiding the transformation of society.

Dewey argued that teaching is inherently an intellectual activity. In the often-cited *How We Think* (1910/1997), Dewey examined how reflective thinking can be encouraged in schools. "But the teacher's problem—as a teacher—does not reside in mastering a subject-matter, but in adjusting a subject-matter to the nurture of thought.... What preparation have my pupils for attacking this subject? What familiar experiences of theirs are available? What have they already learned that will come to their assistance?" (pp. 204–205). For Dewey, pedagogy is rigorous intellectual activity, both for teachers and their students. Careful attention has to be paid to the experiences of the child, problems as they perceive them to be, and the social context in which their understandings emerge. The teacher's task is to flexibly harness emerging intellectual capacities and direct them toward social ends.

Dewey, ever the pragmatist, was troubled by the tradition of dividing the intellectual from the practical, particularly in teaching. "The neglect of deep-seated active and motor factors of experience is a fatal defect of the traditional empirical philosophy" (1916/1966, p. 271). Removing the intellectual from the practical is counter-productive, to Dewey, as he viewed intellectual and practical factors as necessarily interwoven in our making sense of the world. Experimentation is not a random activity, for example, but one guided by experience and fundamentally rational in origin and effect. School is a unique place where practical activities can be elevated beyond the "mundane ... and trivial" level to a theoretical dimension that informs both the original experience and ongoing intellectual constructions of the child (p. 273).

Dewey viewed experience as a great educative storehouse in the classroom, an asset often overlooked by traditional education (1938/1997). Experiences are educative only if they are intelligently linked with past and future experiences in a manner that allows the child to reflect on their meaning. The teacher's role in this conception of pedagogy is to arrange experiences to encourage students learning. "It is his (the teacher's) business to arrange for the kind of experiences which, while they do not repel the student, but rather engage his activities ... (to) promote having desirable future experiences" (p. 27). Dewey's writings are deeply imbued with a commitment to "act intelligently—that is, to formulate plans, to take relevant facts into account, to do what he regarded as particularly difficult: namely, to suspend judgment, hold on to doubt, rethink problems, but never lose sight of the ultimate end in view" (Ryan, 1995, pp. 145–146).

Dewey has been critiqued as being vague, obtuse, and even unreadable. This criticism may be justified with regard to certain ideas, but Dewey is perhaps clearest on the need for an intellectual life among educators. His famous lab school at the University of Chicago provided time and latitude for teachers to discuss the development of individual children, theorize about teaching practice, and make changes in pedagogy based on their experiences (Dewey, 1990). The lab school was founded on the notion that pedagogical principles could be derived and practiced through intellectual activity of teachers.

What emerges from this brief survey of Dewey's contributions to teacher as intellectual? A teacher needs to guide students based on their experiences toward new experiences, helping them to inquire about their world in meaningful ways. Teaching in this manner models thoughtful inquiry, where doubt and confusion are often present, skepticism is healthy and necessary, evidence is gathered and examined, and conclusions are tentative and open to public scrutiny. Teachers are intellectual role models and schools are sites of intelligent discourse. Pedagogy like that described by Dewey is a difficult journey, but one that can be undertaken if teachers are given the time, resources, and space to be community intellectuals.

The notion of community intellectuals falls well short of what critical theorists would find desirable (Freire, 2001/1970; Giroux, 1988, 1984). Although there is a commitment to countersocialization within the idea of community intellectual, there is an equal commitment to negotiation with existing norms and social patterns. In this sense, community intellectuals are constructing a difficult middle ground between the forces of socialization and countersocialization (Engle & Ochoa, 1988). Community intellectuals are those that seek a thoughtful middle way that balances social critique and affirmation and, more importantly, teaches students to critically inquire about the world.

Some may argue that referring to teachers as intellectuals is mistaken, as most do not see themselves in this way nor do they aspire to be intellectuals. I would suggest that this has more to do with the connotation of the word *intellectual* than with the work of teachers. Being an intellectual has come to be regarded as a person who is distant, aloof, and self-absorbed. We imagine hermit-like scholars, whiling away their time refining esoteric theories that will never see the light of day. Clearly this is not what Dewey, and many other educators who have argued for treating teaching as intellectual work, have in mind. Teachers can and should be engaged at the applied level, engaging pedagogical practice as it emerges in real-life situations. Teaching should be concerned, first and foremost, with the activity of teaching and learning. Providing teachers with opportunities to examine the ideational qualities of their work, however, empowers their pedagogy and makes continual recreation of the teaching self possible.

CONCLUSION

I am not too far removed from the daily life of schools to realize how "pie in the sky" some of the ideas presented in this chapter may sound to teachers in the field. Many of the suggestions, though not widely implemented, are being engaged to varying degrees in many schools, however. Teacher in-service is a widely diffused phenomenon. Teachers in certain school districts are given a great deal of autonomy in creating, implementing, and altering the curriculum. Research by teachers is increasingly being recognized as an important contribution to pedagogical knowledge and is supported to varying degrees in schools.

Schools that embody all three areas of professional development (in-service, curriculum author, and researcher), and, thereby the notion of *community intellectual*, are the Central Park East schools of New York City (Meier, 1995). Teachers are continually involved in collegial dialogue about individual students, teacher methodology, and content ideas. Teachers create a curriculum around central questions (i.e., What do we know? Who believes that and why? What causes that and what effect does it have? Why does it matter? and How might things have been different?) and draw on the life experiences of the students in responding to these questions (p. 50).

Teachers are given the time to problematize their own classrooms and collect relevant evidence to improve their work and the lives of their students. Teachers define what constitutes students achievement based on portfolio evidence and make decisions about graduation on this basis. As community intellectuals, teachers are revered by parents and community members for their exemplary work and are active participants with students in the community of East Harlem.

Central Park East schools, though not an educational utopia and still a work in progress, are committed to the notion of *teacher as community intellectual* and live out this pledge in the daily life of the school. The school harkens back to Dewey's laboratory model of one hundred years ago. These schools, situated in very different eras with different students, communities, and faculty on which to draw, are identical in at least one respect: a commitment to schooling as an exciting and invigorating intellectual activity.

Can schools be, in the words of Meier (1995), educationally inspiring and intellectually challenging? Clearly the answer is yes. This is not an easy solution to educational problems, but rather an arduous process that is never complete and always imperfect; a process that requires a great deal of human and material resources. Still, it is in the intellectually inspired school and teachers that we see the greatness of our human capacity and the potential of our greatest assets, our children, to build a compassionate and intelligent global society.

9

A New Way to the World? Global Times, Global Citizens

> The concept of a global civic culture requires the acceptance at some level of a shared identity with other human beings. Species identity ... will rather be a crowning awareness of how all social identities crafted throughout a lifetime by each of us come together in our common humanity.
>
> —Boulding (1988, pp. 56, 73–74)

The conversation of this book draws to a close on a logical point, that of global civics. What is global civics? What does it mean to be a global citizen? Society is moving inexorably toward a global reality, a paradigmatic shift equivalent to the emergence of the modern nation-state system or the industrial revolution. The change that we find ourselves immersed in is so fundamental and enormous that it undermines our ability to understand. As contemporaries of globalization's early life, we lack the vocabulary, categories, and master images to make sense of the change (Sassen, 1996, p. 29; Soysal, 1994, p. 165). Globalization is beyond our cognitive grasp, making those who work in this area feel like carnival soothsayers or Hollywood scriptwriters, attempting in vain to ascertain the blurry future unfolding around us.

The purpose of this chapter, the final one in our extended conversation about global education, is to illuminate the process of building a vocabulary, categories, and master images that will allow us to engage in global civics discourse. A variety of scholars have begun the difficult task of constructing a dialogical space for the conversation of global civics (Boulding, 1988; Castles & Davidson, 2000; Falk, 1994; Garii, 2000; Hanvey, 1976; Howard & Gill, 2001; Ohmae, 1995; Parker et al., 1998; Sassen, 1996;

Soysal, 1994). My plan is not to summarize these important contributions, but rather to synthesize relevant aspects of this emergent body of knowledge toward illuminating the manner in which we can co-construct a global civics discourse. My purpose here is clearly exploratory, as I endeavor to reconceptualize the manner in which we talk of civics and citizenship, cognizant that the analytical "nation-state container" is no longer singularly sufficient for understanding our complex world (Sassen, 1996, p. 28).

What are the salient aspects of global civics? I propose five dimensions of global civics in this brief exploration: (a) population movement, (b) economics, (c) rights and responsibilities, (d) cultural diversity, and (e) contact. Because these cannot encompass all of the possibilities in such a vast area as global civics, this again is only an initial offering. In each area, I briefly discuss the rationale (Why is this issue/phenomenon integral to global civics?) and implementation (How can this dimension be engaged by students and teachers of global education?). The five dimensions are treated independently for clarity's sake. Overlaps among the categories are plentiful, however, and are periodically highlighted.

ASSUMPTIONS

Prior to developing the argument of this final chapter, the assumptions that undergird this exposition deserve brief disclosure. These assumptions include (a) globalization, or the increasing interdependence of human and nonhuman systems across the planet, is an emerging and imminent reality; (b) globalization, thus defined, has implications for many aspects of humanity, especially civic spheres; and (c) globalization's paradigmatic shift requires a new way of reconceptualizing ourselves and societies that is fundamentally lacking.

The fact of globalization, or the compression of the world and intensification of world consciousness, is inevitable. The contemporary debate about globalization's effects on workers, ecosystems, traditional values, and leaders, to name a few, demonstrates the saliency of the phenomenon. Those on the Left view globalization as a ruse by which multinational corporations manipulate labor, resources, and indigenous populations all in the exploitative pursuit of capital accumulation (Roddick, 2000). Left protests crystallized recently in demonstrations directed at the World Trade Organization meetings and related international conferences in Seattle, Quebec, and Genoa. These anti-globalization activists empathize with the imperiled voiceless: indigenous people, impoverished persons, endangered species, and the environment. People at the margins in developing countries frequently see globalization as yet another example of Western infiltration and exploitation. For them, globalization is the wolf of neo-colonialism in sheep's clothing.

Globalization is also opposed, coincidentally, by those on the Right who cling to romanticized notions of national self-determination and sovereignty to counterbalance their shibboleth: one-world government whose power supersedes national authority. The Right's anti-globalization efforts, politically, include tactics such as limiting the powers of the United Nations by postponing dues from the largest funding agent, the United States. Some corporate leaders and capitalists view globalization as an economic free-for-all, where the old world of national regulation and restrictions on commerce have been replaced by millisecond accumulations of capital that know no political boundaries. Others fear this change because it disrupts the previous economic system that they mastered.

Granted there are legitimate reasons for concern about globalization's multifarious implications, but attempting to prevent the compression of the world is akin to hoping the sun will not rise. Indeed, the first light of day has been clearly visible for quite some time. Globalization is both inevitable and ubiquitous (Ohmae, 1995). There are scarcely few places to go "away" from the influences of a shrinking planet. We live in a 24-hour epoch, where goods and people can move virtually anywhere on the planet in the course of a single day, a time period likely to be further compressed in the years to come by technological changes.

Environmental problems make this assumption most evident. Global warming is now widely believed by environmental scientists to be occurring as a result of human activity (U.S. Environmental Protection Agency, 1997). The implications of what this means for our planet are still speculative, but few, if any, places on the Earth will be unaffected. The intensification of industrialization over the past century has caused significant environmental damage that knows no political boundaries. Though we often choose to behave as though we act alone or as self-determined nations, we are all part of the web of human and nonhuman systems (Pike & Selby, 2000).

Our final assumption in discussing global civics is with the nation-state system. Though significant now and for the foreseeable future, nations are gradually being reconfigured. Nation-states that function as independent, inviolable entities with little regard for how they are perceived by others or how they manage to cohere are generally a historical artifact of the early 20th century. Following the collapse of the Soviet Union, the world witnessed the reconfiguration of many political entities and the external and internal forces that shaped their development.

China's problems over the past 15 years are illustrative of these external and internal disruptions in the new age of the nation-state. The stir that was caused by the Olympics being awarded to China in 2008 illustrates the importance of public image and human rights advocacy throughout the world, or external forces. Though China's horrendous human rights record did not prevent Beijing from receiving the event, the resultant discussion demonstrates that even renegade nations like China are somewhat beholden to global values and norms. The political upheaval during the summer of 1989 at Tiananmen Square demonstrates how political leaders feel compelled to coercively and violently put down centrifugal forces in the nation-state, demonstrative of the "pressures within."

This assumption is made even more problematic in that we are inheriting a global system about which we have little knowledge to effectively manage. Fuller (1969) metaphorically referred to Spaceship Earth. Though he focused on ecological systems in his metaphor, the same can be said of the civic sphere. Global civics is like piloting a space ship without an instructional manual, with no flying experience, with little sense of who has the controls, and with no one to ask for guidance but ourselves. It is no wonder that government leaders, policymakers, academics, and political activists are afraid of the strange new world that globalization portends. If these assumptions are allowed, namely, globalization as imminent, changing all aspects of life, and reorienting the nation-state system without clear instruction, then our task is clear: to begin a dialogical conversation about the more salient dimensions of a global civic and how global civic education can occur. The purpose of this dialogue is to help young people come to terms with emerging obligations and responsibilities toward a global civic culture.

FIVE DIMENSIONS OF GLOBAL CIVICS

Population Movement

An essential dimension of globalization is the number of people that move around the globe. Population shifts, either of a temporary, semi-permanent, or permanent nature, are unprecedented in human history. According to 1995 statistics, 23% of Australia's population, 17% of Canada, and 9% of the U.S. population is "foreign born" (Castles & Davidson, 2000, p. 64).

Each of these nations has witnessed approximately a 3% to 4% increase in foreign born populations since 1981 (p. 65). Evidence of the movement of people in the global village is not limited to historically hospitable immigrant nations. Soysal (1994) documented the migrant population in three societies not historically known for their hospitality to foreigners: Switzerland (16.3%), Belgium (9.1%), and Germany (8%; p. 24).

The general pattern of population movement is northward, as people from developing countries seek access to the economic and educational opportunities available in developed nations. Sassen (1991) illustrated a distinct pattern in three global cities (London, New York, and Tokyo) regarding immigration: rapid growth of migrants from poorer nations taking jobs in cities that are otherwise undesirable to local populations. Migrant workers generally are employed in what has been referred to as "3 D jobs (dirty, difficult, and dangerous"; Castles & Davidson, 2000, p. 186). What is most remarkable about immigration patterns is the unabated influx of southern immigrants regardless of the economic situation in their northern destination. Soysal (1994) explored the reasons for this paradox, asserting that nation-states are both less inclined and less able to prevent guestworkers from arriving, or removing them after arrival, because of the emergence of universal standards of human rights, particularly in Europe. "In the postnational model, universal personhood replaces nationhood; and universal human rights replace national rights" (p. 142). People innately have rights that transcend national boundaries and traditional conceptions of civics, emanating from a human rights discourse about the rights and responsibilities of all people. Indeed, it is often the guestworkers themselves who advocate on these grounds, appealing to a higher authority of rights than the nation in which they work (p. 154).

The nature of population migration is of interest to global civics discourse in at least two ways: (a) the diffusion and negotiation of cultural diversity and (b) the transcendence of the individual vis-à-vis the nation-state. These factors have shaped, and will increasingly continue to affect our lives in the decades to come. We can encourage the next generation to have meaningful conversations about this global phenomenon, through the perspective of immigrant peers who are creating new understandings of what it means to be a global citizen.

Implications for Global Education.   Students who have experienced immigration, either directly or through the lives of a loved one, are a tremendous resource to global teachers. I frequently ask immigrant students to share their life histories with peers. One of the most memorable examples from my teaching is the story of Glodil, an "illegal" immigrant from El Salvador. She spoke through tears about fearing for her life in El Salvador, hiding in the back of trucks with her mom, riding for days on dusty roads to *el norte*, and the trauma of adjusting to a White, suburban school where she was treated by teachers and peers as the Other.

This approach must be engaged with a great deal of care and caution, however, as recent immigrant children often feel especially vulnerable. If one's classroom is considered a safe place where trust and caring is actively engendered, than revealing these narratives can be a rich experience for all students. In addition, it validates the most vulnerable students, recent immigrants, rather than implicitly "Othering" them by ignoring their situation, enjoining them to common projects with their peers. Merryfield (1997) has successfully implemented this approach with her teacher education students at Ohio State University, pairing international students with those in teacher education to promote cross-cultural communication and understanding (pp. 7–11).

Global teachers might also consider exploring immigration through inquiry research. Students often have strongly held views about immigration, migrant workers, and citizenship, yet based on little evidence. Students could be guided in the development of a question about these issues and encouraged to explore the evidence, develop a short paper or creative presentation, and present their tentative findings to the class. Along with this inquiry, teachers should have students analyze their own assumptions about citizenship and nation-states. While most adolescents view nation-state boundaries as impermeable and discreet, a careful study of the evidence suggests a more realistic picture: increasingly fluid boundaries, decreasing nation-oriented conceptions of civics, and emergent universal standards of human rights. Recognizing the complex interactions of people and nations will contribute to students' ability to engage global civics in the future.

Economics

It may seem odd to include a discussion of economics within the realm of civics, but global economics is a driving force, as evidenced by the fact that most people migrate around the globe for financial reasons. With regard to globalization, the boundaries of what is economic and what is political have become increasingly blurred. If the recent clashes over economic globalization are an indication of things to come, economic considerations may indeed be the centerpiece of future considerations in what it means to be a global citizen. Global economics is too complex to be given adequate attention herein, so I limit the discussion to the interplay between citizenship and economics in a global context.

The origins of globalization are largely economic, though the impacts are felt throughout society. Four significant economic developments since the Cold War ended have opened the global floodgates of capital flow: the internationalization of the bond market in the late 1980s, the diffusion of information technology, the increasing flow of foreign direct investment (FDI), and the establishment of foreign exchange markets. With the internationalization of the bond market, the old nation-state boundaries for raising capital, both in the public and private spheres, are no more. Financiers can gain capital from a much wider array of investors, as bonds are floated in a global, rather than national, context. In the United States alone, international sale and purchase of U.S. Treasury bonds has grown from $30 US billion to $500 U.S. billion in the period 1988–1993, a staggering 16-fold increase (Sassen, 1996, p. 41).

These remarkable increases have been due in large part to the speed at which computer-based financial operations are possible and the vast amount of financial information now available. Investing in markets outside one's nation prior to the advent of information technologies in the 1980s, was a risky proposition by any measure. An investor could not ascertain the viability of the company, and therefore, the risk ventured. The diffusion of information technology has completely changed these rules. Instead of investment (or as Keynes would say, casino-like speculation) being the domain of elite financiers, it is now within the reach of the adolescent Internet surfer, the retiree, and the stay-at-home mom.

Foreign direct investment (FDI), the amount of capital that flows into corporations from foreign sources, is perhaps the most important sign of economic globalization. Global FDI in 1980 stood at $100 U.S. billion, increasing by 1996 to $350 U.S. billion, more than three times greater (Reinicke, 1998, p. 18). By 1998, global FDI nearly doubled again, to $645 U.S. billion, a 27-fold increase since 1973 (World Trade Organization, 2000). Much of this trade occurs within multinational corporations, when, for example, General Motors-UK ships materials to General Motors-Brazil. Trades such as these are evidence of increased capital flow across international borders, with little if any, regulation.

The ease by which corporations engage intracorporate global trade is proof of just how ubiquitous multinational corporations have become. Currently there are over 45,000 corporations with operations in two or more countries, which facilitates FDI capital flows (Reinicke, 1998, p. 19). Approximately 75 trillion dollars annually is involved in cross-border capital flows, and many assume that that actual number is much higher (pp. 40–41). These figures and the rapidity of their increase are staggering by any measure.

The growth of foreign exchange markets, particularly after the end of the 1971 Bretton Woods agreement which previously pegged currency exchange, have also contributed to opening up global capital flow (Ohmae, 1995; Reinicke, 1998). In the previous system, foreign exchange rates were established against the international standard of the U.S. dollar. After 1971, currency became an international commodity to be bought and sold like stocks, bonds, and other investments. This significant change offered corporations, private investors, and governments a barometer as to the economic health of a particular country based on its currency, allowing meaningful international economic comparisons. Although the factors examined are by no means the only phenomena related to economic globalization (global bond markets, information technology, FDI, and foreign currency exchange), taken together, they significantly contribute to sustained and progressive economic globalization.

But what does economic globalization mean in terms of civic life? The implications of this shift from nationally bounded to globally oriented markets in terms of civic life are significant. Economic activity transcends national borders, destabilizing the "national industrial society," and thereby, simplistic notions of citizenship solely defined by national affiliation (Castles & Davidson, 2000, p. 7). To be successful politically in the era of globalization requires a great deal of attention to the wishes of corporate heads. Sassen (1996) provocatively asserts that firms and corporations are themselves "economic citizens," or capital investors amounting to a political electorate, voting with their feet by leaving inhospitable nations (pp. 38–40). If nation-states are to maintain economic viability and a high standard of living, they need to be concerned with their business climate.

Domestic initiatives, such as welfare policies, are now beholden to global markets and the economic ebb and flow of the nation vis-à-vis the global marketplace. As such, even political leaders who claim to be concerned with social justice need to pursue the investment of global capital to fuel their domestic programs. Prime Minister Blair and President Clinton typify this neo-liberal agenda that is now common among formerly left-leaning parties, like Labour in Great Britain and the Democrats in the United States. As Roddick (2000) contends, "Leaders in world business are the first true global citizens," though she laments their lack of attention to issues of social justice, environmental protection, and universal human rights (p. 14).

The focus on maintaining a productive and competitive business environment, even among neo-liberals like Blair and Clinton, has been the source of much contention among those of the far Left. Cases of multinational corporate abuse of indigenous populations, labor, and the environment in which they transact business are well-documented. Shell Oil's environmental disaster among the Ogoni people of Nigeria has led to contamination of water supplies and sharp increases in cancer rates among children (Roddick, 2000). Disney's outsourcing of the production of souvenirs to Haiti, paying workers only $.28 per hour has contributed to the widespread mistrust of multinational corporations. On this salary, a Haitian would have to work 166 *years* to equal Disney CEO Eisner's *daily* income (p. 8). Reinicke (1998) suggested that although we live in a global village, it is one increasingly divided by a sharp North–South divide of haves and have-nots, an "inequity that is too great to survive" (p. 9).

Economic citizenry suggests the need for increased awareness among individuals with respect to their purchasing power. Just as multinational corporations can vote with their feet in a globally integrated marketplace, so can consumers. Information technology makes consumer awareness more widely available, though the digital divide serves as a barrier to truly democratized information. Roddick (2000) explained a variety of consumer activist strategies that have shown some effectiveness in changing multinational corporate policy: boycotts and awareness campaigns, for example. At the microeconomic level, individuals can change corporate policies, acting in concert, voting with their pocketbooks.

Globalization requires that policymakers attend to the quasi-citizenship functions of multinational corporations as well. As capital flows rapidly and dramatically increase, little has been done to reign in the authority of corporations to do as they wish. This is not sustainable, however, as any polity that cedes all rights and no responsibilities to its citizens cannot last. Multinational corporations as economic citizens is an even more troubling phenomenon in light of the lack of political will and authority of national leaders in global governance and the absence of credible global regulation (Ohmae, 1995). Again, I contend that the solution will emerge among future generations once a vocabulary for addressing the changes wrought by globalization emerges.

Implications for Global Education.   Global educators should guide students in studying how their economic activity directly involves them in global economic life. One lesson that I have used is to study student clothing and personal effects. Students begin by cataloging all of their belongings on a particular school day, including the materials, national origin (if indicated), purchase place and price, and reason for purchase. Students then map the geographic data. Once the initial data is displayed, students can develop hypotheses about the types and origins of consumer goods, such as: Why are most clothing articles from Southeast Asia? Why is my leather handbag from Latin America? Why do some articles indicate that they are "assembled" in a particular place? These questions can lead to thoughtful inquiries about the global economy that are directly related to students.

The use of labels of national origin can also be problematized with students. In the 1980s, the "buy American" movement proliferated the mass media, largely in response to the perception that "Japan was taking over" economically. Students might engage in a case study of a complex consumer product, such as an automobile, and examine the manner in which it is produced. I frequently offered paradoxes to my students as beginning points of inquiry, such as "If Honda is a Japanese car, why are so many assembled in Ohio?" Questions like these challenge students to go beyond simplistic notions of "national industries" and come to understand the extent to which the globally economy is integrated and politicized.

Students may, through the course of their research, choose to participate in letter-writing, promoting social awareness, a boycott, or other form of social action. Global teachers should encourage civic involvement, as it illustrates the potential of global citizenship to be active. As long as teachers do not attempt to indoctrinate students into a particular set of beliefs or force them to act against their own beliefs, social action can be an exciting and rewarding activity for students. Time constraints and/or fear of administrative or parental disapproval often thwart teachers efforts in this area. But if we are to engage students in the process of developing a global civic, exploratory social action is crucial to this end.

Rights and Responsibilities

Knowing and exercising rights and responsibilities are an integral part of citizenship. Being part of a polity requires involvement on the part of the citizens, or at least the opportunity to participate. A global polity does not yet exist. Although there are supranational agencies that are quasi-governmental, such as the United Nations and the European Court of Justice, these do not yet act in a sovereign manner. The absence of a single world government does not mean a global civic culture cannot be developed. Indeed, the emergence of global civics has and will continue to germinate within existing institutions, such as the nation-state. Sites of global civics, though orig-inating in nation-state structures, has and will continue to transcend them. The European Court of Justice, for example, came into existence by the ap-proval of European nations, but it now has a degree of superordinate au-thority with regard to human rights law.

The fulcrum on which the transcendental move toward a global civic oc-curs is the evolving notion of universal human rights. The latter half of the 20th century saw the codification of global human rights, beginning with the ratification of the Universal Declaration of Human Rights in 1948. In just over five decades, 21 internationally binding covenants regarding hu-man rights have been established. Although nations still maintain the sover-eign right of choice as to whether they will participate, international pressure to abide by human rights standards is clearly on the rise (Buergental, 1995).

South Africa illustrates the importance of international human rights vis-à-vis national self-determination perhaps better than any other modern case. For more than four decades, the minority population of White South Africans, through the political arm of the National Party, oppressed the ma-jority "Black" (indigenous), and "coloured" (ethnically Southeast Asian), populations of South Africa mercilessly. The National Party hid behind the guise of self-determination in perpetrating this crime against humanity for the better part of their reign. Increasing global attention by the late 1970s, much of it led by activists within and outside South Africa, turned the tide. The media helped to focus attention on the atrocities, such as Soweto in 1976, and global public opinion made South Africa the pariah of the inter-national community. Many lives were lost and South Africa continues to be beset by issues of inequality, but the object lesson is clear: Flagrant viola-tions of human rights within nations can lead to international condemnation and change.

That is not to suggest a Pollyanna view of the potential of international human rights standards to shape a global civic culture. There are many counterexamples where global condemnation on the grounds of human rights discourse changed very little, as Rwanda, Bosnia, China, and Af-ghanistan are painful reminders. Moreover, the case of South Africa was ridden with human tragedy, despite the eventual change. The salient aspect of each of these cases is not the *effectiveness* of the international commu-nity to supersede national self-determination, but rather the *legitimacy* of human rights discourse in each of these cases. The rights of the individual, regardless of their national citizenship, or even without national citizenship, are increasingly recognized as a central component of civic discourse (Soysal, 1994). Additionally, in the genocidal cases of Bosnia and Rwanda, perpetrators continue to be tried by international tribunals for their actions.

An additional problem area with respect to global human rights is the Western bias inherent in notions of citizenship, particularly with regard to rights and responsibilities. Human rights standards are frequently viewed by Asian and Muslim-dominated nations as the imposition of cultural norms (Castles & Davidson, 2000, p. 206; Galtung, 1994). Assertions about the need for universal human rights codes, particularly coming from Western nations who perfected exploitation in the colonial era and continue to profit from these historical legacies, is viewed as just more Western hypocrisy by those in former colonial regions (Castles & Davidson, 2000; Wilinsky, 1998).

Must global citizenship be rooted in democratic principles to be fair and just? Falk (1994) contended that democracy and citizenship are interwoven, and that discussions of global civics must include notions of democracy, and therefore, rights (p. 128). If a normative perspective on rights and responsibilities is assumed, than global civics must also be a point of imposition on ways of life that are not easily reconciled with Western notions of rights and responsibilities or citizenship. Much human rights discourse has centered around imposition of international standards of global ethics, a strategy that I believe will ultimately fail as it is paradoxically anti-democratic. Rather than imposition, creating space for future generations to engage this critical dialogue is the process by which a fair and just global civic culture can emerge.

Implications for Global Education. As stated at the outset, my purpose is not to resolve the paradoxes that creating a global civic culture present, but to focus on the process of encouraging a discourse about global citizenship with future generations, today's students. How do we stimulate students to think responsibly, critically, and globally? Global educators could begin conversations about rights and responsibilities with what students are most familiar: their schools and national contexts. Students can begin by critically reviewing the school's guidelines for student behavior and discuss the origins, purposes, and effects of such policies. Care must be taken in this approach so as not to reinforce oppositional behavior and attitudes toward the school that is typically adolescent. By "critical," I mean a thoughtful engagement of good and bad aspects of school governance, along with a deeper analysis of criteria that determines what is "good" and "bad."

This inquiry might proceed to an analysis of students' rights as derived from state and federal laws. Thereafter, students can begin to examine how rights within their polity compare and contrast with those in other national contexts and with international covenants regarding human rights. A local-to-global orientation such as this will help students to see themselves in a broader context and through multiple lenses, rather than the traditional focus on national citizenship that so dominates curriculum.

Attention should also be paid to people at the civic margins, such as immigrants, resident-aliens, quasi-citizens, refugees, and other civic categories of people. Students can investigate the manner by which people gain national citizenship in various contexts, how these requirements have changed over time, and the rights that exist for various groups who are not national citizens. Global educators can explore the phenomenon of dual citizenship, stateless individuals, and those who hold a United Nations passport, to problematize the simplistic and distorting "nation = citizenship" framework.

Global educators should also encourage students to inquire about the cultural dimensions of civic notions. A case study of civics in diverse societies, perhaps using China, Nigeria, Germany, and Canada as exemplars, would illustrate the tension between cultural differences and notions of rights and responsibilities. Simply asserting that Western-style democracies are self-evidently "right" for the world to adopt would not only be pedagogically ineffective but counter-productive toward the goals of critical thinking. Rather, having students explore and problematize these areas will enhance their ability, now and in the future, to construct a dialogue about global civics. Some questions to frame this inquiry might include: To what extent do human rights impose a cultural norm of civics and citizenship on people? What other forms of civic life, beyond Western-style democracies, exist? What ground might exist for negotiating various conceptions of civics?

Cultural Diversity

Examining global rights and responsibilities naturally leads to the fourth dimension of global civics explored herein: diversity. The human species can be understood as paradoxically similar and diverse: We are fundamentally the same, and yet environmental and social factors lead to adaptations that are as diverse as there are people on the planet. If the human species is seen on a continuum of similarity and diversity, global civics discourses tend toward the pole of similarity. How, then, do we create a global civic culture where so many seemingly incongruent definitions of citizenship exist?

Though globalization tends to be a normative discourse, it is critical that this normativity does not completely subsume the diversity of belief and action. Western societies have historically ascribed to an assimilation model of citizenship where people were melted into the dominant cultural and civic model. Assimilation models, however, have been fundamentally altered and destabilized in an age of globalization (Castles & Davidson, 2000, p. 165). "Globalization ... makes myths of homogeneity unsustainable. Cultural diversity has become a central aspect of virtually all modern societies" (p. 127).

The recognition of diversity has most recently led to increased multicultural national policies in many nations (Ålund & Schierup, 1991, p. 1). In Australia, the National Agenda establishes cultural identity, social justice, and economic utilization as multicultural policy. It is limited, however, in that all Australians are legally required to have a commitment to the nation-state, to accept basic structures and principles of society, and to abide by their societal obligations (p. 166). In a sense, multiculturalism is the merger of diverse identities and normative institutions, or what Robertson (1992) has termed "the universalization of particularities and the particularization of universalities" (p. 100).

Multiculturalism has been the source of great controversy within national discourses. In Sweden, multicultural policy was implemented to create space for immigrants, premised on liberty, equality, and partnership. Ålund & Schierup (1991) argued that despite good intentions at the outset, multiculturalism in Sweden has drifted toward discussions of immigrants as "social problems" (p. 11). Multiculturalism, in this context, has become a "euphemistic ideology" that masks real structures of power underpinning racial, ethnic, and class inequalities (p. 20). Similar reactions to multiculturalism can be found in nations that have adopted such policies, leading to characterizations of nonmajority populations as "special-needs Others," thereby increasing resentment toward them and perpetuating oppression.

Democratic societies have struggled with pluralism, especially as globalization has forced nations to come to terms with rapid population shifts. Perhaps the "social problem" lies not in cultural diversity, but rather, in the vessel of the nation-state in which these identities are being asked to conform. Despite efforts by governments themselves to reconstruct *ius sanguinis* (law of the blood) definitions of citizenship, elements of this doctrine remain in all modern nation-states (Castles & Davidson, 2000, p. 85). When the polity is defined in national terms, citizenship becomes a limited phenomenon that discriminates against non-citizens and quasi-citizens, typically on the basis of ethnic or racial identity. If the unit of analysis for citizenship is reconfigured toward a global civic, however, then either no one can claim *ius sanguinis,* or we can all claim *ius terrus* (law of the Earth).

Thinking of citizenship in global terms is likely to be a more inclusive framework than from a strictly nation-state orientation. Falk (1994) related a conversation with a Dutch businessman, who, when asked how the development of European Union may affect his Dutch identity, claimed, "I am a global citizen" (p. 134). The business conceptualization of "global citizen" has revolved around the homogeneity, or McDonaldization, of capitalist spaces around the world, referred to as the emergence of "airport cultures" (Berger, 2000, p. 420). Global citizenship in this sense is narrowly defined as rooted in cultural similarity and economics. Inclusive of this notion is a yet to be articulated form of citizenship that constructs a workable middle ground between particularistic and universalistic dimensions of humanity: a civics that is both multicultural and global. This common area is one that requires the attention of young people today, in order to create a new language for an inclusive conceptualization of civics tomorrow.

Implications for Global Education.　　Global education has been closely aligned with issues of human diversity since its inception. Discussions about diversity need to be moved, however, toward considerations of diversity within similarity, or, the particular that is universal. One means of inquiring with students about this issue is to examine how different polities have addressed diversity among their citizens at various points in time. A historical comparison of what was required to be a Greek and a Roman citizen or a contemporary case study in national citizenship can serve as entry to a dialogue about what defines citizenship in different times and in diverse contexts. The core question for each investigation can remain the same: How have societies addressed issues of diversity in governance?

Students should also be familiarized with the significant shift in civic discourses in the latter half of the 20th century. Prior to considering what a global civic might look like, they need to analyze how and why the cognitive terrain of citizenship is shifting from the monolithic nation-state to a more amorphous conceptualization that transcends political boundaries. One means of opening this inquiry is through investigating the quasi-governmental functions of transnational relief, advocacy, and religious organizations. Here are some potentially fruitful comparisons that would encourage thinking in this area:

- How is the Roman Catholic Church similar and dissimilar from a national government, such as Mexico or Indonesia?
- How do belief systems, such as Islam, unify people in a manner that transcends national boundaries?
- How are the functions of organizations like the Red Cross/Red Crescent similar and different from those of a nation?
- How is *SOS-Racisme* similar and different from the governments of the nations in which the group is situated, such as France?

The goal of this line of inquiry is to have students examine organizations that are transnational while considering the dimensions of civic belonging that are not nationally based but exert great power over people's lives.

Students should also be encouraged to examine the emergence of human rights standards and the extent to which these are, or could be, universal. Using the Universal Declaration of Human Rights as a basis, students should be made aware of the debate in 1947 and 1948 on the United Nations Human Rights Committee about cultural diversity. A group of anthropologists argued for the inclusion of a right to live within one's own culture to be included in the document. The committee would not include this right because it would allow a group like the Nazis to claim cultural identity, and thereby, use this as protection from external criticism. Students might research and role-play this debate, as it points directly to the inconsistency inherent in global civics. Perhaps from their conversations will emerge a refreshed image of a future global civic. At the very least, rather than ignoring this apparent contradiction, students will be given the space to intelligently grapple with this issue.

Contact

The fifth dimension of this exploratory conversation about global civics is that of contact. What does it mean to have contact in the realm of civics? Contact includes the daily interactions with one's kin, neighborhood and village, exchanges in places of work, and engagements with those who share similar interests. I refer to these forms as personal contacts, while also discussing two, less-recognized types of interaction: temporal and environmental. How these elements of contact will shape an emergent global civic is yet to be determined. Based on the discussion presented herein, I intend to show how each is elemental to global citizenship.

Personal contact, like most other human interactions, is culturally imbued. As someone living in the United States, I am accustomed to acting as though I am alone in public spaces, exchanging fleeting greetings and rapid exchanges of life situations with more intimate colleagues and friends, and maintaining a measure of privacy about home and family. I was pleasantly surprised while studying in Kenya with the sincerity and commitment of time and interest extended to me in daily contacts. Mikwana, a fellow student with whom I worked closely, would travel the city of Nairobi and in his village outside of Kisumu, stopping every few minutes to have extended dialogues with friends.

A great deal of attention is now being paid, particularly in hyper-economically developed nations of the West, to the personal distancing caused by modern life. Putnam (1995, 2000) contended that we are now "bowling alone," rather than joining leagues, a trend that typifies an isolated, lonely existence in this postmodern age. He argues:

> There is reason to believe that deep-seated technological trends are radically "privatizing" or "individualizing" our use of leisure time and thus disrupting many opportunities for social-capital formation. The most obvious and probably the most powerful instrument of this revolution is television. (Putnam, 1995, p. 75)

Putnam (2000) used data about the fall of participation in "democratic" processes of contact to make his case (i.e., attended a public meeting, made a speech, wrote a letter to the paper; p. 45).

The disconnection from meaningful personal contact is frequently blamed on the desire to gain more economically. Sennett (1998) details his conversation with Rico, a financially successful son of an Italian immigrant, and how he "made it" by climbing the career ladder. Sennett argues that contact was missing from Rico's life, despite his economic status. Rico lacked a sense of belonging to his family and community, caused mainly by his obsession with economic success. Western market economies, spurred on by the forces of economic globalization discussed earlier in this chapter, are warping our sense of shared commitment and attachment to anything; or, in corporate lingo, "no long term" (p. 22). Without personal contact, a functional polity is an impossibility.

Contact can also be defined in a temporal manner. We live in a certain time, and as such, our thoughts about civics and citizenship are largely influenced by the norms of our time. The human construct of nation-states illustrates how being in a certain time influences our thinking. Five hundred years ago, nation-states had no meaning at all, whereas today, this construct remains the dominant, but waning, cognitive map with which we understand our world. Recognizing our own time situatedness helps to see that what is now held as "true" has not always been and may not always be valid. An enriched perspective of ourselves in time also helps us to see possibilities that are otherwise obscured from a present-obsessed mindset.

Boulding (1988) offered the idea of a 200-year present as a way of making contact with the past, present, and future. Boulding suggests that on any given day, someone is being born who will live to be 100 years old and someone is currently alive who is 100 years old. Thus, as we are all linked to other human beings, we are all directly linked to the 200-year present, "a continuously moving moment, always reaching out 100 years in either direction of the day we are in" (p. 4). The 200-year present expands notions of "our time" in a manner similar to how global civics expands understandings of "our fellow citizens."

Contact can also be understood in our relationships with the environment and nonhuman animals. Civics is so often defined as a purely human phenomenon. The manner in which we interact with the environment, however, has serious implications for the diversity of flora and fauna with whom we share the planet. Although national civics typically does not involve notions of ecology and other living beings, it is an essential element of global civics. Humane education has "arguably the largest ambition, the longest pedigree and the least visibility" of all progressive curricula (Selby, 2000, p. 268). Environmental education has taken on an increasingly central role in schools, particularly in the past decade.

Although dominion over nature is deeply embedded in the Judaic-Christian-Islam tradition, there has been a shift toward recognizing greater equality among life forms in recent years. The protection of endangered species, the end of international whaling, and the ban on ivory trade all serve as examples of how global consciousness has been elevated with respect to nonhuman animals. The environment has also received increased international attention, as international covenants are now in place to protect the ozone layer (Montreal Protocol) and reduce the production of global warming gases (Kyoto Protocol). Global citizenship requires humans to place nonhuman animals and the environment at the center of our considerations.

Given existing problems regarding contact (personal, temporal, and environmental) in our civic life, it would seem that this dimension of global civics is the most problematic. The means by which a global civic will be established are not yet clear, but as Kenneth Boulding frequently remarked, "What exists is possible" (Boulding, 1996, p. 345). Elements of contact integral to global civic life are already manifest in various ways. It is the place of global education to move these considerations of contact to the fore of the education of future generations.

Implications for Global Education.   One means of helping students make contact with their communities is to make them inquirers in their own contexts. The Mershon Center's Columbus in the World Project at Ohio State University, duplicated in over 50 other cities, offers a great model for students to see international connections in their communities, encouraging personal interactions (Merryfield, 1997; Woyach & Remy, 1982). Students engage in a community-based inquiry of the connectedness of their community to the rest of the world, through immigrant populations, corporations, travelers, relief organizations, and employees in multinational corporations. Projects like these have many benefits, not the least of which is an appreciation for the truly global nature of communities and the personal/community attachments engendered.

Making contact through time is a difficult proposition, as thinking in terms of the 200-year present is strongly countervaliant to the way young people are socialized. One means of having students get beyond a strictly present-orientation is to interview elderly people about significant public issues. Narrative histories are a useful means of making the past come to life for students and helping them to see the parallels from the past to the present through the experiences of individuals. Students can be fascinated by the details of how their communities have changed, providing them with a sense of depth and attachment.

Students should also be encouraged to speculate about the potential impacts of development in their communities and share their views about needed public policy changes with school and community leaders. Such activities promote critical thinking and community involvement, providing students with a richer sense of time in their lives and in the lives of their community. One way of focusing students attention is to work with them in creating a time capsule. Perhaps using a theme like "The World from our Perspective in 2002" to stimulate student thinking and creation of artifacts to include in the time capsule. These can be placed in a community setting and scheduled to be reopened in 50 to 100 years.

Environmental and nonhuman animal contact is readily available to students of all ages. Elementary students can be encouraged to take care of animals in the classroom, although care must be given to avoid neglect. Most schools are situated near natural landscapes, which can be used in demonstrating the interactions of humans and their environments. Working with urban students, one might encourage them to explore and catalog what is "natural" in their neighborhoods, reflecting on the anthropocentric tendency of humans to divide the world into "natural" and "human-made" categories.

A final idea regarding teaching globally to promote contact, and by far the most demanding on resources, is travel. Bringing students to another part of the world for an extended stay and interaction with local people is a tremendous experience that profoundly shapes the way that people see themselves and their global counterparts. Although these experiences are costly and difficult to arrange, they are well worth the effort (Kirkwood, 2001a). In a decade of teaching high school social studies, taking students to Russia for a month in 1992 was one of the best learning experiences in which I was involved. Living with host families, we gained remarkable insights into the daily life of our Russian peers. We spent time with them in school, at home, and on trips, and the students left with sharp insights of life in Russia. Perhaps most importantly was the recognition by the students about their commonalities.

CONCLUSION

Global civics is a challenging notion, one that we lack a sufficient vocabulary to adequately discuss. In this chapter, I have outlined in broad, exploratory strokes five critical dimensions of global citizenship: population movement, economics, rights and responsibilities, cultural diversity, and contact. I do not believe this array of topics is all-inclusive; however, I offer this as a means of illuminating the *processes* by which global civics can be developed. Global education is a vital means by which future generations can create the vocabulary, master images, and categories that will encourage more fruitful discussions about global citizenship.

Throughout this chapter, I have pointed to apparent paradoxes in the discourse of global citizenship (i.e., the universalization of particularism). I presented these as paradoxes, but they may not be. Rather, my situatedness in writing this book, given my own constraints in thinking about the world in terms not yet defined, has limited this discussion. This is why I return to my earlier assertion that our focus in global education should not be on a didactic presentation of what we (i.e., adult community, scholars, teachers, parents) believe the global future ought to be, but a construction emerging from global youths in conversation with other generations.

Our focus should be on posing apparent paradoxes, rich dilemmas, and moral quandaries about global civics to young people. Their task is to create better solutions for similar problems than previous generations have been able to develop. This will not occur through imposition, however, but only through intelligent and wise guidance from other generation. Our common task is to help future generations formulate the questions of our global future, rather than force-feeding them our answers as though they were decided on truths.

One illustration of how this might happen would be an ideal note to bring to a close this conversation of global civics. A paradox that looms on the horizon for global citizenship, a seemingly intractable one, is the divergence of views about democracy as a foundation for civic life. I cannot think of a way out of this dilemma, regardless of how many scholars I read, debates I have, and how much introspection I engage. The terms of the debate may, most probably will, change dramatically, however, in the next 50 years. What is held as sacrosanct by leaders in Germany and China today, respectively, will unlikely be identically held by their children and grandchildren.

An emergent youth culture, who share more in common with other youths from throughout the world than with other generations in their own societies, may be the phenomenon that contributes the most to developing a global civic culture (Ohmae, 1995). I cannot imagine now what type of global civic, if any, they will create. But I have confidence that if we prepare them with the ability to think critically and appreciate one another's diversity, they will resolve it justly. This is purely an article of faith, but one that working in education has and continues to sustain me.

Afterword

Reflecting on this book at its conclusion, my purposes in writing are more apparent now than they were when I began. Writing has a curious way of helping us sort out what we really think and why. The conversation that has unfolded has been wide-ranging. We briefly examined the dialogue among scholars of global education, the context of education in which the New Jersey global education mandate emerged, and the particular contexts of the three secondary schools studied. Teachers and students in these three schools grappled with a variety of problems in global pedagogy: balancing nationalism, addressing cultural relativism, and tensions associated with identity. The remainder of the book provides alternative ways of addressing difficulties embedded in the daily life of global classrooms, along with a discussion about how curriculum is shaped and teachers develop professionally, all leading to an examination of global civic processes.

Illustrating how teachers and students come to understand the world in classrooms is the overarching purpose of this book, as it is in these conversations that global education becomes real. I also hope that the book has compelled you to reexamine your own grasp of this complex place we call home and how we understand ourselves in it. When we get beyond the sloganeering of globalization, global village, Spaceship Earth, and the like, we are left trying to comprehend an emergent curriculum area about a place paradoxically familiar and strange.

My hope in offering this book to the community of global educators and others is to provide a bit more theory, a modicum of research, and perhaps one or two supports in this project of constructing global education. Constructing global education began over 30 years ago and much outstanding work has been done. But a great deal more remains to be done in establishing a curriculum for our common future.

September 11, 2001

The significance of this date is just beginning to be understood, as terrorist attacks against the U.S. homeland triggered a series of events still unfolding. Global civics may seem like a far-fetched notion in the context of a global war on terrorism, but in actuality, the need for conversation about our common future has perhaps never been more apparent. What questions have arisen in the post-September 11 world that deserve our attention? I briefly examine some of those questions in light of these horrific events. The questions serve to focus attention rather than offer prescriptions, in keeping with the style of the book.

How has the world changed as a result of the events of September 11, 2001 and its aftermath?

The attacks, particularly on the World Trade Center, were surrealistic in their devastation, appearing as a cinematic illusion. The images were horrifyingly real, unfortunately, anything but an illusion. The refrain often repeated has been that the world has fundamentally changed as a result of the terrorist attacks. Security at public sites has certainly increased in the wake of the attacks, as anyone who has used the air travel system can attest. Attention to events in Southwest and Central Asia has increased measurably in the media, at least in the months immediately following the attacks. Clearly the economy has changed, as the United States entered its first recession in over 8 years, and prospects for a rapid turnaround continue to dim.

The commitment of the United States to avoiding protracted, "fuzzy" conflicts, a phenomenon scholars refer to as the Vietnam Syndrome, seems to have changed as a result of the attack. One of the central tenets of the syndrome analysis, which has guided U.S. international relations policy since the 1970s, is that the United States will not involve itself in military conflicts which do not have clearly articulated and achievable objectives (Rourke, 1995). The recently declared war on terrorism, however, seems to represent a departure from this policy. Support for the war on terrorism has consistently been above 80%, mirroring President Bush's approval ratings (Gallup Organization, 2002). This represents a unique post-Vietnam situation in international relations: widespread support for a war with unclear objectives and undetermined opponents.

Although much seems to have changed around the periphery, the attacks did surprisingly little to alter the dialogue about global issues. I wrongly assumed that the tragedy would spark interest in international politics, perhaps a silver lining in a very dark cloud. I have not seen evidence of that occurring, however, either in the media, through my interactions with students, and while working in schools. Rather than serving as a wake-up call to attend more closely to the North–South gap, the clash of ideologies and faiths, the rise of fundamentalist thought, and the massive buildup of weapons of mass destruction, I encounter surprisingly little of this dialogue, except among people who were already engaging these issues prior to 9–11–01. The Pew Research Center recently found that the attention of U.S. citizens to foreign news has remained essentially unchanged in the wake of the terrorist attacks (Kurtz, 2002). People are more narrowly focused on homeland defense rather than addressing the sources of discontent that cause such violence.

President Bush's State of the Union Address in 2002 illustrates the extent to which the United States has not changed. When the President referred to Iran, Iraq, and North Korea as an "axis of evil," the bipartisan audience in the House stood in ovation. Among our allies, especially those in Europe, however, the comment was viewed as irresponsible war-baiting toward two nations, North Korea and Iran, which are beginning to reform and open themselves to the community of nations. Watching the speech and in the discussion that followed, I wondered how much has changed concerning U.S. views of the world and the extent to which the conflict has been educative for our society.

It might be somewhat more accurate to say that the world changed for those living in the United States on 9–11–01. Terrorism and other forms of mass violence have been unfortunately typical throughout the world during the 20th century, by the far the bloodiest in history. As Lapham (2002) noted, "Madness has been stalking the Earth ever since an American B-29 dropped an atomic bomb on Hiroshima on the day in August 1945 that Buckminster Fuller marked on his calendar as 'the day that humanity started taking its final exam'" (p. 8). The dreadful day in the autumn of 2001 is yet another example of this mad killing of innocent lives, followed by more violence against innocents, with 3,950 Afghanis killed in the conflict thus far (Harper's Index, 2002). Given the unfolding of events, 9–11–01 seems to indicate a continuation rather than a fundamental change in the world.

What Does it Mean to Be Engaged in a "War"?

The "war on terrorism" is an unofficial "war" as it has not been declared as such by the U.S. Congress. The "war" is vague, perhaps appropriately, because it is one of the first conflicts of the 21st century. It is a nebulous war because it is not precisely clear who is being fought, how long the combat is expected to last, and what the goals of the conflict are. President Bush outlined the breadth of the "war" in his speech to a joint session of Congress:

> Americans should not expect one battle, but a lengthy campaign, unlike any other we have ever seen. It may include dramatic strikes, visible on TV, and covert operations, secret even in success. We will starve terrorists of funding, turn them one against another, drive them from place to place, until there is no refuge or no rest. And we will pursue nations that provide aid or safe haven to terrorism. (The White House, 2002)

Who is the United States battling in Afghanistan? If it is al Qaeda and the Taliban, is the war now over since these forces have been removed from power? Clearly the conflict has just begun, and yet the next foe is still undetermined. If the enemies are terrorists, than certainly the enemy is within. Does that mean that the U.S. military will be conducting search and destroy raids in Brooklyn and other domestic sites where terrorists have been known to operate? If the conflict in Afghanistan is a "war," then why aren't the prisoners of war being treated as such at Guantanamo Bay? And if they are treated as such, will they be repatriated to Afghanistan at the end of the war, as required by international law? If the United States is at war, then why is John Walker Lindh being charged for conspiracy to murder Americans and not treason, as stipulated in the Constitution? Walker Lindh's crimes, given a state of war, are clear: "Treason against the United States shall consist only in levying war against them, or in adhering to their enemies, giving them aid and comfort" (U.S. Constitution, Article III, Section 3).

These are all important questions that surround a larger, even more complex query: What is a "war"? Defining war, with whom the United States is at war, the battlefield, and the goals after September 11 has become increasingly complex. The lack of clarity about this war is evident in the White House official statement defining the war on terrorism: "The American Response to Terrorism is being fought at home and abroad through multiple operations including: diplomatic, military, financial, investigative, homeland security and humanitarian actions" (The White House, 2002). The breadth and nebulous quality of the "war" suggests that simplified notions of state versus state conflict, which typified war in the 20th century, does not make as much sense in this truly 21st-century conflict. The threat of a cyber attack, for example, where international hackers undermine the security of vital Internet resources in the United States, illustrates another novel dimension of the current conflict, further illustrating how our conception of war is antiquated and limited vis-à-vis the present situation.

How Should Teachers Engage Students in Study of Recent Events?

Despite its complexity, the current situation deserves sustained and thoughtful attention by teachers, particularly global educators. *Social Education* dedicated a special issue, *Teaching about Tragedy* (Simpson, 2001) to address pedagogical concerns surrounding this conflict. Authors in this issue provided a variety of suggestions about how to engage students in a study of 9–11–01 and its aftermath. I hope to briefly address the same question in light of the key global education problems identified herein: nationalism, relativism, and identity.

Nationalism

While driving recently, I saw a bumper sticker that expresses the sentiments of some people after the events of 9–11–01: "Kill 'em all, let Allah sort them out!" Antipathy toward Islam has spiked over the past year, along with a measurable increase in nationalistic sentiments in the United States. Certainly a degree of patriotism is to be expected at a time of national crisis, particularly when those who perpetrated the attacks have as their goal the destruction of a way of life. Caution must be exercised, however, especially in global classrooms, as to not allow earnest patriotism to boil over into xenophobic, vitriolic war mongering. Some discussion questions toward that end might include:

- What are the characteristics of patriotism? Nationalism?
- What has history shown regarding when national love becomes a source of violent hatred?
- What contemporary examples have you seen since 9–11–01 that indicate a healthy love of country compared to a dysfunctional rejection of Others?
- What criteria might you develop to ascertain "healthy" and "dysfunctional" love of nation?

Questions like these may give rise to important classroom dialogue where students are challenged to analyze the complexity of national pride in times of global catastrophe.

Relativism

Cultural relativism is a perplexing issue in ordinary times, but in the wake of the terrorist attacks, it presents an even more daunting challenge. A news magazine headline in the weeks that followed 9–11–01 illustrates the importance of this seemingly esoteric debate: Why do they hate us? The question suggests that otherwise uninterested persons to take notice that Hanvey's (1976) dimension of "perspective consciousness" has great currency in this conflict. Mrs. Bratus' comment that "one man's terrorist is another man's freedom fighter" rings eerily in my mind following the autumn of 2001.

Global educators and their students clearly would benefit from a thoughtful recognition of the relativity of perspective and a sustained engagement of this issue. So many news programs have been broadcast around this theme that teachers can draw on a multitude of contemporary examples to illustrate this idea. Discussing the morality of dying for a cause and how that is viewed in different societies, and in various historical periods, would also provide rich insights about these events. The simplification of perspectivity into right/wrong and good/evil dichotomies following 9–11–01 robs this significant historical event of its educative power. If we are not able to transcend these simplifications and learn to think about perspective differently in the wake of this horror, than I fear that many people have died in vain.

Identity

Soon after 9–11–01, Muslim leaders throughout the world, particularly those in the United States, denounced terrorism, al Qaeda, and violence perpetrated in the name of Allah. Islam, they countered, means "submission" in Arabic, or giving in to God. Myriad differences exist among the one billion Muslims about interpretations of the Qu'ran and Hadith and how one is supposed to act as a devout Muslim. The same disputes exist in virtually all faiths, although those in Islam have generated interest in the wake of the attacks. The dispute helps to illustrate the contested nature of human identity and the manner in which power is gained through various constructions of "What does it mean to be a _____?" Realizing how the same identities carry different individual meanings is a valuable lesson that can be gained form this tragedy, one that challenges the simplicity of homogenized, essentialized talk of Others (Seikaly, 2001).

"Othering" has been a persistent pattern, both of public reaction and security policy, following 9–11–01. People, including members of President Bush's security detail, have been summarily removed from aircraft due to their ethnic appearance. Defenders of these actions have argued that because all of the terrorist attackers were of Southwest Asian descent, it is justifiable to profile individuals in this category, particularly young males. Critics have asserted that this level of scrutiny is discriminatory, sowing more negative feelings toward innocent people. Global educators might engage students in a debate about security profiling in light of these events, comparing the public comments of politicians and political commentators prior to and following the terrorist attacks.

Recent intelligence suggests that al Qaeda is locating supporters who do not fit the "Middle Eastern" profile to be used for future attacks, to avoid being detected through profiling. The thwarted attempt by former Chicago gang member and U.S. citizen Jose Padilla, now Abdullah Al Muhajir upon his conversion to Islam, is a case in point (Candiotti & Potter, 2002). Such efforts by terrorist groups challenge not only the security systems in place, but perhaps more importantly, our conceptions of identity. The desire to pigeon hole terrorist participants into particular ethnic groups, religious affiliations, or national origins suggests a 20th-century perspective on a global issuc that is decidedly 21st-century-like in its complexity. Those who think of the identity = terrorist link in this simplistic manner are, in fact, preparing for the last conflict rather than the next one.

I often find myself wondering how the global educators and students reported on in this book, and those who I taught over the past decade, understand these events. One particular question echoes in my thinking: Do they think about their global teaching and learning in the context of these events? Although I cannot empirically answer this query, I suspect that those who viewed their global learning as an academic exercise to be taught (or completed) probably saw little connection or significance beyond the obvious death and mayhem. I remain hopeful, again in belief rather than through data, that those who viewed the local–global connections around them as meaningful, dynamic, and complex, and who saw themselves as an interdependent entity on this planet, could not help but view 9–11–01 with a greater depth of understanding.

Appendix: Methodology

This study employed a qualitative methodology involving an ethnographic approach and the grounded theory method for data analysis. Grounded theory was first articulated by Glaser and Strauss (1967) and elaborated on by qualitative researchers since the late 1960s. It has been used to generate "abstract analytical schema of a phenomenon that relates to a particular situation" where theory does not exist or is not well developed (Creswell, 1998, p. 56). Ethnographic research allows participants to speak with their own voices about the phenomena that they experience.

The context for this type of research is crucial to understanding, as the inquiry attempts to explain and analyze the relationships of seemingly disparate and disconnected behaviors and values in particular settings. Often these relationships are unknown to the participants. As Spindler (1982) suggests, "A significant task of ethnography is therefore to make explicit what is implicit and tacit to informants and participants in the social settings being studied" (p. 7). In ethnographic research, one does not simply record the occurrences in a particular setting; rather, one analyzes and interprets the patterns of beliefs and behaviors as they interact within the social setting.

Grounded theory is a form of qualitative inquiry that does not begin with *a priori* assumptions and hypotheses. Hypotheses emerge *in situ*, and thus, the research process is fluid and contingent on the ongoing analysis of data by the researcher. The researcher is placed in an interactional setting with the participants wherein the researcher acts as a participant, but is in fact an observer. The researcher must make a conscious effort to become familiar to the informants and develop rapport so that the participants' interactions will be as genuine as possible. "Genuine is taken to be behavior that is spontaneously expressed or otherwise naturalistic" (Kilbride & Kilbride, 1990, p. 24).

Qualitative research is unique in the sense that the person conducting the research is the "instrument" by whom the observed phenomena are being understood and analyzed. This can result in disorganized, chaotic data that provides little if any insight into the phenomena being studied. Qualitative theorists, however, offer methods of inquiry which permit a systematic process of study. Because the process of structuring such a study is difficult to mechanize, care must be taken to search for patterns of data and subsequent theoretical relationships within those patterns. As the instrument, the researcher must "listen not only with the tidiest and most precise of one's cognitive abilities, but also with the whole of one's experience and imagination" (McCracken, 1988, p. 19).

After I had collected a series of field documents (i.e., an interview), they were read by two people with extensive research experience outside the study. I asked these individuals to independently analyze the material without discussing my analysis. They then submitted a list of patterns that they found within the data. The patterns identified by my colleagues demonstrated a high degree of correlation with my independent analysis.

SITE SELECTION

I identified three sites that would illustrate to some degree the diversity of New Jersey. In order to represent that diversity, I located a rural school in the south, an urban/inner city school in the north and a suburban school in the central region of the state. I contacted approximately 15 high schools with these criteria in mind and sought permission to conduct the research. I explained in the letter of introduction that the site visits would be extensive, covering approximately a 2-month time period and that students, teachers and curriculum planners in the global education course would be asked to participate.

I received affirmative replies from Bart High School, an urban high school in a northern city, Valley High School, a rural school situated in the south, and Sunny Brook High School, a suburban district in central New Jersey. All of the names of places and people used in this study are fictional to preserve the anonymity of the people included, which I assured to all participants prior to conducting the research.

DATA COLLECTION

The data of this ethnographic study include observation reports, interviews, and document analyses. This process of data collection was selected because it offered the best opportunity to "understand the world from the subjects' points of view, to unfold the meaning of peoples' experiences to uncover their lived world" (Kvale, 1996, p. 1).

Prior to observing any classes, I spent a few days in each school making informal observations and developing rapport with the teachers. I scheduled multiple observations of each teacher in their world studies classes. Some teachers were hesitant to allow me to observe on a "regular day" (i.e., a lecture or textbook assignment) but I assured them that these type lessons were as important as classes which were designed to be more interactive. There was some concern initially in all three schools about being observed, but this soon dissipated as I came to be unnoticed, even ignored, in most classrooms.

The observations were conducted in a "grand tour" style, as suggested by Spradley (1990). Grand tour observations attempt to reconstruct as precisely as possible all that occurred in a particular setting. It was not possible to record all of the events in such a complex interaction as a high school class, but an effort was made to capture as much detail as possible, including student seating arrangements, student movements, teacher movements, teacher actions/statements, student actions/statements, content, and classroom environment. Although Spradley refers to interviews in using this terminology, it best describes the type of observations that were collected in this study.

I conducted teacher and student interviews after initial observations were completed, in keeping with a naturalistic style of inquiry. I was able to identify certain issues and ideas in observations that seemed significant, later confirming or denying their existence with interviewees. Teacher interviews generally lasted between 1 and 2 hours in total duration. This time was divided into three or four segments because most teachers, by the nature of their work, could not spend more than 30 to 45 minutes at any one time being interviewed.

I attempted to include in the teacher interview group as much diversity as possible, employing the inclusiveness criteria offered by Seidman (1991). Inclusiveness is defined herein as those participating in the study reflecting the range of most or all of those outside the sample who could connect to the experiences of those in the sample. For inclusiveness to be achieved, there should be men, women, ethnic minorities, those with different levels of education, age and experience ranges.

The teacher sample had a diverse range of identities, including females, males, 1 to 27 years of teaching experience, White, African American, Latino, Jewish, Christian, and agnostic. I struggled with the question of how many people to interview, but settled on the 15 ± 10 guide suggested in much of the qualitative research literature (see Kvale, 1996). Including the student and curriculum planners, the number of interviews far exceeded the guideline suggested for quantity of interview subjects.

I attempted to provide an isolated environment for each interview and reminded each informant that their identity would be held confidential. The teachers who were interviewed for the greatest length of time demonstrated two criteria in the interviews: maximum variance and responsiveness. Teachers who offered a maximum variance of data were interviewed repeatedly (Strauss & Corbin, 1990). Maximum variance is defined as those who are able to raise the widest scope of new categories accompanied by depth of analysis of these ideas.

Initial student interviewees were selected using similar criteria as used in selecting the teachers; that is, they:

- Were currently enrolled in world studies course.
- Demonstrated active participation in class.
- Contributed to diversity of sample.
- Demonstrated a willingness to participate.

I met with each student for a few minutes prior to the interviews and explained the study, providing them with an interview consent form for parent signature.

The interviews were intentionally not standardized. The open-ended nature was intended to allow the participants to express their thoughts about global education as completely as possible. As Kvale (1996) asserted, "Interviews are conversations where the outcome is a coproduction of the interviewer and the subject" (p. vii). The participants were encouraged to elaborate in as much detail as possible about their views on the phenomena being examined. As the interviewer, I asked very few questions, usually in the format of "To what extent do you ..." and periodically offered prompts such as "Could you illustrate your understanding of that with an example?" This style allowed me to "promote the unfolding of emic cultural knowledge in its most heuristic, 'natural' form" (Spindler, 1982, p. 7).

I transcribed the interviews in their entirety within 48 hours of taking the recording. A digital recorder was used to capture the highest quality sound and notes were taken to supplement the recording. Despite my efforts to maintain the accuracy of the interviews, "transcripts are decontextualized conversations," and should be taken as representations of conversations rather than the conversations themselves (Kvale, 1996, p. 165).

Through the course of the research, documents were used to generate categories of information and confirm or deny the presence of patterns. A range of document types were included in the study, including: course of study guides, teacher-created assignments, student essays, school mission statements, and school policies. Documents were read and the information contained in them coded along with the observations and interviews. I did not seek out specific documents, with the exception of the course of study guides. The documents that were analyzed arose in the context of observations and interviews. This further enhanced the naturalistic quality of the data while enhancing the contextual quality of the inquiry.

Table A.1 summarizes the data collection in this study for each of the sites and as a composite for the entire study.

ANALYTICAL TECHNIQUES

Qualitative research is designed to let the participants speak with their own voices about phenomena that affect their lives, a descriptive endeavor that is achieved through the collection of data. The intermittent steps of analysis, however, are essential in ferreting out patterns and examining how those patterns interact within a context. The local theory that emerges from this inquiry, grounded in literature and practice, can be used to provide insight into new and different circumstances.

Data were collected and open-coding analysis was conducted on a regular basis, either weekly or bi-weekly. Once sufficient data had been collected at each site, a series of categories emerged, usually between 10 and 15, which could be clarified with participants as to their validity and meaning. I define validity as representing the articulated understanding of the participants. A pattern was assumed to exist if it could be triangulated, meaning that it occurred naturalistically in three unique settings (e.g., in a teacher interview, classroom observation and document analysis) by at least two different participants.

Once the categories emerged, axial coding was employed to give greater depth and achieve saturation of the categories. Saturation is defined as finding information that continues to add to the conceptual base until no new information can be found (Creswell, 1998). Using the patterns established in open coding, participants were queried as to their depth of understanding of the category and how these categories interact with other phenomena. Strauss and Corbin (1990) best described these two processes in the following statement: "Open coding fractures the data and allows one to identify some categories, their properties, and dimensional locations. Axial coding puts those data back together in new ways by making connections between a category and its sub-categories" (p. 97).

TABLE A.1

Data Collection

Data Collection	Bart High School	Valley High School	Sunny Brook High School	Totals
Demographics	urban/inner city northern region Latino & African Am.	rural southern region White, Latino, African Am	Suburban Central region Ethnically diverse	—
District Factor Group (DFG)	special needs district/DFG A	special needs district/DFG B	D.F.G. I	—
Course(s) Observed	World History/ World Cultures	World Cultures	Contemporary World Issues	—
Grade Level	9th	9th	12th	
Teachers/ Curriculum Planners Interviewed	5	5	4	14
Students Observed/ Interviewed	60/10	85/9	52/10	197/27
Observations	22 forty-five minute periods	16 forty-five minute periods	12 ninety minute periods	50 class observations
Nonclassroom Observations*	4	7	3	14
Teacher/ Curriculum Planners Interviews	12 hours	10 hours	10 hours	32 hours
Student Interviews	4 hours	3 hours	7 hours	14 hours
Documents Analyzed	10	9	10	29
Days of Field Observation	24	20	19	63
Analysis of Fieldnotes	35 pages	27 pages	32 pages	94 pages

I employed a zigzag method of analysis offered by Strauss and Corbin (1990), also referred to as the constant comparative method by Creswell (1998). By continually transcribing and coding phenomena in open coding and testing their depth, validity, and interaction in axial coding, analysis occurred through all phases of the study, rather than at the end of the data collection. This allows the researcher to develop hypotheses in the field and test them with the participants, insuring that he/she is accurately describing the phenomena from the perspective of the participants.

This study is limited because it examined three high schools. Generalizations about the data collected and analyzed should be engaged cautiously because little is known about the practice in the hundreds of other New Jersey high schools. This study seeks to develop local theory about the practice of world studies in high schools that demonstrate a range of the types found in the state. This local theory, when read in the context of where it was developed, can be applied to new situations when the new context matches the context of this study to some degree. In this sense, the theory generated herein is illustrative of some of the larger issues in the field, but it is not meant to represent the totality of experience and may be limited in its applicability to other situations given changing conditions.

References

Abbott v. Burke, 119 N. J. 287 (1990).

Abbott v. Burke, 135 N. J. 444 (1994).

Aboud, F. E. (1987). The development of ethnic self-identification and attitudes. In J. S. Phinney & M. J. Rotheram (Eds.), *Children's ethnic socialization: Pluralism and development* (pp. 32–55). Newbury Park, CA: Sage.

Ad hoc committee on global education. (1987). Global education: In bounds or out? *Social Education, 51*(3). 242–249.

Adler, S. (1991). The education of social studies teachers. In J. P. Shaver (Ed.), *Handbook of Research on Social Studies Teaching and Learning* (pp. 210–221). National Council for the Social Studies, Washington, DC.

Alger, C. (1968). Some problems in improving international education. *Social Education, 35*(7), 657–666.

Alger, C. (1998). Global connections: Where am I? How did I get here? Where am I going? *Social Education, 62*(5), 272–275.

Allport, G. W. (1979). *The nature of prejudice*. Reading, MA: Addison-Wesley. (Original work published 1954)

Ålund, A., & Schierup, C.U. (1991). *Paradoxes of multiculturalism*. Aldershot, UK: Avebury Press.

Anderson, C. (1982). Global education in the classroom. *Theory into Practice, 21*(3), 168–176.

Anderson, C. C., Nicklas, S. K., & Crawford, A. R. (1994). Global understandings: A framework for teaching and learning. *Association for Supervision and Curriculum Development.* Retrieved May 26, 2002, from http://ascd.org/readingroom/books/anderson94.html

Anderson, C. C., & Anderson, L. F. (1979). A visit to Middleston's world-centered schools: A scenario. In J. M. Becker (Ed.), *Schooling for a global age* (pp. 1–32). New York: McGraw-Hill.

Anderson, C. C., Nicklas, S. K., & Crawford, A. R. (1994). *Global understandings: A framework for teaching and learning*. Alexandria, VA: Association for Supervision and Curriculum Development.

Anderson, L. F. (1968). An examination of the structure and objectives of international education. *Social Education, 35*(7), 639–652.

An-Na'im, A. A. (1992). Toward a cross-cultural approach to defining international standards of human rights. In A. A. An-Na'im (Ed.), *Human rights in cross-cultural perspectives* (pp. 19–43). Philadelphia: University of Pennsylvania Press

Anyon, J. (1997). *Ghetto schooling: A political economy of urban educational reform*. New York: Teachers College Press.

Anyon, J. (2001). Inner cities, affluent suburbs, and unequal educational opportunity. In J. Banks & C. Banks (Eds.), *Multicultural education: Issues and perspectives* (pp. 85–99). New York: Wiley.

Appiah, K. A. (1992). *In my father's house: Africa in the philosophy of culture.* New York: Oxford University Press.

Appleby, J. (1992). Recovering America's historic diversity: Beyond exceptionalism. *The Journal of American History, 79*(2), 419–431.

Asher, N., & Crocco, M. S. (2001). (En)gendering multicultural identities and representations in education. *Theory and Research in Social Education, 29*(1), 129–151

Banks, J. A. (1996a). The canon debate, knowledge construction, and multicultural education. In J. A. Banks (Ed.), *Multicultural education: Transformative knowledge and action* (pp. 3–29). New York: Teachers College Press.

Banks, J. A. (1996b). The historical reconstruction of knowledge about race: Implications for transformative teaching. In J. A. Banks (Ed.), *Multicultural education: Transformative knowledge and action* (pp. pp. 64–88). New York: Teachers College Press.

Banks, J. A. (2001, June 15). *Educating citizens in a multicultural society.* Speech for the Consortium for Social Responsibility, University of Central Florida, Orlando, FL.

Barnes, B., Stallings, W., & Rivner, R. (1981). Are the critics right about MACOS? *Theory and Research in Social Education, 9* (1), 35–44.

Barth, J. (1996). The alternative futures of international social studies. In R. W. Evans & D. W. Saxe (Eds.), *Handbook on Teaching Social Issues* (pp. 327–337). Washington, DC: National Council for the Social Studies.

Becker, J. M. (1979). The world and the school: A case for world-centered education. In J. M. Becker (Ed.), *Schooling for a global age* (pp. 33–57). New York: McGraw-Hill.

Becker, J. M. (1982). Goals for global education. *Theory into Practice, 21*(3), 228–233.

Becker, J. M. (1991). Curriculum considerations in global studies. In K. Tye (Ed.), *Global education: From thought to action* (pp. 67–84). Alexandria, VA: Association for Supervision & Curriculum Development.

Begler, E. (1998). Global cultures: The first step towards understanding. *Social Education, 62*(5), 272–275.

Bell, M. (2000, October 16). Teachers are leaving because the hassles aren't worth the money. *Orlando Sentinel*, pp. A1, A16–17.

Benitez, H. (2001). Effects of a globalized U.S. history curriculum. *Theory and Research in Social Education, 29*(2), 290–307.

Bennett, C. (2001). Genres of research in multicultural education. *Review of Educational Research, 71*(2), 171–217.

Bennett, W. J. (1993). *The book of virtues.* New York: Simon & Schuster.

Berger, P. L. (2000). Four faces of global culture. In P. O'Meara, H. D. Mehlinger, & M. Krain (Eds.), *Globalization and the challenges of a new century: A reader.* Bloomington, IN: Indiana University Press.

Berliner, D. C., & Biddle, B. J. (1995). *The manufactured crisis: Myths, fraud, and the attack on America's public schools.* Reading, MA: Perseus Books.

Bickmore, K. (1999). Elementary curriculum about conflict resolution: Can children handle global politics? *Theory and Research in Social Education, 27*(1), 45–69.

Blankenship, G. (1990). Classroom climate, global knowledge, global attitudes, political attitudes. *Theory and Research in Social Education, 13*(4), 363–386.

Bolin, F. S. (1987). Teacher as curriculum decision-maker. In F. S. Bolin & J. M. Falk (Eds.), *Teacher renewal: Professional issues, personal choices* (pp. 92–108). New York: Teachers College Press.

Boote, D., Wideen, M. F., Mayer-Smith, J., & Moon, B. (1999) . *In-service Education, School Cultures, and the Failure of Curriculum Reforms: An Elementary Science Case Study.* Paper presented at the annual meeting of the American Educational Research Association, Vancouver, Canada.

Boston, J. A. (1997). Professional development in global education. In M. Merryfield (Ed.), *Preparing teachers to teach global perspectives: A handbook for teacher educators* (pp. 168–188).Thousand Oaks, CA: Corwin Press.

Boulding, E. (1988). *Building a global civic culture: Education for an interdependent world.* New York: Teachers College Press.

Boulding, E. (1996). Boston research center for the 21st century. *American Journal of Economics & Sociology, 55,* 337–346.

Boulding, K. E. (1968). Education for spaceship Earth. *Social Education, 35*(7), 648–656; 669.

Boulding, E. (1988). *Building a global civic culture: Education for an interdependent world.* New York: Teachers College Press.

Boydston, J. A. (1977). *John Dewey: The middle works, 1899–1924; Volume 3, 1903–1906.* Carbondale, IL: Southern Illinois University Press.

Breitborde, L. B. (1993). Multiculturalism and cultural relativism after the commemoration. *Social Education, 57*(6), 104–108.

Buergental, T. (1995). *International human rights.* St. Paul, MN: West.

Bullivant, B. M. (1993/89). Culture: Its nature and meaning for educators. In J. A. Banks & C. A. McGee-Banks (Ed.) *Multicultural Education: Issues and Perspectives* (pp. 29–47). Needham Heights, MA: Allyn & Bacon.

Burtonwood, N. (1996). Culture, identity and the curriculum. *Educational Review, 48*(3), 227–235.

Candiotti, S., & Potter, M. (2002). *Feds arrest man linked to 'dirty bomb' suspect.* Retrieved June 24, 2002, from http://www.cnn.com/index.html

Callan, E. (1994, February). Beyond sentimental civic education. *American Journal of Education, 102,* 190–221.

Carson, R. (1962). *Silent spring.* Boston: Houghton-Mifflin.

Case, R. (1993). Key elements of a global perspective. *Social Education, 57*(6), 318–325.

Castles, S., & Davidson, A. (2000). *Citizenship and migration: Globalization and the politics of belonging.* New York: Routledge.

Chagnon, N. A. (1992). *Yanomamö The last days of Eden.* San Diego, CA: Harcourt Brace Jovanovich.

Chinn, P. W. U. (1998). Teacher-student action research: Answering Melissa's question. *Teaching and Change, 5*(2), 99–116.

Cialdini, R. B. (1988). *Influence: Science and practice.* New York: Scott, Foresman.

Clandinin, D. J., & Connelly, F. M. (1992). Teacher as curriculum maker. In P. W. Jackson (Ed.), *Handbook of research on curriculum* (pp. 363–401). Toronto, Canada: Maxwell Macmillan.

Clandinin, D. J., & Connelly, F. M. (1996). Teachers' professional knowledge landscapes: Teacher stories—stories of teachers—school stories—stories of schools. *Educational Researcher, 25*(3), 24–30.

Cochran-Smith, M., & Lytle, S. L. (1993). *Inside, outside: Teacher research and knowledge.* New York: Teacher's College Press.

Cole, A. L., & Knowles, J. G. (2000). *Researching teaching: Exploring teacher development through reflexive inquiry.* Needham Heights, MA: Allyn & Bacon.

Cornbleth, C. (1990). *Curriculum in context.* London: Falmer Press.

Cornbleth, C. (1991). Research on context, research in context. In J. P. Shaver (Ed.), *Handbook of research on social studies teaching and learning* (pp. 265–275). Washington, DC: National Council for the Social Studies.

Cornett, J. (1990). Teacher thinking about curriculum and instruction: A case study of a secondary social studies teacher. *Theory and Research in Social Education, 18*(3), 248–273.

Creswell, J. W. (1998*). Qualitative inquiry and research design: Choosing among five traditions.* Thousand Oaks, CA: Sage.

Cushner, K. (Ed.). (1998). *International perspectives on intercultural education.* Mahwah, NJ: Lawrence Erlbaum Associates.

Cushner, K. (1999). *Human diversity in action: Developing multicultural competencies for the classroom.* Boston: McGraw-Hill.

Darling-Hammond, L. (1988). Accountability and teacher professionalism. *American Educator, 12*(4), 8–13, 38–43.

Davidson, A. L. (1996). *Making and molding identity in schools: Student narratives on race, gender, and academic engagement.* Albany, NY: State University of New York Press.

Dean, J. (1991). *Professional development in school.* Philadelphia: Open University Press.

DeRoche, E. F. (2000, January). Creating a framework for character education. *Principal,* 32–34.

Dewey, J. (1990). *The school and society and the child and the curriculum.* Chicago: University of Chicago Press.

Dewey, J. (1997). *How we think.* Mineola, NY: Dover. (Original work published 1910)

Dewey, J. (1966). *Democracy and education.* New York: The Free Press. (Original work published 1916)

Dewey, J. (1997). *Experience and education.* New York: Touchstone Books. (Original work published 1938)

Diaz, C. F., Massialas, B. G., and Xanthopoulus, J. A. (1999). *Global perspectives for educators.* Boston: Allyn & Bacon.

Donoahue, Z. (2001). An examination of the development of classroom community through class meetings. In G. Wells (Ed.), *Action, talk, and text: Learning and teaching through inquiry* (pp. 25–40). New York: Teachers College Press.

Doolittle, P. E., Hicks, D., & Lee, J. K. (2001, November). *From theory to practice: The synthesis of constructivism, technology, and social studies.* Paper presented at the annual meeting of the College and University Faculty Association of the National Council for the Social Studies, Washington, DC.

Duncan, J. K. (1973). Curriculum director in curriculum change. *Educational Forum, 38*(1), 51–77).

Egan, K. (1978). Letting our presuppositions think for us. *Curriculum Studies, 10*(2), 123–133.

Ehrlich, R. (1968). *The population bomb.* New York: Ballantine.

Engle, S. H., & Ochoa, A. S. (1988). *Education for democratic citizenship: Decision-making in the social studies.* New York: Teachers College Press.

Erikson, E. H. (1968). *Identity: Youth and crisis.* New York: Norton.

Evans, R. W., Newmann, F. M., & Saxe, D. W. (1996). Defining issues-centered education. In R. W. Evans & D. W. Saxe (Eds.), *Handbook on teaching social issues, NCSS Bulletin 93* (pp. 2–5). Washington, DC: National Council for the Social Studies.

Falk, R. (1994). The making of global citizenship. In B. van Steenbergen (Ed.), *The condition of citizenship* (pp. 126–140). London: Sage.

Fuller, R. B. (1970). *Operating manual for spaceship earth.* New York: Pocket Books.

Feldgus, E. G. (1993). Classroom and school studies. In M. Cochran-Smith & S. L. Lytle (Eds.), *Inside outside: Teacher research and knowledge* (pp. 170–240). New York: Teachers College Press.

Flowers, N. (1993). Teaching about international human rights: An annotated bibliography. In R. W. Evans & D. W. Saxe (Eds.), *Handbook on teaching social issues* (pp. 374–376). Washington, DC: National Council for the Social Studies.

Funderburg, L. (1999, November 7). Integration anxiety. *The New York Times Magazine,* 83–87.

Freire, P. (2001/1970). *Pedagogy of the oppressed.* New York: Continuum.

Fuller, R. B. (1969). *Operating manual for spaceship earth.* New York: Simon & Schuster.

Funderburg, L. (1999, November 7). Integration anxiety. *The New York Times Magazine,* 83–87.

Gakouo, K. (1995). *Nyumba ya Mumbi: The Gikuyu creation myth.* Nairobi, Kenya: Jacaranda Designs.

Gallie, W. B. (1964). *Philosophy and the historical understanding.* London: Chatto & Windus.

Gallup Organization. (2002). *Reaction to the attacks on America.* [On-line]. Available: http://www.gallup.com/

Galtung, J. (1994). *Human rights in another key.* Cambridge, UK: Polity Press.

Garii, B. (2000). United States social studies in the 21st century: Internationalizing the curriculum for global citizens. *Social Studies, 91*(6), 257–265.

Gaudelli, W. (2000). *Approaches to global education.* Unpublished dissertation, Rutgers University, New Brunswick, NJ.

Gaudelli, W. (2001a). Identity discourse: Problems, presuppositions, and educational practice. *International Journal of Sociology and Social Policy, 20*(3), 60–81.

Gaudelli, W. (2001b). Pedagogical orientations towards democratic civic life. *Florida Educational Leadership, 1*(3), 26–29.

Gaudelli, W. (2002). *Professional development, global pedagogy, and potential: Examining an alternative approach to the one-shot workshop.* Manuscript submitted for publication.

Gee, J. P. (2001). Identity as an analytic lens for research in education. In W. G. Secada (Vol. Ed.), *Review of research in education: Vol. 25* (pp. 99–126). Washington, DC: American Educational Research Association.

Geertz, C. (1984). Distinguished lecture: Anti anti-relativism. *American Anthropologist, 86,* 263–277.

Germain, M. H. (1998). *Worldly teachers: Cultural learning and pedagogy.* Westport, CT: Bergin & Garvey.

Giroux, H. A. (1984). Teachers as transformative intellectuals. *Social Education, 49*(4), 376–379.

Giroux, H. A. (1988). *Schooling and the struggle for public life: Critical pedagogy in the modern age.* Minneapolis: University of Minnesota Press.

Glaser, B. G., & Strauss, A. L. (1967). *The discovery of grounded theory: Strategies for qualitative research.* Chicago: Aldine.

Goldenberg, C., & Gallimore, R. (1991). Changing teaching takes more than a one-shot workshop. *Educational Leadership, 49*(3), 69–72.

Goodlad, J. I. (1984). *A place called school: Prospects for the future.* New York: McGraw-Hill Publishers.

Grant, C. A., & Sleeter, C. E. (1998). *Turning on learning: Five approaches to multicultural teaching plans for race, class, gender and diversity.* Princeton, NJ: Merrill of Prentice Hall.

Grant, S. G., Derme-Insinna, A., Gradwell, J. Lauricella, A. M., Pullano, L., & Tzetzo, K. (2001). Teachers, tests, and tensions: Teachers respond to the New York State global history exam. *The International Social Studies Forum, 1*(2), 107–126.

Grossman, P. L., & Stodolsky, S. S. (1995). Content as context: The role of school subjects in secondary school teaching. *Educational Researcher, 24*(8), 5–11, 23.

Gutman, A. (1993). The challenge of multiculturalism in political ethics. *Philosophy and Public Affairs, 22*(3), 171–206.

Hahn, C. (1984). Promise and paradox: Challenges to global citizenship. *Social Education, 48*(4), 240–243.

Hahn, C. (1991). Controversial issues in social studies. In J. P. Shaver, (Ed.), *Handbook of Research on Social Studies Teaching and Learning* (pp. 470–480).

Hall, J. A., & Lindholm, C. (1999). *Is America breaking apart?* Princeton, NJ: Princeton University Press.

Hansot, E. (1993). Misperceptions of gender and youth: Learning together, learning apart. In S. B. Heath and M. W. McLaughlin (Eds.), *Identity and inner-city youth: Beyond ethnicity and gender* (pp. 196–209). New York: Teachers College Press.

Hanvey, R. G. (1976). *An attainable global perspective.* New York: Center for War/Peace Studies.

Harper's Index. (2002, March). *Harper's Magazine,* 13.

Hasan, O. E. (2000). Improving the quality of learning: Global education as a vehicle for school reform. *Theory into Practice, 39*(2), 97–103.

Hatch, T. (1999). Dilemmas of theory, design, and practice in curriculum and school improvement: Editor's introduction. *Peabody Journal of Education, 74*(1), 1–11.

Haugaard, K. (1997). Suspending moral judgment: Students who refuse to condemn the unthinkable. *Chronicle of Higher Education, 18,* B4–B5.

Heater, D. (1984). *Peace through education.* London: Falmer Press.

Heath, S. B. & McLaughlin, M. W. (1993). Ethnicity and gender in theory and practice: The youth perspective. In S. B. Heath & M. W. McLaughlin (Eds.), *Identity and inner city youth: Beyond ethnicity and gender* (pp. 13–35). New York: Teachers College Press.

Hirshfeld, L. A. (1996). *Race in the making*. Cambridge, MA: MIT Press.

Horner, E. R. (1998). *The New Jersey municipal data book*. Palo Alto, CA: Information Publications.

Howard, S., & Gill, J. (2000). The pebble in the pond: Children's constructions of power, politics and democratic citizenship. *Cambridge Journal of Education, 30*(3), 357–379.

Hunt, M. P., & Metcalf, L. (1968). *Teaching high school social studies: Problems in reflective thinking and social understanding*. New York: Harper & Row.

Isaacs, H. R. (1975). *Idols of the tribe: Group identity and political change*. Cambridge, MA: Harvard University Press.

Jarvie, I. C. (1984). *Rationality and relativism*. Boston: Routledge & Kegan Paul.

Johnston, M., & Ochoa, A. (1993). Teacher education for global perspectives: A research agenda. *Theory into Practice, 32*(1), 64–68.

Kaplan, J. (2001). Name, rank, and serial number please! A look inside Florida's secondary schools. *Florida Educational Leadership, 1*(2), 26–29.

Keehn, D. (1989). *Global, international and foreign language education: 1988–89 state profiles*. New York: The American Forum for Global Education.

Kilbride, P. L., & Kilbride, J. C. (1990). *Changing family life in east Africa*. Nairobi, Kenya: Kenya Litho.

King, D. C. (1979). Secondary school programs. In J. M. Becker (Ed.), *Schooling for a global age* (pp. 153–184). New York: McGraw-Hill.

Kirkwood, T. F. (2001a). Building bridges: Miami 'ambassadors' visit Russia. *Social Education 65*(4), 236–239.

Kirkwood, T. F. (2001b). Our global age requires global education: Clarifying definitional ambiguities. *Social Studies, 92*(1), 10–16.

Kirschenbaum, H. (2000, September). From values clarification to character education: A personal journey. *Journal of Humanistic Counseling, Education and Development, 39,* 4–20.

Klein, F. (1985). The master teacher as curriculum leader. *Elementary School Journal, 86*(1), 35–43.

Kniep, W. M. (1985). *A critical review of the short history of global education: Preparing for new opportunities*. New York: Global Perspectives in Education.

Kniep, W. M. (1986). Defining a global education by its content. *Social Education, 50*(6), 437–446.

Kniep, W. M. (1987). *Next steps in global education: A handbook for curriculum development*. New York: American Forum for Global Education.

Kochendorfer, L. (1997). Types of classroom teacher action research. *Teaching and Change, 4*(2), 157–174.

Kohn, A. (1997, February). How not to teach values: A critical look at character education. *Phi Delta Kappan*, 429–439.

Kohn, A. (1999). *The schools our children deserve: Moving beyond traditional classrooms and tougher standards*. Boston: Houghton-Mifflin.

Konick, M. (1979). A network for development of global education. *Indiana Social Studies Quarterly, 32*(2), 12–23.

Kubow, P., Grossman, D., & Ninomiya, A. (1998). Multidimensional citizenship: Educational policy for the 21st century. In J. J. Cogan & R. Derricott (Eds.), *Citizenship for the 21st century: An international perspective on education* (pp. 115–134). London: Kogan Page.

Kurfman, D. G. (1991). Testing as context for social education. In J. P. Shaver (Ed.), *Handbook of research on social studies teaching and learning* (pp. 310–320). Washington, DC: National Council for the Social Studies.

Kurtz, H. (2002, June 10). Many in the US still ignore foreign news, poll shows. *Orlando Sentinel,* p. A9.

Kvale, S. (1996). *InterViews*. Newbury Park, CA: Sage.

Kymlicka, W. (1997). *The rights of minority cultures*. London: Oxford University Press.

Ladson-Billings, G. (1994). *The dreamkeepers: Successful teachers of African-American children*. San Francisco: Jossey-Bass.

Ladson-Billings, G. (1995). Toward a theory of culturally relevant pedagogy. *American Educational Research Journal, 32*(3), 465–491.

Lamy, S. L. (1982). Teacher training in global perspectives education: The center for teaching international relations. *Theory into Practice 21*(3), 177–183.

Lamy, S. L. (1987). *The definition of a discipline: The objects and methods of analysis in global education*. New York: Global Perspectives in Education.

Lamy, S. L. (1990). Global education: A conflict of images. In K. Tye (Ed.), *Global education: From thought to action* (pp. 49–63). Arlington, VA: Association for Supervision and Curriculum Development.

Lapham, L. H. (2002, March). Notebook: Spoils of war. *Harper's Magazine*, 8–11.

Lavelle, L. (1999). Shipping lines to remain in Port Newark. *The Bergen Record*. Retrieved May 26, 2002, from http://nl3.newsbank.com/nl-search/we/Archives?p action=list&p topdoc=11&p maxdocs=210

Leach, D. J., & Conto, H. (1999). The additional effects of process and outcome feedback following brief in-service teacher training. *Educational Psychology, 19*(4), 441–462.

Leming, J. S. (1993). In search of effective character education. *Educational Leadership, 51*(3), 63–71.

Leung, Y. W., & Print, M. (1998, April). *A search for rational nationalistic education in Hong Kong*. Paper presented at the meeting of the American Educational Research Association, San Diego, CA.

Levine, P. (1998). The sweetness of Bobby Hefka. In *What Work Is: Poems by Philip Levine* (pp. 72–73). New York: Knopf.

Levine, P. (2001). The sweetness of Bobby Hefka. In J. Chametzky, J. Felstiner, H. Flanzbaum, & K. Hellertein (Eds.), *Jewish American Literature* (pp. 855–866). New York: Norton.

Levstik, L. (1997). 'Any history is someone's history': Listening to multiple voices from the past. *Social Education, 61*(1), 48–51.

Levstik, L., & Barton, K. (2000). *Doing history: Investigating with children in elementary and middle schools*. Mahwah, NJ: Lawrence Erlbaum Associates.

Marcia, J. E. (1980). Identity in adolescence. In J. Adelson (Ed.), *Handbook of adolescent psychology* (pp. 159–187). New York: Wiley.

Massialas, B. G. (1996). Criteria for issues-centered content selection. In R. W. Evans & D. W. Saxe (Eds.), *Handbook on teaching social issues, NCSS bulletin 93* (pp. 44–50). Washington, DC: National Council for the Social Studies.

McCracken, G. (1988). *The long interview*. Newbury Park, CA: Sage.

McDougall, W. A. (2001, Spring). Why geography matters. *American Educator*, 10–15.

McLaughlin, M. W., & Heath, S. B. (1993). Casting the self: Frames for identity and dilemmas for policy. In S. B. Heath & M. W. McLaughlin (Eds.), *Identity and inner city youth: Beyond ethnicity and gender* (pp. 210–240). New York: Teachers College Press.

McLaughlin, M. W., & Talbert, J. E.. (1990). The contexts in question: The secondary school workplace. In M. W. McLaughlin, J. E. Talbert, & N. Bascia (Eds.), *The contexts of teaching in secondary schools: Teachers' realities* (pp. 1–16). New York: Teachers College Press.

McLaughlin, M. W., Talbert, J. E., & Bascia, N. (Eds.). (1990). *The contexts in question: The secondary school workplace*. New York: Teachers College Press.

McLuhan, M. (1964). *Understanding the media: The extensions of man*. New York: McGraw-Hill.

McNeill, William. (1963). *The rise of the West: A history of the human community*. Chicago: University of Chicago Press.

McWilliams, W. C. (1999, September 25). *National and international politics*. Speech for Rutgers University International Educational Forum, New Brunswick, NJ.

Mead, M. (1943). *And keep your powder dry: An anthropologist looks at America*. New York: Morrow.

Meier, D. (1995). *The power of their ideas: Lessons for America from a small school in Harlem.* Boston: Beacon Press.

Merryfield, M. M. (1996). *Making connections between multicultural and global education: Teacher educators and teacher education programs.* Columbus, OH: Mershon Center.

Merryfield, M. M. (1997). A framework for teacher education in global perspectives. In M. M. Merryfield, E. Jarchow, & S. Pickert (Eds.), *Preparing teachers to teach global perspectives: A handbook for teacher educators* (pp. 1–24). Thousand Oaks, CA: Corwin Press.

Merryfield, M. M. (1998). Pedagogy for global perspectives in education: Studies of teachers' thinking and practice. *Theory and Research in Social Education, 26*(3), 342–379.

Merryfield, M. M. (2001). Moving the center of global education: from imperial world views that divide the world to double consciousness, contrapuntal pedagogy, hybridity, and cross-cultural competence. In W. B. Stanley (Ed.), *Critical issues in social studies research for the 21st century* (pp. 179–208). Greenwich, CT: Information Age.

Merryfield, M. M., Jarchow, E., & Pickert, S. (1997). *Preparing teachers to teach global perspectives: A handbook for teacher educators.* Thousand Oaks, CA: Corwin Press.

Merryfield, M. M., & White, C. S. (1996). Issues-centered global education. In R. W. Evans & D. W. Saxe (Eds.), *Handbook on Teaching Social Issues* (pp. 177–187). Washington, DC: National Council for the Social Studies.

Metz, M. H. (1990). How social class differences shape teachers' work. In M. W. McLaughlin, J. E. Talbert, & N. Bascia (Eds.), *The contexts of teaching in secondary schools: Teachers' realities* (pp. 40–110). New York: Teachers College Press.

Metzger, W. P. (1987). The spectre of "professionism." *Educational Researcher,* 16 (August-September, 1987): 10–16.

Molseed, T. R. (2000). Redesigning pre-service teacher practices through staff development: Serendipitous growth for classroom teachers. *Education, 120*(3), 474–478.

Morse, J. (2000, March 6). Sticking to the script. *Time,* 60–61.

National Council for the Social Studies. (1981). Position Statement on Global Education. Retrieved May 29, 2002, from http://databank.ncss.org/article.php?story=20020402120154452/

Naylor, D. T. (1974). *An in-depth study of the perceptions of public school educators and other significant school-related groups concerning aspects of nationalistic instruction.* Unpublished doctoral dissertation, Rutgers University, New Brunswick, NJ.

Neff, R. H. (1990). Research-based finding seldom incorporated in teacher in-service education. *Journal of Instructional Psychology, 17*(1), 46–52.

Nelson, J. L. (1975, November). *On the study of nationalistic education.* Paper presented at the meeting of the National Council for the Social Studies, Atlanta, Georgia.

Nelson, J. L. (1976). Nationalistic vs. global education: An examination of national bias in the schools and its implications for a global society. *Theory and Research in Social Education, 4*(1), 33–50.

Nelson, J. (1996). The historical imperative for issues-centered education. In R. W. Evans & D. W. Saxe (Eds.), *Handbook on Teaching Social Issues* (pp. 14–24). Washington, DC: National Council for the Social Studies.

Nelson, J. L. (1976). Nationalistic v. global education: An examination of national bias in the schools and its implications for a global society. *Theory and Research in Social Education, 4,* 33–50.

Nelson, J. L., Carlson, K., & Palonsky, S. B. (1993). *Critical issues in education.* New York: McGraw-Hill.

Nesbitt, W. A. (1968). Introduction. *Social Education 35*(7), 637–638.

New Jersey Constitution. (1947/1998). *Constitutions of the United States: National and state, binder 3.* Dobbs Ferry, NY: Oceana Publications.

New Jersey Department of Education. (1988). *New Jersey World History/Cultures Curriculum Guide.* (PTM No. 700.34). Trenton, NJ: New Jersey Department of Education.

Nieto, S. (1996). *Affirming diversity.* White Plains, NY: Longman

Noddings, N. (1984). *Caring: A feminine approach to ethics and moral education.* Berkeley, CA: University of California Press.

Noddings, N. (1992). *The challenge to care in schools.* New York: Teachers College Press.

Norlander-Case, K. A., Reagan, T. G., & Case, C. W. (1999). *The professional teacher: The preparation and nurturance of the reflective practitioner.* San Francisco: Jossey-Bass.

Oakshott, M. (1962). *Rationalism in politics and other essays.* New York: Basic Books.

Ogbu, J. U. (1991). Immigrant and involuntary minorities in comparative perspectives. In M. A. Gibson & J. U. Ogbu (Eds.), *Minority status and schooling: A comparative study of immigrant and involuntary minorities* (pp. 3–36). New York: Garland.

Ogbu, J. U. (1998). Voluntary and involuntary minorities: A cultural-ecological theory of school performance with some implications for education. *Anthropology and Education, 29*(2), 155–188.

Ohmae, K. (1995). *The end of the nation-state: The rise of regional economies.* New York: The Free Press.

O'Meara, P., Mehlinger, H. D., & Krain, M. (2000). *Globalization and the challenges of a new century: A reader.* Bloomington, IN: Indiana University Press.

One nation, many peoples: A declaration of cultural interdependence. (1991). New York: Report of the New York state social studies review and development committee.

Palonsky, S. (1986). *900 shows a year.* New York: Random House.

Parker, W., Grossman, D., Kubow, P., Kurth-Schai, R., & Nakayama, S. (1998). Making it work: Implementing multidimensional citizenship. In J. J. Cogan & R. Derricott (Eds.), *Citizenship for the 21st century: An international perspective on education* (pp. 135–154). London: Kogan Page.

Phinney, J. S., & Rotheram, M. J. (1987). Children's ethnic socialization: Themes and implications. In J. S. Phinney and M. J. Rotheram (Eds.), *Children's ethnic socialization* (pp. 274–292).

Phinney, J. S. (1989). Stages of ethnic identity development in minority group adolescents. *Journal of Early Adolescence, 9*(1–2), 34–49.

Phinney, J. S. (1990). Ethnic identity in adolescents and adults: Review of research. *Psychological Bulletin, 108*(3), 499–514.

Pierce, B. L. (1926). *Public opinion and the teaching of history in the United States.* New York:. Knopf.

Pike, G. (2000). A tapestry in the making: The strands of global education. In T. Goldstein & D. Selby (Eds.), *Weaving connections: Educating for peace, social and environmental justice,* (pp. 218–241). Toronto, Canada: Sumach Press.

Pike, G., & Selby, D. (1988). *Global teacher, global learner.* London: Hodder & Stoughton.

Pike, G., & Selby, D. (2000). *In the global classroom: Volumes 1 & 2.* Toronto, Canada: Pippen.

Pinar, W. F., Reynolds, W. M., Slattery, P., & Taubman, P. M. (1995). *Understanding curriculum: An introduction to the study of historical and contemporary curriculum discourses.* New York: Peter Lang.

Plaintiff's Trial Brief, Marilyn Morheuser, Educational Law Center. In Abbott v. Burke Superior Court of New Jersey Chancery Division Mercer County General Equity Part Docket No. 91-C-00150.

Popkewitz, T. S. (1980). Global education as a slogan system. *Curriculum Inquiry, 10*(3), 303–315.

Purpel, D. E. (2000). Moral education. In D. A. Gabbard (Ed.), *Knowledge and power in the global economy: Politics and the rhetoric of school reform* (pp. 247–254). Mahwah, NJ: Lawrence Erlbaum Associates.

Putnam, R. D. (1995). Bowling alone. *Journal of Democracy, 6,* 65–78.

Putnam, R. D. (2000). *Bowling alone: The collapse and revival of American community.* New York: Simon & Schuster.

Ravitch, D., & Finn, C. (1987). *What do our 17-year-olds know? A report on the first national assessment of history and literature.* New York: Harper & Row.

Reardon, B. A. (1988) *Comprehensive peace education: Educating for global responsibility.* New York: Teachers College Press.

Redfield, R. (1959). Social anthropology and the nature of man. *Anthropological Quarterly, 32,* 2–21

Redwine, S. (1973). *Big Blue Marble song.* New York: Alphaventure Music.

Reinicke, W. H. (1998). *Global public policy: Governing without government?* Washington, DC: Brookings Institution Press.

Remy, R. C. (1982). This issue (introduction). *Theory into Practice 21*(3), 154.

Robertson, R. (1992). *Globalization: Social theory and global culture.* London: Sage.

Robinson, E. H., Jones, K. D., & Hayes, B. G. (2000, September). Humanistic education to character education: An ideological journey. *Journal of Humanistic Counseling, Education and Development, 39,* 21–29.

Roddick, A. (2000). *Business as unusual.* London: HarperCollins.

Rogers, C. R. (1969). *Freedom to learn.* New York: Merrill.

Rothman, R. (1987, May 20). Report urges schools to think globally in a changing world. *Education Week,* 15–16.

Rourke, J. T. (1995). *International politics on the world stage, 5th edition.* Guilford, CT: Dushkin.

Ryan, A. (1995). *John Dewey and the high tide of American liberalism.* New York: Norton.

Sassen, S. (1991). *The global city: New York, London, and Tokyo.* Princeton, NJ: Princeton University Press.

Sassen, S. (1996). *Losing control? Sovereignty in an age of globalization.* New York: Columbia University Press.

Schlesinger, A. M. (1991). *The disuniting of America: Reflections on a multicultural society.* New York: Norton.

School board will recognize other cultures, but as inferior. (1994, May 13). *New York Times,* p. A16.

Shukar, R. (1993). Controversy in global education: Lessons for teacher educators. *Theory into Practice, 32,* 52–57.

Schwartz, S. J. (2001). The evolution of Eriksonian and neo-Eriksonian identity theory and research: A review and integration. *Identity, 1*(1), 7–58.

Seidman, I. E. (1991). *Interviewing as qualitative research.* New York: Teachers College Press.

Seikaly, Z. A. (2001). At risk of prejudice: The Arab-American community. *Social Education, 65*(6), 349–351.

Selby, D. (2000). Humane education: Widening the circle of compassion and justice. In T. Goldstein & D. Selby (Eds.), *Weaving connections: Educating for peace, social and environmental justice* (pp. 268–296). Toronto, Canada: Sumach Press.

Sennett, R. (1998). *The corrosion of character: The personal consequences of work in the new capitalism.* New York: Norton.

Shiman, D., & Fernekes, W. R. (1999). The Holocaust, human rights, and democratic citizenship. *The Social Studies 90*(2), 53–62.

Simon, R. L. (1997). The Paralysis of Absolutophobia. *Chronicle of Higher Education, 43*(42), B5–B6.

Simpson, M. (Ed.). (2001). Teaching about tragedy: Special issue about 9-11-01. *Social Education 65*(6).

Sorokin, E. (2002). No founding fathers? That's our new history! *Washington Times.* Retrieved May 28, 2002, from http://nl9.newsbank.com/nl-search/we/Archives?p=_action=list?p_topdoc=21

Soysal, Y. N. (1994). *Limits of citizenship.* Chicago: University of Chicago Press.

Spindler, G. (1982). *Doing the ethnography of schooling: Educational anthropology in action.* Prospect Heights, IL: Waveland Press.

Spradley, J. P. (1990). *Participant observation.* New York: Holt.

Steinberg, J. (1999; November 26). Teachers in Chicago schools follow script from day 001. *New York Times,* pp. A1, 12.

Strauss, A., & Corbin, J. (1990). *Basics of qualitative research: Grounded theory procedures and techniques*. Thousand Oaks, CA: Sage.

Sweeney, A. E., Bula, O. A., & Cornett, J. W. (2001). The role of personal practical theories in the professional development of a beginning high school chemistry teacher. *Journal of Research in Science Teaching, 38*(4), 408–441.

Tanner, D., & Tanner, L. (1975). *Curriculum development: Theory into practice*. Upper Saddle River, NJ: Merrill of Prentice Hall.

Tatum, B. D. (1999). *"Why are all the black kids sitting together in the cafeteria?"* New York: Basic Books.

The White House. (2002). *America responds to terrorism*. Retrieved May 27, 2002, from http://www.whitehouse.gov/

Thomas, M. (1993, November). *Teaching patriotism as a moral matter*. Paper presented at the Comparative and International Education Society's Western Regional Conference, Los Angeles, CA.

Thornton, S. (1991). Teacher as curricular-instructional gatekeeper in social studies. In J. Shaver (Ed.), *Handbook of research on social studies teaching and learning* (pp. 237–240). New York: Macmillan.

Thornton, S. J. (2001, November/December). From content to subject matter. *The Social Studies, 237–242*.

Torney, J. (1977). The international knowledge and attitudes of adolescents in nine countries: The IEA civic education survey. *International Journal of Political Education, 1*, 3–20.

Torney, J. (1979). Psychological and institutional obstacles to the global perspective in education. In J. M. Becker (Ed.), *Schooling for a global age* (pp. 59–93). New York: McGraw-Hill.

Torney-Purta, J. (1982). The global awareness survey: Implications for teacher education. *Theory into Practice 21*(3), 200–205.

Torney-Purta, J. (1985). *Predictors of global awareness and concern among secondary school students*. Columbus, OH: Mershon Center of The Ohio State University.

Torney-Purta, J. (1989). Measuring the effectiveness of world studies courses. In R. B. Woyach. & R. C. Remy (Eds.), *Approaches to world studies: A handbook for curriculum planners* (pp. 209–247). Boston: Allyn & Bacon.

Tucker, J. L. (1982). Developing a global dimension in teacher education: The Florida International University experience. *Theory into Practice, 21*(3), 212–217.

Tucker, J. L. (1996). NCSS and international/global education. In O. L. Davis (Ed.), *NCSS in Retrospect* (pp. 00–00). Washington, DC: National Council for the Social Studies.

Tye, B. B. (1990). Schooling in America today: Potential for global studies. In K. A. Tye (Ed.), *Global education: From thought to action*, (pp. 35–48). Alexandria, VA: Association for Supervision & Curriculum Development.

Tye, B. B., & Tye, K. A. (1992). *Global education: A study of school change*. Albany, NY: State University of New York Press.

Tye, K. A. (1999). *Global Education: A Worldwide Movement*. Orange, CA: Interdependence Press.

Tye, K. A. (2001, March 12). The challenges of teaching globally. Speech to the World Teaching Institute, University of Central Florida, Orlando, FL.

U.N. Convention on the Rights of the Child. (1989).

UNICEF. (2001, August 13). Young people and social change. www.unicef.org/voy/misc/chforum.html

Universal Declaration of Human Rights. (1948).

U.S. Census Bureau. (2001). *Overview of race and Hispanic origin*. Retrieved June 19, 2001, from http://blue.census.gov/

U.S. Constitution. (1787).

U.S. Environmental Protection Agency. (1997). *Cool facts about global warming* (EPA Publication No. 230-F-97-001). Washington, DC: Author.

Vulliamy, G., & Webb, R. (1993). Progressive education and the national curriculum: Findings from a global education research project. *Educational Review, 45*(1), 21–41.

Wade, R. C. (1994). Conceptual change in elementary social studies: A case study of fourth graders' understanding of human rights. *Theory and Research in Social Education, 23*(1), 74–95.

Wells, G. (2001). The development of a community of inquirers. In G. Wells (Ed.), *Action, talk, and text: Learning and teaching through inquiry* (pp. 1–22). New York: Teachers College Press.

Werner, W., & Case, R. (1997). Themes in global education. In I. Wright & A. Sears (Eds.), *Trends and issues in Canadian social studies education* (pp. 176–194). Vancouver, Canada: Pacific Education Press.

Weston, B. (1975). Education for human survival. *Annals of the New York Academy of Science, 261*(1), 115–125.

Whitman, C. T. (1999, March 3). *Remarks to International Conference of Conservative Women Parliamentarians*, Washington, DC.

Willinsky, J. (1998). *Learning to divide the world: Education at empire's end*. Minneapolis, MN: University of Minnesota Press.

Wilson, A. (1982). Cross-cultural experiential learning for teachers. *Theory into Practice, 21*(3), 184–192.

Wilson, A. H. (1985). Exchange students as bridges between cultures. *Intercom, 106*(1), 5–8.

Wilson, A. H. (1993). *The meaning of international experience for schools*. Westport, CT: Praeger.

Wilson, A. H. (2001). Growing towards teaching from a global perspective: An analysis of secondary social studies preservice teachers. *The International Social Studies Forum, 1*(2), 127–144.

World Cultures: A global mosaic (2nd ed.). (1996). Englewood Cliffs, NJ: Prentice Hall.

World Trade Organization. (2000). *FDI flows and global integration*. Available: http://www.wto.org/english/thewto_e/minist_e/min99_e/english_/about_e/_22fact_e.htm

Woyach, R. B., & Remy, R. C. (1982). A community-based approach to global education. *Theory into Practice, 21*(3), 177–83.

Woyach, R. B., & Remy, R. C. (1989). *Approaches to world studies: A handbook for curriculum planners*. Boston: Allyn & Bacon.

Wu, Sen-Yuan (1997). The estimates of foreign-born population in New Jersey: 1997. New Jersey Department of Labor http://www.state.nj.us/labor/lra

Yuen-Kwan, W. L. (1998). How sustainable are in-service teacher training courses? *Asia-Pacific Journal of Teacher Education, 26*(1), 65–74.

Zygouris-Coe, V., Pace, B., Malecki, C., & Weade, R. (2001). Action research: A situated perspective. *International Journal of Qualitative Studies in Education, 14*(3), 399–412.

Author Index

Subject Index